1989

MATTHEW ARNOLD
and the Betrayal of Language

MATTHEW ARNOLD
and the Betrayal of Language

by
David G. Riede

UNIVERSITY PRESS OF VIRGINIA
Charlottesville

This is a title in the series

THE UNIVERSITY PRESS OF VIRGINIA

First published 1988

Library of Congress Cataloging-in-Publication Data

Riede, David G.
Matthew Arnold and the betrayal of language.

(Virginia Victorian studies)
Bibliography: p.
Includes index.
1. Arnold Matthew, 1822–1888—Criticism and interpretation. I. Title. II. Series.
PR4024.R5 1988 821'.8 87-13693
ISBN 0-8139-1149-4

Printed in the United States of America

For Benedict and Austin

Contents

	Acknowledgments	ix
	Introduction	1
I.	The Early Poetry: Distant Voices	30
II.	Romantic Voices and Classic Form	72
III.	The Poetry of the Wilderness	117
IV.	Love Poetry: Sincerity and Subversive Voices	163
	Conclusion	204
	Notes	221
	Index	235

Acknowledgments

Though it is somewhat surprising that, one hundred years after Arnold's death, so much primary work remains to be done in collecting and editing his papers and letters, it is also true that Arnold has attracted the attention and diligence of exceptionally gifted editors and scholars. I am grateful to all of them, but especially to Professor R. H. Super, whose magnificently edited and annotated edition of the prose works has been invaluable to me, and to Kenneth and Miriam Allott, whose splendid edition of the poetry I have chosen to use in place of the previously standard (and also excellent) edition by C. B. Tinker and H. F. Lowry. I have also been greatly aided by Park Honan's recent biography and by the numerous critical works cited in the notes. I would also like to thank Natalie Tyler, Veronica Leahy, and Professors Cecil Lang, George Ford, Daniel Albright, and George Landow, who read all or part of the manuscript and offered helpful suggestions. And I would like to thank the University of Rochester and the John Simon Guggenheim Memorial Foundation for making the time available for me to finish the book.

Unless otherwise noted, references to Arnold's poetry are cited by line numbers in the text, and refer to *The Poems of Matthew Arnold,* edited by Kenneth Allott, 2d ed. by Miriam Allott (New York: Longman, 1979), and references to prose works, cited by volume and page number in the text, refer to *The Complete Prose Works of Matthew Arnold,* 11 volumes, ed. R. H. Super (Ann Arbor: Univ. of Michigan Press, 1960–77).

MATTHEW ARNOLD
and the Betrayal of Language

Introduction

Matthew Arnold is properly regarded as nineteenth-century England's greatest spokesman for culture, classical education, the great literary tradition, the study of humane letters, and the saving power of poetry. For students in the humanities he has been a defender of the literary faith, of belief in the "ennobling power of great literature."[1] His insistence on the "pursuit of perfection" and on such absolutes as "the best that is known and thought in the world" has been, in his time and ours, a stay against artistic, intellectual, and moral anarchy. From the beginning to the end of his career, Arnold insisted that however rapidly the world changed, however completely old beliefs and faiths became outmoded and discarded, great literature would endure as a source of continued value. Whatever else happens in human affairs, and "in spite of momentary appearances," literature will endure because it is essential to the continued existence of humanity: "currency and supremacy are insured to it . . . by the instinct of self-preservation in humanity" (9:188). In his own age, an age that had lost religious certainty, that was struggling to be modern without breaking entirely with the past, Arnold offered culture, and especially poetry, as a source of comfort and security, and he did so with an almost astonishing confidence:

> *The future of poetry is immense, because in poetry, where it is worthy of its high destinies, our race, as time goes on, will find an ever surer and surer stay. There is not a creed which is not shaken, not an accredited dogma which is not shown to be questionable, not*
> (9:161) *a received tradition which does not threaten to dissolve. Our religion has materialised itself in the fact, in the supposed fact; it has attached its emotion to the fact, and now the fact is failing it. But for poetry the idea is everything; the rest is a world of illusion, of divine illusion. Poetry attaches its emotion to the idea; the idea* is

> *the fact. The strongest part of our religion to-day is its unconscious poetry.*

Poetry, in other words, has a power over us akin to the best and strongest power of religion.

But "other words" do not do Arnold's words justice. His assertions are memorable less because of their paraphrasable content than because they are beautifully—poetically—expressed. Indeed, Arnold himself must have felt this, since he is avowedly quoting (actually misquoting and improving) his own earlier words.[2] In fact, despite his frequent insistence on the importance of "content" in literature, or on the need for overall architectonic form, he often finds the source of power and moral efficacy in literature less in what is said than in how it is said, in how it is expressed in pithy and telling language. All his life he filled notebooks with aphoristic quotations, precise verbal formulations that seemed to have an almost talismanic power, and one of his methods for judging poetry was to compare, not whole works, but severed phrases, with "touchstones" from the great masters. Further, Arnold's own essays are best remembered, not for their paraphrasable content, but for their famous aphoristic formulas: "sweetness and light," "reason and the will of God," "the pursuit of perfection," "the best that is known and thought in the world," "to see the object as in itself it really is," "the grand style," "the best self," and so on. It is because of the mysterious power inherent in language that Arnold regarded poetry as "more of a stay to us" than the other arts, or than science, or than religion (9:62–63). Nor is this surprising—words of power *must* bear the burden of poetic argument within themselves because the poetic language is not "attached to the fact." Because the facts of religion and the systems of religion become outworn, and because the truths of science are inadequate to satisfy the emotional needs of humanity, literature, as Ruth apRoberts has recently argued, becomes all-important to Arnold: "All dogma is vulnerable because presented as absolute. But what is blessedly *in*vulnerable is literature (or poetry, or art), because it acknowledges its fictionality." Therefore, "in spite of all the shifting provisional impermanence, [language] is nevertheless man's best and most characteristic capacity. In the beginning of man, there is language, his power to make himself by the metaphorical word."[3] Arnold himself takes for granted that language, that a certain style of expression, has the power to "form the character" (1:38). All of this would seem to imply that what Arnold believed in above all was the power and plenitude of language, that, as Douglas Bush has said, "he had a sincere and practical faith in the *directing and energizing power of pregnant statements* of human experience and aspiration—a faith reflected in the repeated key phrases of his published works."[4]

Despite this manifest insistence on the power of words, however, recent critics have regarded Arnold's faith in language as much more limited than Bush and apRoberts indicate. Where apRoberts states that Arnold saw man's capacity to create with words as his saving grace, Howard Fulweiler has said that "Arnold's problem . . . is a basic and shattering disillusionment with the creative and formative power of human beings, especially as that power is employed in the poet's use of imaginative language."[5] And J. Hillis Miller argues that Arnold's key phrases are not at all "pregnant" but are "empty linguistic shells": "They are scrupulously empty phrases. Their repetition empties them further of meaning, and testifies to the fact that though there is something to which the words refer, that something is not named by the words."[6] Similarly, W. David Shaw calls Arnold's description of God as "the Eternal, not ourselves, that makes for righteousness" an example of an "empty signifier," and argues that "Arnold's plight is that of his own Stagirius, who empties his language, finally, of all analogies and symbols, in order to keep his words open to some higher truth," but whose words, nevertheless, do not signify that truth.[7] Of course, ever since F. H. Bradley, critics have been aware of the frequent emptiness of important phrases in Arnold's religious writing, but the empty language occurs throughout all of Arnold's writings, and tends to undermine him at his most impassioned moments. Like Bradley before them, Miller and Shaw are referring primarily, though not exclusively, to Arnold's religious phrases, but even in his most emphatic statement about the power of poetry, Arnold's language, strangely empty, describes a circle with nothing inside it: poetry does not attach its emotion (what is poetry's emotion?) to the illusory fact but to the idea (what idea?) and "the idea *is* the fact" to which poetry does not attach its emotion.

The point here is not to ridicule Arnold but only to show that his language has nothing to refer itself to but itself. Nor do I want to imply that Miller and Shaw are right and that Bush and apRoberts are wrong—Arnold does indeed assert the saving power of language, but in words that, ironically, are often self-referential and only enclose an empty space. Arnold is at odds with himself—he describes an inspired and almost magically full language, but he describes it with a sadly empty language. In his ideas about language, as in so many other ways, Arnold was a man caught between two worlds, a past in which language generated "a world of illusion, of divine illusion," and a future for which an adequate vocabulary was yet unborn. Naive language, the language of the past, was forceful because apparently unproblematical. As Rousseau, Wordsworth, Emerson, and others argued, the language of primitives and peasants is powerful because no insuperable gap is perceived between mind and nature, thought and the objects of thought, words and things. And even for sophisticated thinkers, faith in God ensured the harmonious union of the mind and the principle of creation, so that language was sanctioned by religion and fulfilled with the revelation of God. But for the sophisticated and agnostic Arnold, both the primitive and religious language theories were illusive. In his transitional age, it seemed to Arnold that the only languages available were the powerful but misleading language of the past, and the language of science, arid and inadequate, but pointing, as it seemed, to objective truth. The old language could give comfort and joy, and the new could give truth, but Arnold sought, in a well-known phrase, "Joy whose grounds are true."[8] And in another famous phrase he repeatedly affirmed the need to see objectively, to "see the object as in itself it really is."

Because objective truth was of paramount importance to Arnold, he was far more undermined by the "shifting provisional impermanence" of language than apRoberts suggests, and that is why his elevation of poetry over science is in uneasy alliance with his desire for objectivity. In his essay on Maurice de Guérin, he has no trouble in stating that poetry has "the power of so dealing with things as to awaken in us a wonderfully full, new, and intimate sense of them" and that "the interpretations of science do not give us this intimate sense of objects as the interpretations of poetry give it; they appeal to a limited faculty, and not to the whole man" (3:13). But in this apparently straightforward discussion the phrase "intimate sense" becomes an empty signifier because Arnold never defines it, but instead repeats "intimate sense," "this sense," "this feeling," "this sense," "this sense," "this intimate sense," over and over within the space of five sentences, and calmly moots the question of what "this sense" is by blandly stating that "I will not now inquire whether this sense is illusive, whether it can be proved not to be illusive, whether it does absolutely make us possess the real nature of things" (3:13).

The phrase becomes rhetorically effective through sheer repetition as it develops the concreteness of a "fact" to be counted on. But the calm of this utterance is perhaps belied by its defensiveness—obviously it is of some consequence if poetry compels us to see the object as "in itself it really is not,"[9] and if the function of poetry, like that of dogmatic religion, is to comfort humanity with illusions. When Arnold finally does define not what the sense *is* but what it *does,* he can only refer to a very possibly delusive "feeling": "When this sense is awakened in us, as to objects without us, we feel ourselves to be in contact with the essential nature of these objects, to be no longer bewildered and oppressed by them, but to have their secret, and to be in harmony with them" (3:13). Arnold is confident that language has power over the feelings, but he is not able to assert that the grounds of these feelings "are true." Poetry appeals to feeling, but fact, the object as it really is, remains in the domain of science.

Arnold's uncertainty about the sources of power and authority in language is perhaps nowhere more clearly evident than in his attempts to respond to Thomas Henry Huxley's attack on his most cherished positions. In his essay "Science and Culture," Huxley asserted that "the best that is known and thought in the world" is assuredly not an exploded medieval religion and its literary offshoots but the truths of science. And with Arnold very much in mind he wittily associated the "Levites in charge of the ark of culture" with the high priests of Christianity and other "scholarly and pious persons" who continue to indulge in a "medieval way of thinking."[10] Huxley's central argument hit Arnold where he was most vulnerable by emphasizing that science sees and describes the object as in itself it really is, whereas humanism depends upon mere words: "scientific 'criticism of life' presents itself to us with different credentials from any other. It appeals not to authority, nor to what anybody may have thought or said, but to nature. It admits that all our interpretations of natural fact are more or less imperfect and symbolic, and bids the learner seek for truth not among words but among things."[11] Huxley's argument was hardly novel—it is a staple of Baconian thought and of rationalist thought generally—but it bluntly stated that only two views of language were possible, the correct scientific view that regarded language as secondary and derivative, and the false religious view that had gone out in the middle ages. Huxley's argument had peculiar force in mid-Victorian England because, like most of his writings, it compelled people to take sides either with science or religion, and allowed no middle ground. Indeed, Huxley's argument was essentially a crystallization of the debate about language that had been stirred up in 1844 by science's assertion, in the form of Robert Chambers's *Vestiges of the Natural History of Creation,* that language was not of divine origin but was merely mankind's gradual improvement over the gestures and signals of animals. And the religious establishment, of course, responded by arguing that mankind could not possibly have invented language, so it must have been revealed by God—or at the very least, the capacity for language must have been implanted in man's brain.[12]

Arnold's difficulty in countering Huxley's argument resulted, characteristically, from his being caught in the middle. In his essay "Literature and Science" he simply argued that though science does indeed add to our knowledge and that though everyone should be aware of scientific modes of thought, science cannot put ideas into relation with one another or into relation with human experience and aspiration. But when he further argued that language, in the form of "poetry and eloquence," has a "fortifying, and elevating, and quickening, and suggestive power" (10:68), he found that he could not explain this power beyond saying that experience demonstrated it to be so: "Experience shows that for the vast majority of men, for mankind in general, [poetry and eloquence] have the power. Next, do they exercise it? They do. But then, *how* do they exercise it so as to affect man's sense for conduct, his sense for beauty? And this is perhaps a case for applying the Preacher's words: 'Though a man labour to seek it out, yet he shall not find it; yea, farther, though a wise man think to know it, yet shall he not be able to find it' " (10:67). In appealing to experience Arnold thought he was being empirical and therefore scientific, but of course he was only referring the matter back to his own impressions. Poet that he was, his language refers to "feelings," not to the object as it is. He clearly trusts the power of words sufficiently to excuse his lack of explanation, not on scientific or logical or philosophical grounds, but simply with a quotation from Ecclesiastes. And he is confident enough about the power of language to support his assertions by simply quoting phrases from literature and allowing them to display the power he attributes to them. In fact, Arnold does not argue his points at all, but merely asserts them and trusts that the eloquence of his prose and the beauty of his quotations will be sufficient argument. But of course as in his comments in the Maurice de Guérin essay, the points that he blandly declines to inquire into are of fundamental importance if he desires, as of course he does, that his assertions be not only convincing but also true—he plainly needs to refer his language to something other than his own experience and to itself, and yet he cannot do so without referring it either to mere things or to a sacred origin.

Arnold's dilemma becomes somewhat clearer when the competing language theories of his age are considered in more detail. The antagonism between the advocates of science and of religion had polarized the issue to such an extent that no middle ground was possible—either God had created the world and given man speech, or there was no God and language was merely man's inadequate invention to designate material things and to gesture at what he cannot understand, let alone name. From this perspective it was clear that the theory of Arnold's romantic predecessors was plainly religious. Coleridge, and, for that matter Wordsworth and Emerson, both of whom Arnold especially admired, all believed in a plenitude of language that results from the preexistent because divinely ordained correspondence of the mind with nature: as Emerson puts it in his essay on language, the "relation between the mind and matter is not fancied by some poet, but stands in the will of God." Consequently, "good writing and brilliant discourse are perpetual allegories. This imagery is spontaneous. It is the blending of experience with the present action of the mind. It is proper creation. It is the working of the Original Cause through the instruments he has already made."[13] By the time Arnold began writing, the religious content in the romantic idea of language was being thoroughly Christianized by such writers as R. C. Trench, Tennyson's fellow Apostle and the future Archbishop of Dublin. Trench eulogized the wonderful power of words, even adopting Emerson's aphoristic definition of words as "fossil poetry," and he did so by rejecting the materialistic notion about the evolution of language, "which is contradicted alike by every page of Genesis, and every notice of our actual experience." This observation, disconcertingly like Arnold's refutation of Huxley by appeal to experience and Ecclesiastes, anticipates a definitive statement that Arnold could not have made: "But the true answer to the inquiry how language arose, is this, that God gave man language, just as he gave him reason, and just because he gave him reason (for what is man's word but his reason coming forth, so that it may behold itself?) that he gave it to him, because he could not be man, that is a social being, without it." For this reason Trench could refute the scientific or materialistic conception long ago set forth by Hobbes, and insist that "there is a reality about words, that they are not merely arbitrary signs, but living powers; that, to reverse the words of one of England's 'false prophets,' they may be the fool's counters, but are the wise man's money."[14]

Trench's orthodoxy made his praise of the plenary power of language easy and inevitable, but similar arguments were offered even by the liberal, "higher critics" who, like Arnold, wanted to eulogize the power of language without defending the literal truth of the Bible. Arnold's friend Max Müller, for example, accepted the Emersonian idea of fossil poetry, observing that "there is a petrified philosophy in language," but despite his "scientific" study of roots, he ended up tracing the source of power in language, like Arnold, to "human nature" and ultimately, unlike Arnold, to God: the fundamental linguistic elements, he said, are "produced by a power inherent in human nature. They exist, as Plato would say, by nature; though with Plato we should add that, when we say by nature, we mean by the hand of God."[15] But Arnold, once again, was not willing to take the final and seemingly inevitable step, was not willing to answer the modern, scientific arguments of Huxley with a medieval assertion that simply referred language back to a divine first cause.

In fact, Arnold could scarcely refute Huxley's view of language effectively because, not believing in a transcendental and all-creating God, or even in a supernal Platonic ideal, he naturally rejected the metaphysics of Christianity, almost casually dismissing the primary textual authority for Christian and romantic faith in the divine Logos by rejecting as mere theory the Gospel of St. John, with its famous opening verses that conflate the initial creative fiat of Genesis with the incarnation of the Word, or Logos, in Jesus. So central, indeed, is this text to the logocentric view that the lifelong ambition of Coleridge, the greatest of English romantic theorists, was to justify the Christian and romantic faith in the power of the word to unify man and nature by writing "a large volume on the LOGOS, or the communicative intelligence in nature and man, together with, and as preliminary to, a Commentary on the Gospel of St. John."[16] But Arnold, despite his sense that poetry has "the power of so dealing with things as to awaken in us a wonderfully full, new, and intimate sense of them," could nevertheless not accept the "identification of Jesus with the divine hypostasis known as the Logos" because it was based on words, not things—it was based on "scholastic theology," on metaphysics, and not on experience and fact (6:40–41).[17] Consequently he could not easily refute Huxley's agnostic view of language because, agnostic himself, he held a similar view. His own higher criticism of the Bible in *St. Paul and Protestantism* (1870), *Literature and Dogma* (1873), and *God and the Bible* (1875) repeatedly denies the divine origin of language, and insistently reduces words to "things." Indeed, in a lecture delivered shortly after the writing of "Literature and Science," Arnold praised the scientific attitude that elevates "things" above the words that arbitrarily designate them: "We labour at words and systems, and fancy that we are labouring at the things for the sake of which those exist. But in truth we are often only labouring at the artificial and difficult forms under which we choose to try to think things, and the things themselves must be seen simply if we are to see them at all" (10:82). Further, Arnold always regarded his own religious teachings as "scientific": "What essentially characterizes a religious teacher, and gives him his permanent worth and vitality, is, after all, just the scientific value of his teaching, its correspondence with important facts and the light it throws on them. Never was the truth of this so evident as now. The scientific sense in man never asserted its claims so strongly; the propensity of religion to neglect those claims, and the peril and loss to it from neglecting them, never were so manifest" (6:8). Strict scientific analysis of the Bible and of the theology based on it insists upon judging language that presents itself as scientific and accountable to fact by rigorous empirical standards, but it also insists upon judging language that presents itself as figurative and poetical by the standards, not of empirically verifiable reality, but of literary criticism. In this way Arnold could strip away the "false science" of theological teachings about a supernatural deity who is like an enlarged person in the next street, about personal immortality, about heaven and hell, about miracles, and about Christ's resurrection, but at the same time retain the poetry of the Bible and its moral efficacy. Further, by retaining the humanizing tact of literary criticism, he could avoid the excessive rigor of scientific thought, which he caustically characterized as "that formidable logical apparatus, not unlike a guillotine, which Professor Huxley speaks of somewhere as the young man's best companion," and could be grateful that "the good of letters may be had without skill in arguing," and can be had by those who are not "athletes of logic" (6:168–69). Since the Bible itself, unlike the metaphysics grafted on to it, was mostly literary and poetical, the murderous dissecting power of science could be diverted from it almost entirely, while literary criticism exposed its enduring and real import.[18] As apRoberts has said, Arnold, recognizing the shifting and provisional nature of language, intended to use his experience as a literary critic to salvage a rational religion for the modern world: he "proceeds toward the discovery of religious phenomenology by his searching analysis of literary phenomenology: how figures work."[19]

Certainly Arnold, seeing himself as a "dissolvent," but not an "acrid" one (3:109–10), plainly wanted not to destroy but to show the enduring and positive value of the Bible and its language by stripping away the encumbering excrescence of dogma. Echoing the faith expressed at the end of "The Function of Criticism at the Present Time" that criticism will lead humanity out of the wilderness, he declared in *Literature and Dogma* that "the great work to be done for the better time which will arrive, and for the time of transition which will precede it, is not a work of destruction, but to show that the truth is really, as it is, incomparably higher, grander, more wide and deep-reaching, than the *Aberglaube* [Arnold's polite word for superstition] and false science which it displaces" (6:384–85). Unfortunately, Arnold's contention, however ironically intended, that this could be accomplished without skill in argument and without rigorous logic, is unsettling. As critics in his own day recognized, Arnold's only basis for determining whether particular Biblical phrases were meant as fact or as poetry was what he would call critical tact, and what others might call idiosyncratic impression. In an 1873 review article cuttingly entitled "Amateur Theology," John Tulloch noted Arnold's contention that the Hebrew idea of God as a personal power was poetry but their idea of righteousness was an experiential fact, and wondered "on what principle can we pronounce the one to be poetry and the other experience or fact?"[20] To put the matter in modern critical terminology, Arnold's exegesis of the Bible plainly hinges upon a blatant intentional fallacy, a belief that he can determine not what was said, but what was meant. He differentiates between language that is meant to be understood "poetically" and language that is meant to be taken "literally." He declares, for example, that when the language of the Old Testament is used in the New, "The disciples use it literally, Jesus uses it as poetry" (8:139), so the disciples mean exactly what they say, and Jesus does not. Because poetry acknowledges its own fictionality, because "poetry nothing affirmeth," Jesus' teachings do not have to be accepted literally. Arnold could, therefore, interpret them in any way he saw fit, could insist for example, that when Jesus *said* "God," he actually *meant* not a personal God, but "a vast object of consciousness not fully covered" by the "term of common speech" (6:285).

As E. K. Brown long ago pointed out, "Arnold was wholly sincere—it need scarcely be said—in his belief that in his theological works the negative was secondary, the positive primary. But the negative was grounded in scholarship, the positive was arbitrary and personal."[21] Consequently, he was always more convincing when emptying out poetical language than when trying to refill it with a more strictly denotative or scientific language. Despite his stated intentions, and despite apRoberts's assertion that his examinations of literary language enabled him to formulate a phenomenology of religion, he might more accurately be described as a failed nominalist, for his criticism of theological, metaphysical, and poetic language takes the essentially nominalist position that words are understood in relation to other words, not in relation to things, or reality. But his insistence that "scientific" language can refer to things and even to universal laws breaks down the coherence of his position. Or to put it in more modern terms, Arnold's study of religious language led him to a deconstruction of literary language. In fact, one could go a step beyond W. David Shaw's statement that Arnold is a "demythologizer, who deconstructs the metaphors of the Bible in order to found a religion of culture,"[22] for Arnold's emptying of poetic language seriously calls into question the power of language upon which the religion of culture crucially rests. And further, as I will argue, the deconstruction of Biblical language makes explicit a distrust of his medium that had undermined his poetry even early in his career.

Before considering how Arnold attempted to salvage a faith in language from the wreck of his analyses, it is worth while to consider just how thoroughly destructive those analyses had been. In the first place, though he hoped eventually the "truth of science and truth of religion" would be "made to harmonise" (3:74), and though he regarded poetry as having a hold over the imagination, his initial acceptance of a dichotomy between poetic and scientific language nevertheless accorded to science an exclusive hold over *verifiable* truth. Indeed, in order to establish the truth of the Bible's "imaginative language" at all, Arnold's method was to "translate" it into "positive language" (6:69). By calling God "simply *the stream of tendency by which all things seek to fulfil the law of their being*" he claims, however oddly, to translate the "language of figure and feeling" into the "language of literal fact and science." Because this language does not inspire emotion, it is "inadequate" and falls "*below* what we feel to be the truth," but it is "a *scientific* definition" which is, unlike figurative language, "admittedly certain and verifiable" and which refers "to a certain and admitted reality." "This, at least," Arnold remarks, "is an advantage" (6:189–90). The end result of differentiating between two different kinds of language is that though poetic language is defined in phenomenological terms, by its effect on the perceiving mind, scientific language is defined in absolute terms by its ability to render verifiable "reality." The truth of poetic language is subjective and arbitrary, but the truth of scientific language is absolute, and enables the writer to fulfil the purpose of Arnoldian criticism—to describe the object as in itself it really is. Scientific language, Arnold says over and over again, is "inadequate," yet it is so far preferable to poetic language for getting at the truth of things that Arnold makes it—or aspires to make it—the medium of his criticism and, wherever possible, "translates" religious language into it. But the important point is that once language is split in two, with one language corresponding to the mind, and the other to external reality, both are "inadequate" to bridge the gulf between mind and nature, between self and other. The logocentrism of romanticism and religion is denied, or to put it in more Arnoldian terms, no "adequate" language exists. And of course, the possibility of finding an adequate language is even slighter than Arnold realizes, since the "scientific" language he employs is itself highly metaphoric, and can therefore point only to analogies of the object, not to the object as in itself it really is. It refers only to other words, not to things.

Arnold argues, in fact, that the poetry of the Bible is generated precisely from a sense of the limitations of language. The Bible speaks poetically of "the high and lofty One that inhabiteth eternity, whose name is holy" because "the spirit and tongue of Israel kept a propriety, a reserve, a sense of the inadequacy of language in conveying man's ideas of God" and so "keeps to the language of poetry and does not essay the language of science" (6:187). But, committing the intentional fallacy, Arnold somewhat arbitrarily asserts that "Israel knew . . . that his words were but *thrown out* at a vast object of consciousness, which he could not fully grasp" (6: 187–88). The theory of language attributed to Israel was, of course, Arnold's own, and one which, significantly, is at the furthest possible extreme from either the high romantic or the religious idea of a language of plenitude. Rather it is exactly in accord with contemporary agnostic thought, since, according to Shaw, the "agnostic metaphysical theories of Sir William Hamilton and of his Victorian disciples Henry Mansel, Herbert Spencer, and T. H. Huxley" all "contend that our words for God are merely equivocal signs, gestures in the direction of an unknowable Power which surpasses all the philosopher or theologian can think or say about Him."[23] Arnold reiterates the idea insistently, as here in *Literature and Dogma*: "In truth, the word 'God' is used in most cases as by no means a term of science or exact knowledge, but a term of poetry or eloquence, a term *thrown out,* so to speak, at a not fully grasped object of the speaker's consciousness, a *literary* term, in short; and mankind mean different things by it as their consciousness differs" (6:171). Arnold is, of course, not out to discredit such language but rather to proceed "toward the discovery of religious phenomenology by his searching analysis of literary phenomenology: how figures work." Or, to paraphrase Andrea del Sarto, he is arguing that a man's speech should exceed his grasp, or what's a Bible for? But on the other hand it might be suggested that, in the terms Arnold himself used to describe the British College of Health, language that is "thrown out" may offer us only "the grand name without the grand thing" (3:280).

Though Arnold clearly intends to preserve the phenomenology of religion by paring away dogma, his arguments about language draw him, perhaps inevitably, beyond phenomenology and into something very like modern deconstruction. His agnostic denial of the verifiable existence of anything beyond or above material nature, beyond or above the world of things, leads him to a distrust of all words that can not be referred back immediately to something "concrete," and ultimately to a distrust of a metaphysics of presence or being in language:

> *To such a degree do words make man, who invents them, their sport! The moment we have an abstract word, a word where we do not apprehend both the concrete sense and the manner of this sense's application, there is danger. The whole value of an abstract term depends on our true and clear conception of that which we have abstracted and now convey by means of this term.* Animal *is a valuable term because we know what breathing,* anima, *is, and we*
> (7:188) *use animal to denote all who have this in common. But the* être *of Descartes is an unprofitable term, because we do not clearly conceive what the term means. And it is, moreover, a dangerous term, because without clearly conceiving what it means, we nevertheless use it freely. When we at last come to examine the term, we find that* être *and* animal *really mean just the same thing:* breather, *that which has vital breath.*

The attempt to do away with metaphysics by reductive etymology, however, is less an anticipation of the twentieth century than a return to the eighteenth—and even earlier. In fact, this theory of language has been a staple of rationalist thought ever since Locke noted "how great a Dependance our *Words* have on common sensible experience" and observed that words which are "made to stand for *Ideas* that come not under the cognizance of our Senses" are all "taken from the Operation of sensible Things, and applied to certain Modes of Thinking. *Spirit,* in its primary Signification, is Breath; *Angel* a Messenger."[24] As Hans Aarsleff has said, Condillac, following Locke, had used this idea to discredit "all metaphysics, except the Lockian kind," and to argue that by removing language from its concrete origins, philosophy had only made it more obscure and difficult.[25] Condillac's idea that primitive languages were superior because closer to material origins is not far from Arnold's suggestion that the strong, figurative language of the Bible resulted from Israel's "inaptitude to express even abstract notions by other than highly concrete terms" (6:187). The crucial difference, however, is that for Condillac the original, primitive languages had been perfect; for Arnold they were, like modern language but for different reasons, inadequate.

Arnold's refusal to accept the idea of a perfect primal language once again separates him from both the religious and romantic views of a language of power and plenitude. When he derided the "home-grown theory of the One Primeval Language" (7:304), he may well have been thinking of Max Müller's theory that originally the roots of modern languages were the words of an original common source language, so that "the Science of Language thus leads us up to that highest summit from whence we see into the very dawn of man's life on earth; and where the words which we have heard so often from the days of our childhood—'And the whole earth was of one language and of one speech'—assume a meaning more natural, more intelligible, more convincing, than they ever had before."[26] The notion of a perfect primal language, which finds some sanction in Wordsworth's praise of the untutored speech of peasants, had been very much a part of romantic thought, perhaps most clearly and emphatically expressed by Emerson:

> *Savages, who have only what is necessary, converse in figures. As we go back in history, language becomes more picturesque, until its infancy, when it is all poetry; or all spiritual facts are represented by natural symbols. The same symbols are found to make the original elements of all languages. It has moreover been observed, that the idioms of all languages approach each other in passages of the greatest eloquence and power. And as this is the first language, so is it the last. This immediate dependence of language upon nature, this conversion of an outward phenomenon into a type of somewhat in human life, never loses its power to affect us. It is this which gives that piquancy to the conversation of a strong-natured farmer or backwoodsman, which all men relish.*[27]

Arnold, however, reduces words to things not to praise figurative language but to disparage transcendental metaphysics. He attacks the whole modern philosophical tradition, from Descartes through Hegel and on, rather heavy-handedly referring to "those great men, those masters of abstruse reasoning, who discourse of being and non-being, essence and existence, subject and object" (7:182), on the grounds that its terminology has become meaningless because detached from its material roots. Following the etymologies of Curtius and Renan, he observes that "those terrible abstracts, *is, be,* and *exist*" arose from "these harmless concretes, *breathe, grow,* and *stand*" (7:184). Consequently, words which, originally, were obviously figurative have been wrongly granted the status of actualities and have become the basis of a metaphysics of presence: "The original figure . . . was soon forgotten; and *is* and *be,* mysterious petrifactions, remained in language as if they were autochthons there, and as if no one could go beyond or behind them. Without father, without mother, without descent, as it seemed, they yet were omnipresent in our speech, and indispensable. . . . And *being* was supposed to be something absolute, which stood under all things." Evidently for Arnold petrifactions or fossils only interfered with the lucidity of language. Confused by these petrifactions, and ignoring their origins, philosophers "thought they had in pure *being,* or *essence,* the supreme reality, and that this *being* in itself, this *essence* not even serving as substance, was God" (7:187–88). Properly understood, Arnold sarcastically states, "metaphysics, the science treating of *être* and its conditions, will be the science treating of breathing and its conditions. But surely the right science to treat of breathing and its conditions is not metaphysics, but physiology!" And waxing still more sarcastic, he concludes that "perhaps the one man who uses that wonderful abstract word, *essence,* with propriety, will turn out to be, not the metaphysician or the theologian, but the perfumer" (7:188–89). Arnold's sarcasm does not diminish the serious import of his argument: words are simply signs for things, and if we forget the primacy of things and give words a reality of their own, we do so at our peril. Huxley could not have said it better.

Nineteenth-century etymology and philology could, of course, be used not to reduce language to things but rather to fulfil it with a renewed sense of its historical density. Even without referring language back to divine revelation and an initially perfect state, one could see the word as "fossil poetry" and recognize the innumerable accretions of historical usage instead of stripping them away. Much of Trench's celebration of words, for example, does not in any way depend upon metaphysical ideas, as when he states that "language is the amber in which a thousand precious and subtle thoughts have been safely embedded and preserved" and that its enrichment by the usage of previous generations has made the present language "a receptacle of choicest treasures, a storehouse of so much unconscious wisdom, a fit organ for expressing the subtlest distinctions, the tenderest sentiments, the largest thoughts, and the loftiest imaginations, which at any time the heart of men can conceive."[28] And it was with some such notion that agnostic writers like Carlyle and, after his loss of faith, Ruskin, often used etymological definitions to give authority to their words; Ruskin, especially, used the historical accretions of language to generate secular and humanistic myth.[29] But Arnold deliberately rejected such a procedure, calling Ruskin's use of etymology "fanciful" (6:30) and extravagant (3:252). Indeed, in an unpublished letter to Müller he declared that he had not had any intention "of chaffing etymology, but of chaffing *Ruskin* and the incredible nonsense he has permitted himself to talk about it." Arnold's definitions are almost invariably reductive, almost invariably for the purpose of demythologizing language.[30]

Aside from his definition of "being," perhaps the clearest example of reductive etymological definition in Arnold is his Lockian derivation of "spirit" from "breath": "Spirit . . . means literally, we know, only breath" (7:181). But this is a far cry from Locke's statement that spirit *originally* meant breath, for it denies any validity to meanings attached after the word has fallen away from its original material referent. Denying the capacity of language to speak of anything beyond the physical, reducing spirit to breath, Arnold adopts the materialistic vocabulary of Tennyson's blood-red Nature:

> She cries, "A thousand types are gone;
> I care for nothing; all shall go.
>
> "Thou makest thine appeal to me:
> I bring to life, I bring to death;
> The spirit does but mean the breath:
> I know no more."

(*In Memoriam*, section 56)

Whatever his intentions, the effect of Arnold's treatment of language, far from providing a comforting "religious phenomenology" by showing how figures work, empties the figurative vocabulary of religion of its meaning. In religious matters there is no solace in words. Far from clearing the way for a new religion of culture, the establishment of a language that can speak with verifiable accuracy only of *things* legitimizes the Iagoesque epistemology that reduces all abstractions to physical causes, love to "a lust of the blood."

If words have no reality apart from things, they most certainly have no independent authoritative power, and insofar as they are regarded as beyond nature, and therefore magical, they are insidious. Arnold approvingly quoted Joubert to this effect: "Instead of 'grace,' say help, succour, a divine influence, a dew of heaven; then one can come to a right understanding. The word 'grace' is a sort of talisman, all the baneful spell of which can be broken by translating it. The trick of personifying words is a fatal source of mischief in theology" (3:200–201). ApRoberts, commenting on this passage, notes that Arnold approves because "we must know our metaphors for what they are, metaphors; must know our fictions for fictions, or they cease to be useful and make mischief."[31] This is certainly true, but Arnold's rejection of the talismanic power in language more seriously undercuts the possibility of even a phenomenological effectiveness in language than apRoberts realizes. She elsewhere maintains that "Arnold's theory [of language, metaphor, and myth] is antireductive" because "we do not speak of *mere* metaphor, or *mere* myth,"[32] yet Arnold *does* speak of *mere* words when rejecting myths of supernaturalism: "The miracles of our traditional religion, like other miracles, did not happen; its metaphysical proofs of God are mere words" (8:153). He similarly rejected St. Paul's talismanic theory of language, his characteristic method of using profuse quotations from the Old Testament "in order to invest his doctrine with the talismanic virtues of a verbal sanction from the law and the prophets" (6:60): "A Jew himself, he uses the Jewish Scriptures in a Jew's arbitrary and uncritical fashion, as if they had a talismanic character; as if for a doctrine, however true in itself, their confirmation was still necessary, and as if this confirmation was to be got from their mere words alone" (6:22). Evidently this is no more than the Huxleyan and, indeed, universally modern rejection of the ancient and medieval idea that one could prove one's doctrine by the citation of authoritative prior texts, but it does not do much to justify the practical faith in extensive quotations that is evident on every page of Arnold's published works, and even more emphatically in his habit of filling notebooks with choice phrases.

If he had ever found it necessary to justify his technique, Arnold might well have given the same argument he used to defend the retention of hallowed, though poetic and therefore illusive, phrases in the Prayer Book: it was the practice of Jesus himself to use extensive allusions, to adopt the "materialising language and imagery" of the too credulous believers in supernaturalism, even though "it cannot have been because he shared their illusions" (8:138). Indeed, Arnold's description of the language of the Gospels seems perfectly to describe his own rhetorical technique: "And the more we examine the whole language of the Gospels, the more we shall find it to be not language all of the speaker's own, and invented by him for the first time, but to be full of reminiscence and quotation" (8:138–39). This is a *necessary* method because "the power of religious ideas over us does not spring up at call, but is intimately dependent upon particular names and practices and forms of expression which have gone along with it ever since we can remember, and which have created special sentiments in us." This attribution of the power of language over us to "the wonderful force of habit" (8:134) helps to explain Arnold's constant reiteration of key phrases and quotations, but it does not even attempt to establish any power inherent in the words themselves. In fact, even when using Jesus as a precedent, Arnold does not attribute any special fullness or even truth to his words, but actually finds them inaccurate and misleading: "The great reason for continuing to use the familiar language of the religion around us as approximative language, and as poetry, although we cannot take it literally, is that such was also the practice of Jesus. For evidently it was so. And evidently, again, the immense misapprehension of Jesus and of his meaning, by popular religion, comes in part from such having been his practice" (8:137). Even the language of Jesus does not correspond to truth, or even to "things," but only to other words. Allusive and illusive, it draws on misunderstood words and leads to further misunderstanding. Obviously, for Arnold, since Jesus is not Logos, his word is not the Word, and indeed it has no special authority. Once again, even when Arnold sets out to defend or explain the power or force in language, the full implications of his argument reveal that although language may be powerful, even talismanic and magical, it is a baneful magic to the extent that it is illusive.

Arnold's most rigorous, rational, systematic thought about language, found in his writings about religion, tends to demythologize and deconstruct the Word, but in his discussions of poetry and defenses of culture, Arnold nevertheless *assumes* the power in words to cultivate the mind. Arnold, in fact, never presents a sustained analysis of how language may have power, never even analyzes the language of literary texts. Despite apRoberts's contention that Arnold was prepared to analyze religious language by his prior experience with literary language, his first really rigorous discussion of "how figures work," and his first and almost only "close reading" of a text, is his analysis of Paul's Epistle to the Romans in *St. Paul and Protestantism*. Still, from beginning to end he did emphatically believe, as we have seen, in the solacing power of "letters," and especially of poetry. In 1853, for example, he advised Clough to "stick to literature—it is the great comforter, after all,"[33] and repeatedly, over several decades, he exalted poetry as the supreme form of language: "Poetry is nothing less than the most perfect speech of man, that in which he comes nearest to being able to utter the truth" (9:39). And even if, as in "Literature and Science," he could not show *how* poetry worked to ennoble mankind, he never doubted that it did—for Arnold it was an indubitable fact, an eternal law, that poetry, like God, makes for righteousness. He says elsewhere: "First, let us remark the law—the beneficent law—which, in the region of grave and serious composition, connects bad poetry with false moral sentiments. Good rhetoric may consist, in this region, with false moral sentiments, but good poetry, poetry which satisfies, never" (7:10). Arnold further proceeds to connect bad literary criticism with failure "to ponder this law, which is eternal" (7:10). But this is itself rhetoric, no different in structure, if less obviously ludicrous in sense, than, say, Carlyle's affirmation of the eternal law of the gods, who "wish besides pumpkins, that spices and valuable products be grown in their West Indies."[34]

Arnold dogmatically affirms the saving quality of the highest form of human utterance, but does not demonstrate it. Yet though he never, in his entire career, supported his faith by analysis of particular examples, he did continually refer in general terms to two ways in which language may have the power: it may have it by being in "the grand style," or it may have it by possessing "natural magic." But a brief examination of what Arnold meant by these phrases reveals that each is entirely undercut by application of his own critical principles in the religious criticism.

Arnold's first reference to the "grand style" occurs as early as 1849, in a letter to Clough, where it is already associated with both the "nobility of the poet's character" and the "moral effects produced by *style*." One function of poetry, "to add to one's store of thoughts and feelings," can apparently be accomplished by "a sustained tone, numerous allusions, and a grand style."[35] And almost forty years later, in 1888, Arnold was still insisting on the same point—and still unable to account for it: "The mighty power of poetry and art is generally admitted. But where the soul of this power, of this power at its best, chiefly resides, very many of us fail to see. It resides chiefly in the refining and elevation wrought in us by the high and rare excellence of the great style. We may feel the effect without being able to give ourselves clear account of its cause, but the thing is so" (11:331).

In fact, Arnold attempted to explain what he meant by the term just once, in his 1860–61 lectures *On Translating Homer,* and there it was in response to complaints that he had left it too vague. Even then he confessed that, though he could give examples, he could not adequately define it: "Alas! the grand style is the last matter in the world for verbal definition to deal with adequately. One may say of it as is said of faith: 'One must feel it in order to know what it is.' But, as of faith, so too one may say of nobleness, of the grand style: 'Woe to those who know it not!' " (1:188).

Arnold, of course, is craftily turning the tables on his critics—if they do not know what the grand style is, the fault is with *them,* not with his failure to explain. He does, however, venture upon a definition, but the definition says nothing whatever about style, but only about the poet and his subject matter: "Let us try, however, what *can* be said. . . . I think it will be found that the grand style arises in poetry, *when a noble nature, poetically gifted, treats with simplicity or with severity a serious subject.* I think this definition will be found to cover all instances of the grand style in poetry which present themselves. I think it will be found to exclude all poetry which is not in the grand style" (1:188). Clearly, this does not explain how works can communicate the poet's nobility or seriousness, and neither does the subsequent discussion of the "grand style simple" represented by Homer, and the "grand style severe" represented by Milton. Arnold makes a great show of demonstration and explanation, but ultimately it all comes down to the same dogmatic assertion he later used to answer Huxley: "letters," poetry, "the grand style" have a power over us—he cannot explain it, but he knows it by experience, and if we do not, we must take it on faith. Obviously this is hopelessly at odds with Arnold's arguments in the antidogmatic religious books and essays that we must never accept anything on merely verbal authority.

But Arnold does have one other explanation for the effectiveness of the "grand style," an argument that draws it into close affinity with his second famous phrase, "natural magic"—the "grand style" itself is "magical," though the simple is "more *magical*" than the severe. Not surprisingly, Arnold is as hesitant to explain "natural magic" as to explain the "grand style"—it was the natural magic of Guérin, in fact, that he described as providing an "intimate sense" of things, but without explaining whether it enables one to see the object as in itself it really is, or is "illusive." And in "On the Study of Celtic Literature" he defined the "magical way of handling nature" in the emptiest verbal manner possible—by tautology: "in the magical, the eye is on the object, but charm and magic are added" (3:377). Elsewhere, however, he provided a little more substance to his definition, assimilating it to his conception of the "grand style" by once again tracing it to the temperament of the poet: "This faculty always has for its basis a peculiar temperament, an extraordinary delicacy of organisation and susceptibility to impressions" (3:30). But this too is ultimately tautological: natural magic in poetry is produced by poets with a faculty for natural magic.

Obviously, one is tempted to say, the term "natural magic" cannot be defined because, as Arnold would say, it is figurative, "approximative," a term "thrown out." But then, what does it approximate? What is it thrown out at? Either it is thrown out at nothing at all, and is therefore an "empty signifier," or at a kind of sacred mystery and is therefore itself magical, a kind of talisman. The rationalist in Arnold, of course, rejects the idea of talismanic language, but then again he also rejects the logocentric, religious view of a sacred language that he nevertheless sets forth in his most compelling description of "natural magic": "in Keats and Guérin, in whom the faculty of naturalistic interpretation is overpoweringly predominant, the natural magic is perfect; when they speak of the world they speak like Adam naming by divine inspiration the creatures; their expression corresponds with the thing's essential reality" (3:34).[36] This, no doubt, is poetic also—and illusive. The crucially important point is that Arnold's demystifying of language leaves him with no possible arguments—no possible language—for setting forth the faith in poetic language that he nevertheless clings to. He has accepted what Kenneth Burke describes as "the typically scientist view of the relation between science and magic," in which "scientific knowledge is . . . presented as a terminology that gives an accurate and critically tested description of reality; and magic is presented as antithetical to such science." The inevitable result of these assumptions is that "one . . . confronts a flat choice between a civilized vocabulary of scientific description and a savage vocabulary of magical incantation."[37] Arnold's simultaneous acceptance of the scientific language and use of the mystifying term "natural magic" indicates just how thoroughly he was caught between two worlds. He certainly entertains the belief that the magic in language, its undoubted power over the feelings, *may* correspond to some kind of truth, that intuition and imagination *may* be valid ways of knowing, but he is uncomfortable without scientific certitude. Conversely, he is convinced of the truth of scientific language, but uncomfortable with its aridity. In another time and place,

Arnold might well have been able to adopt a moderate position concerning the nature of poetic language, but in Victorian England the great debate between the religious faithful and the "men of fact" polarized the issue of language. One could, it seemed, believe in the power of words, or in the power of facts. Arnold wanted to believe in both, but found it difficult to reconcile the apparent opposition between mind and nature, words and things.

Analysis of Arnold's simultaneous mystification and demystification of poetic language suggests, I think, three general implications for the study of his poetry. First, as a poet and lover of poetry he felt himself to have been born, as he always said, into a difficult age, an age of "*blankness* and *barrenness,* and *unpoetrylessness.*"[38] The charge against the age is unfair, of course, and merely reflects Arnold's incapacity to see how other writers responded richly and fully to the challenges of postromanticism, but it indicates his sense of oppression in an empirical age. It is not surprising that the four lines he set forth as an indisputable example of the grand style were Milton's description of the plight of the poet in bad times:

> Standing on earth, not rapt above the pole,
> More safe I sing with mortal voice, unchanged
> To hoarse or mute, though fall'n on evil days,
> On evil days though fall'n, and evil tongues.

Arnold has usually been recognized, as he expected to be, as the very embodiment of the mid-Victorian Zeitgeist, but the extent to which he epitomizes the pathos of the poet's irremediable loss of linguistic plenitude has perhaps not been appreciated. It was in the nineteenth century, as Michel Foucault argues, that the loss of an authoritative, primal Word condemned literature to turn in upon itself, and to reveal "not the sovereignty of a primal discourse, but the fact that we are already, before the very least of our words, governed or paralysed by language."[39] Or, as Foucault again says, in words that almost seem to echo Arnold's sense of the critic in the wilderness, starting in the nineteenth century, "we no longer have that primary, that absolutely initial, word upon which the infinite movement of discourse was founded and by which it was limited; henceforth, language was to grow with no point of departure, no end, and no promise. It is the traversal of this futile yet fundamental space that the text of literature traces from day to day."[40] Caught in this historical fold, Arnold wanted still to refer his language outward, toward truth and purposiveness, and so he fought against the recognition he could not wholly avoid, that poetic language can only point to itself or throw itself outward into the void. Above all Arnold desired literature to have a powerful, clear effect on the world, but his analysis of language made him very much a part of what Foucault calls the nineteenth-century's dissolution of the link between knowledge and language: in a scientific understanding, *things,* not words, are primary. And though Arnold could not see this far, the ultimate result of such thinking was to generate a confrontation between "a knowledge closed in upon itself and a pure language that had become, in nature and function, enigmatic—something that has been called, since that time, *Literature.*"[41] Inevitably, Arnold's formula to unite words and things in a criticism that sees "the object as in itself it really is" becomes qualified with Pater's phenomenological addition that "the first step . . . is to know one's own impression as it really is," and becomes entirely turned in upon itself in Wilde's reversal: "the primary aim of the critic is to see the object as in itself it really is not."[42]

The second important implication of Arnold's analysis of language is closely related. Cutting himself off from the original, primal, sacred word, he also cut himself off as a poet from his immediate poetic predecessors. Arnold's complex relationship with the romantic poets has been much discussed, often to make the point that his failure to accept romantic models was his poetic downfall. Critics have occasionally been rather censorious: because Arnold "would not or could not see" the need to develop the high romantic mode, "the spiritual unity proclaimed by the great Romantic writers is broken in his hands. Poetry and science, imagination and thought, knowledge and being, fall apart, and no centre is left."[43] Certainly it is true that Arnold could not accept the logocentric romantic epistemology that fused perception and object in language, but he is hardly to be blamed for that—from the perspective of mid-Victorian scientific thought, Wordsworthian romanticism and Wordsworthian language were simply impossible. Arnold was not a belated poet in the sense that he was coming at the end of an exhausted poetic tradition in which everything had been said, but in the sense that he was born into an age in which a modern, skeptical, "scientific" epistemology divided sharply between pointless verbal delusion and strict empirical veracity. The modern sense expressed in the closing years of the romantic period by Peacock and Macaulay had become pervasive: sadly, mankind had become too knowledgeable to believe in the comforting illusions of poetry—language should express the truth insofar as it is able, and the most truthful language is scientific.

Other poets were able to write brilliantly and copiously under these circumstances: Browning by concerning himself more with limited human perceptions than with objective truth, Tennyson by retaining a faith in the intuitive truths of the imagination, Swinburne by self-conscious mythmaking, and others such as Rossetti and Morris by frankly accepting a split between objective truth and aesthetic purpose. Nevertheless, it was all but inevitable that Arnold, with his empirical rationalism and his emphatic faith in the moral purposiveness of "letters," should see the task of his age as criticism, not poetry.

The third general implication of Arnold's vacillation between faith in the power of language and doubt as to how it comes about is that, obviously, he had no strong theory of language, and that this is likely to affect him profoundly as a practicing poet. Indeed, I have concentrated entirely, in this chapter, on Arnold's more and less explicit comments about language in his prose writings, but it is in his poetry—written mostly before the prose—that Arnold had to struggle not just to describe poetic language, but to use it. It was in his poetry that he had to face the question he always avoided in prose: *how* can poetic language be effective? Uncertainty in such matters ends up creating a degree of confusion for the writer of prose, but if Harold Bloom is right, it should be fatal for the poet. Bloom asserts that "either one can believe in a magical theory of language, as the Kabbalists, many poets, and Walter Benjamin did, or else one must yield to thoroughgoing linguistic nihilism, which in its most refined form is the mode now called Deconstruction." It does not matter which the poet chooses, as long as his "theory of language be extreme and uncompromising enough": "Either the new poet fights to win freedom from dearth, or from plenitude, but if the antagonist be moderate, then the agon will not take place, and no fresh sublimity will be won."[44] Bloom has little respect for Arnold as a poet, perhaps because, caught as always in the middle, he could not assume the Bloomian role of poet-warrior. But the tensions and conflicts that arise in his poetry as a result of his very uncertainties, his very tentativeness about language, seem to me more paradigmatic for the modern poet's plight than does Bloom's image of a battlefield between strong poets armed with strong theories of language. Arnold is a poet of the modern world in its lack of strong beliefs, its uncertainty and confusion. Not a heroic poet-warrior, he is perhaps a confused straggler on the modern darkling plain, where ignorant armies clash by night.

My argument, in the following chapters, will be that the best in Arnold's poetry results from a tension between his poetic ambition and his doubts about his medium. In chapter one I argue that Arnold's poetry, from the very beginning, incessantly demonstrates a need to find an infallible, authoritative language, a voice of God or at the very least a voice that would harmonize with the natural world, and that of course it consistently fails to find it. The next chapter examines Arnold's attempt to employ classical themes and forms, to exploit the great tradition, in order to find a way to avoid entrapment in a merely verbal order. The third chapter looks at some of Arnold's best poems as experiments in the mode of romance, defined here as a kind of errantry or questing, and sees him as entrapped within a language and tradition that is inevitably self-referential, self-enclosed. The final chapter considers Arnold's most earnest attempts to escape the claustrophobic confines of intertextual entrapment in his love poetry, and argues that the more he attempts to be entirely sincere, to speak from himself, the more he is subverted by a language that cannot escape the contamination of the tradition. The third and fourth chapters both argue that in poem after poem Arnold sets out to say one thing, acknowledges its inevitable fallaciousness, and deliberately undercuts himself. Further, to a greater extent than has been recognized, Arnold's poetry is still more deeply undermined as the poet is unconsciously betrayed by his doubts about poetry and the poetic tradition. The result, in most of the best poems, is that his overt purposes are subverted by a corrosive subtext and that he finds himself constantly struggling, unsuccessfully, to find words that will refer not just to other words, but to *things,* to *reality.* The tension produced in Arnold's poetry, whether deliberate or not, is a major source of its strength and, further, the peculiar dynamics of this poetry make it of particular interest to the postmodernist criticism that has more often than not disparaged Arnold as the spokesman of an outmoded traditionalism. Ironically, Arnold, as a poet, is largely disabled by an overwhelming tradition that he cannot avoid and cannot control.

I

The Early Poetry: Distant Voices

ARNOLD'S LIFELONG concern with defining the modern role of the poet and of poetry began to appear in his earliest work and became the dominant thematic interest of his first book. *The Strayed Reveller, and Other Poems* (1849) returns over and over again to questions about the poet's relation to his age, his relation to nature, his vision, his voice, his language. Either directly or indirectly almost every poem in the volume reflects what critics have generally recognized as Arnold's persistent determination "to discover what poetry in his age could be."[1] Arnold established his primary interest at the outset with a Greek motto that laments the fate of the belated poet. The motto, from a fragment by Choerilus of Samos, has been translated by E. H. Coleridge: "Yea, blessed is the servant of the Muses, who in days of old ere the meadow was mown, was skilled in song. But now, when all is apportioned and a bound is placed to the arts, we are left behind like stragglers who drop in at the tail end of a race."[2] The epigraph seems clearly to suggest the familiar problem of the belated poet, a dearth of fresh material—as D. G. Rossetti was to say, "It has all been said and written."[3] But the problem of how to become a skilled servant of the Muse in the nineteenth century turns out, for Arnold, to have little to do with whether the Muse has squandered all her gifts on earlier generations. The question is whether she ever had or could have a gift of song worth having in the modern world.

Arnold suggested in a letter to Clough that the modern poet is not troubled by a lack of unused material, but by a glut: "The poet's matter being *the hitherto experience of the world, and his own,* increases with every century. . . . For me you may often hear my sinews cracking under the effort to unite matter."[4] The problem, for

Arnold, was to reduce the chaos of modern experience to something comprehensible and meaningful. Failure to do so was the bane of modern poetry—Browning and Keats, he told Clough, failed because they did not "understand that they must begin with an Idea of the world in order not to be prevailed over by the world's multitudinousness."[5] And somewhat later he accused Clough of failing for the same reason: "You would never take your assiette as something determined final and unchangeable for you and proceed to work away on the basis of that: but were always poking and patching and cobbling at the assiette itself—you could never finally, as it seemed—'resolve to be thyself.' "[6] As Arnold's quotation from his own "Self-Dependence" makes clear, the principle of organization, or "Idea of the world," or "assiette," had first to organize the self before it could organize the world. Arnold's analysis of Clough was, as often, veiled self-analysis. In an 1849 letter to his sister he stated bluntly that his own problems as a poet came from his inability to overcome or control multitudinousness in either himself or his poetry: "The true reason why parts suit you while others do not is that my poems are fragments—*i.e.* that I am fragments, while you are a whole; the whole effect of my poems is quite vague & indeterminate—this is their weakness; a person therefore who endeavored to make them accord would only lose his labor; and a person who has any inward completeness can at best only like parts of them; in fact such a person stands firmly and knows what he is about while the poems stagger weakly & are at their wits end."[7]

Modern critics have tended—with good reason, I think—to agree with Arnold's self-assessment, remarking on the poet's "characteristic tone of indecision" and on the "vitiating uncertainty of tone within the poems."[8] The problem for Arnold as a belated or postromantic poet was not to find material but to find a consistent, meaningful point of view that would integrate his subjective personality, organize the chaos of the outside world, and bring self and other into harmony. He needed both an "Idea of the world" that would enable him to see life steadily and see it whole, and a justification of it that would save him from endless patching and cobbling. Consequently, as E. D. H. Johnson has said, much of his early poetry "is the record of the author's search for a principle of authority conformable alike to his subjective consciousness and to some mode of belief sanctioned by tradition."[9] He needed a trustworthy Muse, a voice that would come from without, yet speak from within.

Early Voices

Arnold's most pressing problem as an aspiring poet was not the difficulty of choosing between competing philosophies or faiths but the difficulty of finding authoritative expression in a multitudinous and skeptical age. He was, in other words, an author in need of an authorized vision, or style, or—in the word he most favors in the early poems—an authorized and authoritative "voice." As W. S. Johnson has argued, Arnold was characteristically Victorian in his uncertainty about how to find and use his own voice, and even about how to find out what his own voice was: "The great era of prophetic poets and poetic prophets is almost unanimous in its desire for a largely impersonal voice, whether its source be revelation, ecclesiastical authority, the world-soul, physical science, or some other eternal 'not ourselves' which makes for knowledge and perhaps for righteousness. But along with this desire goes an ineluctable urge to examine and project the writer's personality."[10]

In some obvious ways the problem of finding an appropriate tone and voice was immediate, practical, and pressing for a young poet. Arnold's uncertainties appear dramatically in his treatment of a very early fragment (probably written in 1844):

> Night comes; with Night comes Silence, hand in hand;
> With Night comes Silence, and with that, Repose;
> And pillows on her cold white breast and locks
> Within the marble prison of her arms
> The Poet's fond and feverish melancholy;
> Cuts short the feignings of fantastic grief,
> Freezes the sweet strain on the parted lips,
> And steals the honied music of his tongue.

The self-conscious echoing of an earlier poetic tradition is, of course, characteristic of the juvenilia of most poets—a kind of poetic lalling—but the personification, alliteration, and especially the flat, echoic repetition in the first two lines all seem to exaggerate the apprentice poet's attempt to summon the profundity of a bardic voice. The speaker here is plainly "The Poet," and his formulaic language lacks the suppleness, the interiority, and especially the tact to "project the writer's personality." Of course Arnold was aware of this as he mocked the "fond and feverish melancholy" and the "fantastic grief" of his poet, but the full significance of the piece extended, perhaps, beyond his conscious control. The Poet's utterance, however false, has at least the authenticity of emanating from within, of living on his parted lips and in his voice, but Night, like the writing of the lines, silences, freezes, and imprisons the utterance. The written lines, in their fixedness and monumental impersonality, have little resemblance to actual communication in speech—if spoken to someone they would, of course, sound ridiculous.[11] Consequently when Arnold did address himself to a real audience, when he was trying to convey something of his own personality in a letter to Clough, he revised the lines to distance himself so far from his real concern about poetic utterance that they ceased to describe his own poetic apprenticeship, and became a whimsical, supercilious, class-conscious burlesque of "The 'Usher's' rash and feverish Melancholy."[12] Clearly, Arnold was embarrassed by his bardic mask and conscious of how close his profundity had already come to burlesque. But the crucial point is that the lines, now frozen as a text, hardly represent the Wordsworthian conception of poetry as words spoken by a man to his fellow man—rather they have become an object from which the poet can ironically detach himself. If he is really to be a man speaking to mankind—or even just to Clough—he must find a speaking voice. If he does not, he is as trapped in his own silence as his poet-usher is in the silence of Night.

Arnold could write a kind of poetry by impersonally adopting traditional poetic language, but such language lacked the authenticity of his own voice, and was useless in communicating anything genuine. He certainly came to realize this quickly—perhaps in the act of writing to Clough—and at some later point he still further revised the lines, allowing the Poet to remain in place of the lowly Usher, but now writing in "false breath" over "sweet strain" and "shallow" music over "honied" music. Significantly, though, he left the original phrases uncanceled, perhaps because he was aware that the "sweet strain" was simultaneously "false breath," that "honied music" was simultaneously "shallow."

Arnold's apprentice poems show in various ways his difficulties in finding an authentic, distinctive voice. In his Rugby prize poem, "Alaric at Rome," his tone was boldly confident, and so was his voice. A schoolmate recalled that he recited the poem with a "roll and vigour . . . unlike the timid utterance of the ordinary school poet."[13] But the poem is so obviously Byronic that the voice can hardly be called Arnold's own. Similarly, "Cromwell," the Newdigate prize poem of 1843, gains its confident tone largely by mimicry of Tennyson, Wordsworth, and others. But "Cromwell" also raises the issue in a thematic way by repeatedly referring to authoritative voices in nature. Admittedly borrowing from a sonnet by Wordsworth, Arnold described the voices of sea and mountain and their call to freedom. The sea's is a "voice of fear," a "mystic tone" (ll. 2, 4), and the "high sounds that mountain children hear" are "Freedom's mystic language" (ll. 27, 29). The authoritative language of nature adds authority to the utterance of the poet. But even the very young Arnold seems to have been somewhat ambivalent about such voices. In the first place, since Cromwell did not grow up near either the sea or the mountains, the point of the poem is that he did not hear any voices, but loved freedom anyway—the voices are unheard and unnecessary. Further, the description of the sea's voice is ambivalent:

> Sounds of deep import—voices that beguile
> Age of its tears and childhood of its smile,
> To yearn with speechless impulse to the free
> And gladsome greetings of the buoyant sea!
>
> (ll. 5–8)

The voice produces not profound human speech but profound human speechlessness, and it does not inform but beguiles. Obviously it is unfair to emphasize the uncontrolled and very likely unintended implications of poetic juvenilia, but the sense that authoritative voices have become either silent or misleading soon became a major theme for Arnold, and a concern with the relation between transcendent voices and human knowledge was clearly already worrying him in 1843.

Arnold was evidently vaguely aware even earlier that the modern poet's inability to find an authoritative voice was ultimately related to the loss of the voice of God, the spoken Word that Christian and romantic poets, in different ways, could echo to find harmony between the inner self and outward reality. As early as 1836 he was aware that any "voice" heard in nature is only supplied by "Fancy's power,"[14] and by 1838 he was writing a poem explicitly about the withdrawal of God's voice. The subject of the poem was supplied by Flavius Josephus' *The Jewish War,* part of which is quoted in an epigraph: "The Spirit of God was said during the Siege of Jerusalem by those who kept watch there to have departed from the Temple at night with a rushing noise." Arnold immediately associated the withdrawal of God with song: "Land of the East! Around thy shores are flung / By fancy's hand the glittering stores of song" (ll. 1–2). Song is still present, but only as fancy puts it there, and it is, oddly, not heard, but *seen,* "glittering." The visual adjective is no accident—the whole of the first section (ll. 1–26) describes the *visions* of the past that fancy conjures up to sight, and the following section is emphatic about the silence of the actual present: "But all is silent now. On Salem's hill / God's voice, that talked of old with man, is still" (ll. 27–28). And the result is confusion and destruction, "wild eddyings of the whirling storm" (l. 29). Even though the poem ends with "Hope" that "still would *picture* dreams" (l. 51, my emphasis), no reassuring voice is available in the present. Rather, as is characteristic of Arnold from beginning to end of his poetic career, humanity is left between a past authenticated by God's presence manifested in his voice and an unreachable future. But the present is a wasteland in which God's voice is not heard.

Arnold's early interest in the relation of God's voice to human utterance can perhaps be best understood with reference to a later manifestation of the same concern. In his 1844 sonnet "Written in Butler's Sermons" Arnold wrote of the vanity of Butler's efforts to find the hidden sources of human identity, and over thirty years later he took up the same topic in "Bishop Butler and the Zeit-

Geist." In the essay he accused Butler of making the assumption—unscientific, un-Newtonian, and "fantastic" because unverifiable—that God put his benevolent nature into man and that compassion is therefore a law of human nature. He countered with the explanation—scientific, because he empirically felt it to be so—that compassion is an instinct. Obviously, Arnold's case was Butler's from the start, since both assumed an innate benevolence in mankind, but Arnold, eager to de-anthropomorphize the deity, explicitly denied the grounds of Butler's assertion, explicitly denied, that is, that God is the "author of our being." Arnold's problem, however, was that his quasi science gave him no effective vocabulary, so he used Butler's language "poetically" and agreed that human nature is "the voice of God within us." The result is an interesting but disconcerting implication that the ground of our being is an unauthored voice. With no author there can be no authority; with the "voice of God" reduced to an empty signifier, we become hollow men, pipes for any passing wind to play upon. If Arnold's argument is logically extended to its full implications, as it must be if his real difficulties are to be fully understood, the human voice neither resonates with the truth of an Eternal Verity nor even expresses the unutterable ultimate identity of the speaker.

Arnold's explicit concern with finding an authenticating voice—or at the very least, an appropriate voice for himself—is not isolated to a few juvenile pieces, but surfaces with remarkable frequency throughout his works. Indeed, as one fairly obvious quantitative indication, the word *voice* appears no less than 107 times in the Arnold concordance.[15] One reason for this may be that despite his lifelong insistence on the power of "letters," Arnold shared the general view that what is written in letters is secondary, and what is oral is primary. He would have agreed with Newman that when words "have to be conveyed to the ends of the earth, or perpetuated for the benefit of posterity, they must be written down, that is, reduced to the shape of literature." But as Newman said, though literature necessarily silences voice, it is distinguished from other forms of the written word by its attempt to simulate voice, to imitate the power and intimacy, the presence, of the spoken word.

Though literature must accept the impersonality of print, it must nevertheless express the personality, the individual "ideas and feelings personal to" the author, "proper to himself, in the same sense as his voice, his air, his countenance, his carriage, and his action are personal." It is precisely in its possession of something like voice that the language of literature differs from the language of science—as Newman said also of slang, literature "breathes of the personal." It would seem that Arnold, later in life, might have made an analogous case to defend literature against science, might have agreed with Newman that in its approximation to voice, "literature expresses, not objective truth, as it is called, but subjective; not things, but thoughts."[16] Unlike Newman, however, Arnold could not hear the voice of God, and so could not be sure that "subjective" truth was truth at all, or that there could be any truth apart from "things." If such a merely personal voice is the distinguishing mark of literature, then how is literature to achieve the transpersonal authority that Arnold sought for it?

Many of the poems in the 1849 volume are explicitly concerned with this question, but it is especially central to those written in 1843 and 1844, particularly "Stagirius," "The Voice," "Written in Emerson's Essays," "Shakespeare," "Mycerinus," and "The New Sirens." Perhaps the most straightforward poetic expression of the need for a transcendent voice and the feebleness of the merely human voice is offered in "Stagirius," aptly described by Alan Roper as "an unremarkable piece whose chief interest lies in its summary enumeration of almost every pessimistic topic in the 1849 volume."[17] Though poetically unremarkable, the poem *is* doctrinally central, and not just in its list of woes but in its sense of their cause. Much as in his fragmentary lines about the Poet's "feverish melancholy," Arnold sets out a voice of romantic despair and ironically detaches himself from it even as it expresses his own malaise—the ascetic monk, after all, is not Arnold, and so presumably his Shelleyan voice is not Arnold's either. Nevertheless, the desire for a calming, healing voice from God *is* entirely Arnoldian:

(ll. 49–56) O let the false dream fly,
Where our sick souls do lie

Tossing continually!
O where thy voice doth come
Let all doubts be dumb,
Let all worlds be mild,
All strifes be reconciled,
All pains beguiled!

And even more emphatically Arnoldian is the sense that without the voice of God, other voices are not merely ineffectual but demonic and idolatrous:

When the soul, growing clearer,
Sees God no nearer;
When the soul, mounting higher,
To God comes no nigher,
But the arch-fiend Pride
Mounts at her side,
Foiling her high emprise,
Sealing her eagle eyes,
(ll. 14–29) And, when she fain would soar,
Makes idols to adore,
Changing the pure emotion
Of her high devotion,
To a skin-deep sense
Of her own eloquence;
Strong to deceive, strong to enslave—
Save, oh! save.

The sentiment is, however, not merely Arnoldian but Victorian generally: the subjectivity of romanticism is too turned inward, too lacking in outward validation, and so becomes narcissistic, self-idolatrous. It is the fate of the soul, for example, in Tennyson's "The Palace of Art," and of his St. Simeon Stylites, and of the much later Dorian Gray. But perhaps the most intriguing analogy is to Hopkins, a monk like Stagirius who sometimes sensed that his own voice may not be in harmony with God's, and that his utterance may therefore be of narcissistic pride, the sin of Lucifer who struck a false note in the choirs of heaven by singing of himself and not of

God. Lucifer's fall from harmony with the voice of God was the first sin of pride, "a dwelling on his own beauty, an instressing of his own inscape, . . . a sounding, as they say, of his own trumpet and a hymn in his own praise," and of course all subsequent singing that fails to harmonize with God's voice is demonic, a repetition of the sin of the fallen angels, who "would not listen to the note which summoned each to his own place . . . ; they gathered rather closer and closer home under Lucifer's lead and drowned it, raising a countermusic and countertemple and altar, a counterpoint of dissonance, and not of harmony."[18]

Obviously, Arnold is not Hopkins and would not use these terms, but the themes of "Stagirius" suggest that for him, too, the language of romantic aspiration is self-indulgent, self-deceptive, and idolatrous—self-singing. The ideal of voice in poetry, as opposed to the merely labeling vocabulary of science (words for things) ought to be that it is, or seems to be, immediate, alive, and integrative. Because voice emanates from within, it links the inner world of the speaker with the outside; it reverberates from within to sound the depths without, and so goes beyond and behind the visual world of surfaces.[19] But for Stagirius, and for Arnold, the voice does not resonate with the harmony of the spheres or find an echo in the eternal I Am—far from piercing the superficial, it is itself superficial, devoted only "To a skin-deep sense / Of her own eloquence."

The sense of a demonic element in voice emerges in a somewhat different fashion in the poem aptly entitled "The Voice." The poem describes an attractive, tempting voice, heard in the past and occasionally welling up into present consciousness to disturb the gloom with an apparently inappropriate joyousness, like

A wild rose climbing up a mouldering wall—
(ll. 20–22) A gush of sunbeams through a ruined hall—
Strains of glad music at a funeral.

The poem is enigmatic to the extent that the original owner of the voice is never identified, and criticism of it has tended to be concerned with biographical speculations, most of which suggest Newman or Thomas Arnold as the original speaker. But in any case the voice represents a temptation to acquiescence (in whatever fixed belief) that has been and must continue to be sternly resisted:

Those lute-like tones which in the bygone year
    Did steal into mine ear—
(ll. 35–40) Blew such a thrilling summons to my will,
    Yet could not shake it;
Made my tossed heart its very life-blood spill,
    Yet could not break it.

Perhaps whom the voice belonged to is less important than the fact that the voice is perceived as both enticing and deceptive. Certainly it is enticing—it seems to offer precisely the "assiette," and precisely the authority that Arnold sought. Further, its musical tones are seductive in ways that an unspoken language could never be, especially since, having been internalized, the voice seems to have mysterious origins within the self:

O unforgotten voice, thy accents come,
(ll. 29–31) Like wanderers from the world's extremity,
    Unto their ancient home!

The voice is resisted, but at considerable cost, since resistance means to stand alone, isolated—separated from both inner impulses and the convictions of others. By implication, no voice, however beautiful, should be able to sway the analytic reason. But if this is so, poetry and eloquence are seductions to be wary of.

The speaker of the poem has deliberately and sternly resisted the seductive summons of the voice, and yet in other ways the poem implies, even if only accidentally, that voices are not always resistible. To begin with, the speaking voice of the poem is plainly influenced by another voice from the past: the voice of Shelley is heard throughout, though most clearly in the first four lines:

As the kindling glances,
    Queen-like and clear,
Which the bright moon lances
    From her tranquil sphere.

As Allott notes, the lines echo Shelley's "To a Skylark":

Keen as are the arrows
Of that silver sphere
Whose intense lamp narrows
In the white dawn clear.
(ll. 21–24)

My point is not just that this is a case of literary borrowing, but that even though the speaker prides himself on resisting other voices, his utterance is dependent upon an "unforgotten voice" that has become so interiorized as to seem his own. Arnold himself realized—at least in 1869—that he was not in control of his own voice: "In 'The Voice' the falsetto rages too furiously; I can do nothing with it; ditto in 'Stagirius.'"[20] Language works in far more complicated ways than the poem explicitly states, and is far more difficult to control. Alien voices are not merely seductive, but insidious. The mysterious origin, the "ancient home," of any interiorized voice is inaccessible to reason or even consciousness. The poet cannot always choose what to accept and what to reject: language has a vitality beyond his reach and influences him in mysterious ways.

Indeed, one passage in the poem strangely emphasizes the uncontrollable vitality of language. The final stanza describes the ultimate ineffectuality of the immaterial voice:

In vain, all, all, in vain,
They beat upon mine ear again,
Those melancholy tones.

It is probably less than deliberate but more than coincidental that the poem in which Shelley's "falsetto" rages uncontrollably anticipates Arnold's famous characterization of Shelley as a "beautiful and ineffectual angel, beating in the void his luminous wings in vain" (9:237). The association of the resisted voice with the fallen angels in Chaos is at the very least suggestive, especially since Arnold repeatedly used the image to describe heretical writings. J. A. Froude's *Nemesis of Faith,* for example, was "mere fume and vanity": he was "beating the air."[21] Francis Newman, heretically disagreeing with Arnold about Homer, was also "beating the air" (1:175), and even John Wesley "beat his wings in vain" (6:46). Arnold was not, of course, reacting to any particular doctrine but to the inevitable ineffectuality of any attempt to speak of a noumenal realm. The text that apparently lies behind all of Arnold's uses of the figure (though it is ultimately traceable to St. Paul: "so fight I, not as one that beateth the air" [1 Cor. 9:26]) makes this abundantly clear, for it is Joubert's ambivalent description of the beauty but ultimate ineffectuality of Plato. Arnold admiringly translated the passage in 1863: " 'Plato loses himself in the void' (he says again); 'but one sees the play of his wings, one hears their rustle.' And the conclusion is: 'It is good to breathe his air, but not to live upon him' " (3:203). Despite the admirable beauty of some of their writings, these beaters of the air have in common with Shelley "the incurable fault . . . of unsubstantiality." Their words, detached from things, can at best achieve the ephemeral being of voice. However beautifully a voice disturbs the air, it remains insubstantial—one could not live upon it any more than Hamlet could "eat the air, promise-crammed."

Some of the early poems show somewhat more hope that a sustaining voice, a truthful voice, might be heard. The sonnet "Shakespeare," for example, ends with the affirmation of a triumphant utterance—triumphant at least in honesty and comprehensiveness:

All pains the immortal spirit must endure,
(ll. 12–14) All weakness which impairs, all griefs which bow,
Find their sole voice in that victorious brow.

But even here the poet's uncertainty is perhaps revealed in the incongruity of a brow's voice (Arnold did not much improve the situation by changing "voice" to "speech" in 1877). Obviously, Arnold has visualized the brow, not heard the voice. Despite the present tense, Shakespeare's voice, unlike his portrait, has no living presence for the poet. But the main point of the sonnet is that the source of Shakespeare's oracular knowledge is mysterious (rather like the voice in "The Voice"), and that the oracle is now mute:

Others abide our question. Thou art free.
We ask and ask—Thou smilest and art still,
(ll. 1–8) Out-topping knowledge. For the loftiest hill,
Who to the stars uncrowns his majesty,

Planting his steadfast footsteps in the sea,
Making the heaven of heavens his dwelling-place,
Spares but the cloudy border of his base
To the foiled searching of mortality.

Once again, the portrait is seen, but the voice is not heard. Very strangely in a poem celebrating a poet, Shakespeare's most notable trait is an inscrutable silence. The point is reinforced by a submerged voice within the text, for Arnold's echo of Cowper's "Light Shining out of Darkness" assimilates the silence and mystery of Shakespeare with the inscrutability of God, who

moves in a mysterious way,
His wonders to perform;
He plants his footsteps in the sea,
And rides upon the storm.
(ll. 1–4)

Even Shakespeare's smile, apparently only conjectured at since it is above the clouds, may derive from the hidden smile of Cowper's God: "Behind a frowning providence / He hides a smiling face" (ll. 15–16). Whether or not Arnold intended it, the authority of Shakespeare's voice is analogous to the authoritative voice of God, and is fraught with the same problems: both voices are now silent and their truth must be taken on faith. Even Shakespeare's voice, if it is detached from a human source as it virtually is in the sonnet, becomes a kind of mystery of faith. Of course Arnold presumably intended to suggest that Shakespeare's grasp of human affairs transcended ordinary human subjectivity and bias, that it represents genuine objective *truth*—but deifying the bard only returns Arnold to the problem that the voice of God is withdrawn from the world, that there are no oracles.

Nevertheless, in the remarkable sonnet "Written in Emerson's Essays" an oracular voice is exactly what the poet claims to hear:

"O monstrous, dead, unprofitable world,
That thou canst hear, and hearing hold thy way!
A voice oracular hath pealed to-day,
To-day a hero's banner is unfurled;

Hast thou no lip for welcome?"—So I said.
Man after man, the world smiled and passed by;
A smile of wistful incredulity
As though one spake of life unto the dead—

Scornful, and strange, and sorrowful, and full
Of bitter knowledge. Yet the will is free;
Strong is the soul, and wise, and beautiful;
The seeds of godlike power are in us still;
Gods are we, bards, saints, heroes, if we will!—
Dumb judges, answer, truth or mockery?

The sonnet insists upon the orality of oracles—the *voice* of Emerson, the *speech* of his prophet, the *silence* of a world that has "no lip for welcome." And indeed, even many years later, in his 1884 essay on Emerson, it was as a living voice that Arnold remembered Emerson and the other oracles of his youth:

> *Forty years ago, when I was an undergraduate at Oxford, voices were in the air there which haunt my memory still. . . . there came to us in that old Oxford time a voice, also, from this side of the Atlantic,—a clear and pure voice, which for my ear, at any rate, brought a strain as new, and moving, and unforgettable, as the strain of Newman, or Carlyle, or Goethe. . . . [Emerson] was your Newman, your man of soul and genius visible to you in the flesh, speaking to your bodily ears, a present object for your heart and imagination. That is surely the most potent of all influences! nothing can come up to it.* (9:165, 167)

Underlying the flight of rhetoric is the notion of the incarnate word, the word made flesh. The Christian resonance is present in the sonnet as well, in an echo of a passage in Proverbs understood by Christians as a prefiguration of Christ's mission: "Wisdom crieth without; she uttereth her voice in the streets: She crieth in the chief place of concourse, in the openings of the gates: in the city she uttereth her words, *saying,* How long, ye simple ones, will ye love simplicity? and the scorners delight in their scorning, and fools hate knowledge? Turn you at my reproof: behold, I will pour out my spirit unto you, I will make known my words unto you. Because I have called, and ye refused . . ." (Proverbs 1:20–24). But despite this strong subtextual injunction to accept the call of wisdom, when Arnold later looked back on his early oracles he realized that "it is not always pleasant to ask oneself questions about the friends of one's youth; they cannot always well support it" (10:168). In retrospect, the potent voice of Newman had only attempted to solve modern "doubts and difficulties" with "a solution which, to speak frankly, is impossible" (10:165), and Emerson, the American Newman, is also found wanting, is found, in fact, occasionally "unsound" (10:172).

Arnold's late reservations about the absolute potency of Emerson's voice are already abundantly present in the sonnet, though more as a troubling undercurrent of uncertainty and contradiction than as a reasoned assessment. There is a clear disparity between the sonnet's insistence on orality and its title's awareness that the poem "Written in Emerson's Essays" is at least two removes from the spoken word. Also the quotation marks around the opening speech and the laconic distancing of them in the past tense ("So I said") removes the sonnet still further from the presence of the living word—even the "speaker's" own. And of course the sonnet acknowledges that the supposedly living word fails to resurrect the "dead," and further that it is the scornful world that has "knowledge," however "bitter" it may be. The skeptics, in fact, seemed at first to be entirely in the right, since the original wording of the last line had seemed to dismiss the oracle: "O barren boast, o joyless Mockery." For that matter, even the final line Arnold retained insists on the continued silence of the skeptical world and leaves unanswered whether the oracle is "truth or mockery." As W. S. Johnson has well said, the sonnet on Shakespeare "moves from questioning to victorious silence" and that on Emerson "moves from proclamation to questioning, but for each poem the end is silence."[22] In each the oracle, whether truthful or deceptive, is silent—no authoritative voice continues to peal by the end of the sonnets. Both poems finally must be said to side—tacitly, of course—with the silent and scornful world.

A dubious oracle of a somewhat different sort is the subject of "Mycerinus," arguably Arnold's first fully successful poem. "Mycerinus" is, at the very least, the best of Arnold's poems of 1844, perhaps because in it he was able to objectify and dramatize the issues that obsessed him. In the 1849 volume Arnold simply cited his source for the poem as Herodotus 2.133, but in 1853 he charitably added a note pulling together relevant sentences from 129 and 133: "After Cephren, Mycerinus, son of Cheops, reigned over Egypt. He abhorred his father's courses, and judged his subjects more justly than any of their kings had done.—To him there came an oracle from the city of Buto, to the effect that he was to live but six years longer, and to die in the seventh year from that time." The poem consists of a speech by Mycerinus, who bitterly resigns himself to a life of pleasure, and a narrative, which briefly describes the king's revelry and speculates on his true state of mind. The themes, then, are divine injustice, the relation of the gods to mankind, the impulse to hedonism—but above all, the poem is concerned with the oracle itself, the voice of an absolute authority.

An interesting echo of Wordsworth implies that the king's choice of hedonistic revelry over duty is directly related to a sense that the voice of the oracle, however authoritative, is not the voice of God but only an inscrutable destiny. As has often been noted, the king's speech is in the stanza form of "Laodamia," while the subject matter, as Allott observes, is "in blunt opposition to Wordsworth's acceptance of heavenly 'justice.'"[23] But Wordsworth's "Ode to Duty" also lies behind "Mycerinus," for Arnold's poem counters Wordsworth's personification of Duty as the "Stern daughter of the voice of God," with the ungodly voice of the oracle, the "dread voice from lips that cannot lie, / Stern sentence of the Powers of Destiny" (ll. 5–6). The dutiful exercise of justice becomes meaningless when disconnected from any authority higher than man, when the notion that "Man's justice from the all-just Gods was given" (l. 20) becomes a mockery. Indeed, Mycerinus speculates, if there are any gods at all, they are the indifferent Lucretian gods, withdrawn to "Where earthly voice climbs never" (l. 44). In a universe without a ruling moral principle, human action becomes futile; in a universe without an authoritative moral voice, human speech becomes meaningless. It is the same idea that made the somewhat later poem "The Sick King in Bokhara" so bleakly despairing. In that poem a man who has broken the law demands, essentially, that the king speak with the authority of Allah to sentence him to death. The king evidently does not hear the voice of Allah, though he must submit to the will of the priests and fulfill his duty as Allah's substitute by pronouncing the sentence. His official, oracular voice—his voice of authoritative power—comes from nondivine sources and is hopelessly counter to his own moral impulses. As an oracle the king is a sham. In "Mycerinus," too, the king sees that the aspiration of human speech to divine truth is an empty mockery:

Stringing vain words of powers we cannot see,
(ll. 51–53) Blind divinations of a will supreme;
Lost labour!

Inevitably, Mycerinus comes to the conclusion that, much as he feels there ought to be something to say, further speech is pointless:

Into the silence of the groves and woods
(ll. 67–69) I will go forth; though something would I say—
Something—yet what, I know not.

And so Mycerinus, without a sustaining voice of God, lapses into silence.

The second section of the poem, a reflective narrative in blank verse, is a significant formal break from the public oratory of the first section. It consists in large part of speculation about what the king is really thinking, now that he is no longer speaking. Critics have generally focused their attention on this final section, trying to find the true Arnoldian ethical position. That position is generally regarded as one of aloof moral stoicism and spiritual retreat:

It may be on that joyless feast his eye
Dwelt with mere outward seeming; he, within,
(ll. 107–11) Took measure of his soul, and knew its strength,
And by that silent knowledge, day by day,
Was calmed, ennobled, comforted, sustained.

But it has also been argued, at least as plausibly, that the poem never really undercuts Mycerinus' hedonism or suggests a better alternative, that it is philosophically open-ended, that the narrator's thrice-repeated "It may be" reflects a tentative, skeptical attitude, not a fixed creed.[24] The poem that began with reference to an absolutely authoritative utterance ends with futile attempts to find meaning in the enigmatic silence of the king.

The beautiful closing lines, however, tell not of silence, but of inarticulate sound:

> So six long years he revelled, night and day.
> And when the mirth waxed loudest, with dull sound
> Sometimes from the grove's centre echoes came,
> To tell his wondering people of their king;
> In the still night, across the steaming flats,
> Mixed with the murmur of the moving Nile.
>
> (ll. 122–27)

As often in Arnold's poetry, the ending emotionally distances the reader by placing the poem's human action within a larger than human context—the fate of one man is absorbed in the stillness and timelessness of nature. But despite their beauty and tranquillity the lines emphasize not harmony with nature but the indifference of time and nature to mortal concerns, and they emphasize both the inarticulateness of nature's voice, a "murmur," and the inextricably linked pointlessness of human utterance, reduced to a "dull sound" and distanced to an echo. His people are left "wondering . . . of their king," cut off from his example and authority just as he is cut off from the example of "Some better archetype, whose seat was heaven" (l. 22). The only oracle left to the people is hollow laughter from the "grove's centre," an echo of their withdrawn king, and an ironic echo of the withdrawn gods.

Though Arnold never fully undercut Mycerinus' hedonism within the poem, he did write, in about the same period, a poem in explicit refutation of the call to the life of pleasure. But it is perhaps because the case for Mycerinus' view of life is so strong that "The New Sirens: A Palinode" is itself somewhat inarticulate—as Arnold admitted to Clough, "it is exactly a mumble."[25] Whether "The New Sirens" was intended as a palinode to "Mycerinus" is unclear, but it is certainly an attempt—though not very successful—to spurn the hedonistic call to pleasure, the siren song that calls the natural man to love and beauty. And interestingly the call to pleasure that renders Mycerinus inarticulate is here explicitly an enticement away from poetry. The speaker of the poem, himself a poet, has abandoned the frowning Muse for the "mad sallies" of the Sirens, and has "Left our awful laurels hanging, / And came heaped with myrtles to your throne" (ll. 31–32). The potential seriousness of this gesture is evident in its anticipation of Empedocles' later rejection of his "laurel bough! / Scornful Apollo's ensign" (*Empedocles* 2.191–92), but for now the act is merely temporary, as the poet will proceed to resist the seductive Sirens.

He is able to resist the New Sirens partly because he recognizes them as a merely updated version of the old ones, and the "hitherto experience of the world," and especially of Ulysses, has taught him the dangers of their sweet song. But Arnold's Sirens, more plainly sexual than those of the *Odyssey,*[26] are also rejected out of a general sense that the pleasures of love lead only to a cold awakening, an "Unlovely dawning" (l. 265) of bitter regret. And this is so even though the New Sirens are not the cold-blooded killers of Ulysses' day:

The uncouthness
Of that primal age is gone,
And the skin of dazzling smoothness
(ll. 49–56) Screens not now a heart of stone.
Love has flushed those cruel faces;
And those slackened arms forego
The delight of death-embraces,
And yon whitening bone-mounds do not grow.

The increased gentility of the Sirens, however, does not conceal that they remain cruel, however flushed, and that sensual love takes place in the shadow of death. Further, their lack of primitive savagery makes the Sirens rather dreary. Anticipating the Swinburnean sense that the fierce and deadly passions of the past can scarcely exist in our time "of famished hours, / Maimed loves and mean," Arnold's speaker sees that

The wingéd fleetness
(ll. 251–54) Of immortal feet is gone;
And your scents have shed their sweetness,
And your flowers are overblown.

There is no grandeur about these Sirens, nothing superhuman, nothing divine. In fact, it is precisely because their voice is so clearly *not* the voice of God that the poet is so easily able to resist their charms:

> Can men worship the wan features,
> The sunk eyes, the wailing tone,
> Of unsphered, discrownéd creatures,
> Souls as little godlike as their own? (ll. 247–50)

The song of the Sirens is just another human voice, with no particular authority, no particular power.

The Sirens are full of doubts and uncertainties that make it seemingly impossible to follow a clear path in the multitudinous confusion of modern life, but it is significant that they state the difficulties best themselves, and that they offer the most coherent philosophy in the poem:

> "Come," you say, "opinion trembles,
> Judgment shifts, convictions go;
> Life dries up, the heart dissembles—
> Only, what we feel, we know.
> Hath your wisdom felt emotions?
> Will it weep our burning tears?
> Hath it drunk of our love-potions
> Crowning moments with the wealth of years?" (ll. 81–88)

The argument and tone anticipate some of Arnold's best later poetry, and even now he—or at least the speaker of the poem—cannot find a better response to the modern malaise: "—I am dumb. Alas, too soon all / Man's grave reasons disappear!" (ll. 89–90). Faced with a clear and emphatic summary of modern difficulties, of the inevitable vacillation among too many uncertainties, the poet is struck dumb, is left without a voice. The point could not be more emphatic. Yet the poet struggles on, hoping that eventually the voice of God may be heard: "Yet, I think, at God's tribunal / Some large answer you shall hear" (ll. 91–92). But this is a faint and forlorn hope, as even the poet admits: "Yes, I muse!" And he muses in a day when the Muse can no longer sustain him, when the world has grown too knowing to believe in anything more than immediate sensation, and too old to take pleasure in that.

In a slightly later poem, "Fragment of a Chorus of a 'Dejaneira,'" Arnold had a Greek chorus lament that the "frivolous mind of man" (l. 1) accepts a state of vacillating uncertainty rather than seeking the truths of divine revelation. In prosperity men do not seek truth, and so

> In profound silence stern,
> Among their savage gorges and cold springs,
> Unvisited remain
> The great oracular shrines.
> (ll. 8–11)

And those in trouble are incapable of understanding the oracles;

> Thither in your adversity
> Do you betake yourselves for light,
> But strangely misinterpret all you hear.
> (ll. 12–14)

But the insistent point of Arnold's early poems, especially those of 1843–44, is that oracles are always either silent, incomprehensible, or demonic. If there is a just God, he is now silent, and in his silence the poet's utterance of any "large answer" must reverberate hollowly. For a moment, in "The New Sirens," Arnold seemed to have found his most distinctive voice, the voice in which he later analyzed the perplexities of his age in such poems as "The Scholar-Gipsy," "Stanzas from the Grande Chartreuse," and "Dover Beach," but he attributed the voice to the Sirens, and rejected it. His effort in the poetry that followed was to find his voice again after being struck dumb in the absence of an authoritative, divine voice.

Inharmony with Nature

For the romantic or transcendentalist, the authoritative power of language is connected with the creative fiat of God, the all-creative Logos that resonates in both human reason and nature. The harmony between the mind and nature can be expressed in poetry, which echoes the Logos in its dual meanings of "reason" and "word." Among the clearest of the many romantic expressions of this philosophy is Coleridge's in "Frost at Midnight":

so shalt thou see and hear
The lovely shapes and sounds intelligible
Of that eternal language, which thy God
(ll. 58–63) Utters, who from eternity doth teach
Himself in all, and all things in himself.
Great universal Teacher!

But to the agnostic imagination there is no authoritative word that links mind and nature, so there is no possibility of harmony and of course no intelligible, eternal language reverberating such a harmony.

Arnold's most explicit rejection of the high romantic idea of nature is the sonnet "In Harmony with Nature: To a Preacher," which insists that humanity must rise above the merely natural:

"In harmony with Nature?" Restless fool,
Who with such heat dost preach what were to thee,
When true, the last impossibility—
To be like Nature strong, like Nature cool!

(ll. 1–8)

Know, man hath all which Nature hath, but more,
And in that *more* lie all his hopes of good.
Nature is cruel, man is sick of blood;
Nature is stubborn, man would fain adore.

This is, of course, characteristic of the Victorian reaction against what was perceived as romantic nature worship and is very much of a piece with Tennyson's horror at a nature "red in tooth and claw," but the explicit denial of "harmony" also undercuts the romantic image of the poet as a kind of aeolian harp, resonating to the breeze that is also the breath of God.

No particular preacher has been identified with the fool of the sonnet, but G. Robert Stange and others have noted the relevance of a passage that Arnold would have known in Epictetus. God, said Epictetus, "brought man into the world to take cognizance of Himself and His works, and not only to take cognizance, but also to interpret them. Therefore it is beneath man's dignity to begin and end where the irrational creatures do: he must rather begin where they do and end where nature has ended in forming us; and nature ends in contemplation and understanding and a way of life in harmony with nature."[27] Clearly, Arnold has accepted and even paraphrased the point that humanity must surpass irrational creatures, but he goes further by denying higher powers to nature and giving them to man alone. If Epictetus' passage is the source for the sonnet, as it seems to be, the implication is that Arnold was concerned with the desire to *interpret* God and his works, to understand God's message. But by eliminating anything in nature analogous to the higher human attributes of compassion and reverence, Arnold entirely eliminated nature as a way to understanding of God—certainly the word of God is not to be found in nature, and perhaps that is why the poem is addressed as a corrective "To a Preacher."

It may well be that Arnold was thinking less of Epictetus than of Emerson, for the sonnet seems an evident repudiation of a passage he had read in the section on language in *Nature*: "A life in harmony with nature, the love of truth and of virtue, will purge the eyes to understand her text. By degrees we may come to know the primitive sense of the permanent objects of nature, so that the world shall be to us an open book, and every form significant of its hidden life and final cause."[28] Once again, the possible source links the phrase "in harmony with nature" to the possibility of interpreting God's word, and in this case, to the possibility of a fully authentic language. Yet it seems beside the point to look for any one particular source, since the phrase "harmony with nature" and the idea it describes was a commonplace of pre-Victorian thought. The important point is that Arnold was among the first to refute the idea that mind could be in harmony with nature, among the first to insist that mind, human consciousness, is not only alienated from nature but is the cause of that alienation. Consequently Arnold's separation of humanity from nature sternly denies the possibility of a naturally authoritative language. Nature is not a "text" that can teach the primal language.

The sonnet "Quiet Work," which Arnold liked well enough to use as the opening poem in his first volume, at first seems to contradict "In Harmony with Nature." The eminently romantic point of the sonnet is that the poet should follow nature's example, working silently, inevitably, and without fuss to achieve his purposes. The sestet offers an evident tribute to nature:

> Yes, while on earth a thousand discords ring,
> Man's fitful uproar mingling with his toil,
> Still do thy sleepless ministers move on,
> Their glorious tasks in silence perfecting;
> Still working, blaming still our vain turmoil,
> Labourers that shall not fail, when man is gone.
>
> (ll. 9–14)

The language itself is patently romantic, echoing, as Allott suggests, Keats's "Bright Star" and, more emphatically, Wordsworth's "Gipsies": "Life which the very stars reprove / As on their silent tasks they move!" (ll. 23–24).[29] More generally, "ministers" in this sense is a word so Wordsworthian as to deserve copyright protection, and the sleepless, silent ministry of nature seems plainly a recollection of the "secret ministry of frost" and the "silent icicles" of Coleridge's "Frost at Midnight."

Yet despite all of the romantic catchwords, the passage is at best ambivalent about the possibility of learning from nature. In the first place, on earth all that can be heard are "a thousand discords . . . Man's fitful uproar"—and perhaps this is evident in the Babel of romantic voices making themselves heard. Further, the romantic, personified nature of the poem is something of a *deus absconditus,* above the fray, silent, and indifferent. Although the poet asks, in the opening lines, to learn a lesson from Nature, she is certainly not the "Great universal Teacher" that she is in "Frost at Midnight." She is simply silent, and the only lesson to be learned from her example is to work silently. This is of course the point of the sonnet, as it is the point of Plotinus in a passage translated by Coleridge and read by Arnold in 1846: "Should any one interrogate her [Nature], how she works . . . she will reply, it behoves thee not to disquiet me with interrogations, but to understand in silence even as I am silent, and work without Words."[30] The advice is perfectly suited to the earnest Victorian—it is perfectly Carlylean, in fact—but advising a poet to "work without Words" is likely to be disheartening. In this essential respect, at least, "Quiet Work" and "In Harmony with

Nature" are in agreement—both discourage the romantic notion that language is somehow inherent in the natural order, and that it is therefore more than an artificial and arbitrary labeling of things.

Much the same point is made in yet another sonnet, "Religious Isolation," in which the speaker scolds a friend (or, as is generally assumed, Arnold scolds Clough) for childishly believing in a correspondence between his idiosyncratic feelings and any universal law. The "holy secret" that molds the human mind is not spoken by nature: "never winds / Have whispered it to the complaining sea" (ll. 10–11). Consequently every individual mortal lives alone, alienated from nature and apparently even from the rest of humanity: "To its own impulse every creature stirs; / Live by thy light, and earth will live by hers!" (ll. 13–14). Despite the hearty exhortation to self-reliance, the poem presents a bleak view of man's place in nature and has discouraging implications for the poet. Not only is he cut off from the prospect of a universal voice in nature, but he is left with no knowledge except his "own impulse"—the poem, in fact, adopts the position of the New Sirens that "Only, what we feel, we know." And what we feel is not necessarily of interest to anyone else. The poem is not explicitly about poetry, but it is addressed by one poet to another, so its implications along these lines ought to be taken seriously, and they are very grim indeed. The poet has nothing to work with but subjective feelings, and if he attempts to speak of these he may be scornfully compared to a child who, "Too fearful or too fond to play alone" (l. 5), babbles of his "swarming thoughts" (l. 4) to an "incurious bystander" (l. 3). The implicit advice to the poet is the same as that of the other sonnets: "be silent."

Arnold's lack of faith in a benevolent nature was, of course, a major cause of his reaction against the romantics, and especially against Wordsworth. All his life Arnold believed that Wordsworth—a neighbor and family friend for much of Arnold's youth—was among the greatest of all English poets, but he could not accept either the older poet's faith in nature or his conception of the role of poets and poetry. Eventually Arnold spelled out his ideas about Wordsworth in critical prose, but several poems in the 1849 volume work out a response to Wordsworthian romanticism—

both incidentally and programmatically. One of the earliest poems in the volume, "To a Gipsy Child by the Sea-Shore," pointedly rejects the idea that children and peasants live in close communion and harmony with a joyful nature. The gipsy child knows no "superfluity of joy" but only the hunger and pain of poverty (ll. 9–12), and far from being in communion with nature and rural life, he is an exile and an outcast. Wordsworth believed he could get closer to the fundamental truths of Nature by sympathy with those who lived close to Her; Arnold did not even believe that the feelings of the outcast child—let alone the secrets of nature—could be fathomed: "Glooms that go deep as thine I have not known: / Moods of fantastic sadness, nothing worth" (ll. 17–18).

The point that is made deliberately in "To a Gipsy Child" is perhaps made accidentally—and so all the more revealingly in a very different sort of poem, "The Hayswater Boat." The poem, describing an abandoned boat on a mountain tarn, is an apparent effort to invest a solitary scene with Wordsworthian significance, grandeur, and mystery:

A region desolate and wild.
Black chafing water: and afloat,
And lonely as a truant child
In a waste wood, a single boat:
No mast, no sails are set thereon;
It moves, but never moveth on:
And welters like a human thing
Amid the wild waves weltering.
(ll. 1–8)

The rest of the poem consists of further description and speculation about how the boat came to be there—including a rather bizarre surmise that a "pigmy throng" has been behaving mischievously. But the dangerous plight of a boat that is associated with "a truant child," a "human thing," does not imply a benevolent sense of nature. Indeed, as A. Dwight Culler has excellently said, the poem's "final question, 'What living hand has brought it here?' is not a Romantic fancy implying beneficent powers, but a metaphysical demand as to who placed this lonely child in this intolerable situation."[31] Like "To a Gipsy Child," the poem echoes Wordsworth only to suggest the alienation of humanity from a nature that is at best indifferent and at worst actively hostile.

The alienation of humanity from nature is evident in the descriptive style of the verse:

> Behind, a buried vale doth sleep,
> Far down the torrent cleaves its way:
> In front the dumb rock rises steep,
> A fretted wall of blue and grey.
>
> (ll. 9–12)

Wordsworth's descriptions suggest the interconnections and fusion of disparate elements in a landscape; for him, the steep rock would be likely to "connect / The landscape with the quiet of the sky." But Arnold separates the various elements, putting each neatly in its place: the vale is "behind," the torrent is "far down," and the rock (significantly "dumb"), is "In front." Each item is even provided its own carefully end-stopped line. As J. Hillis Miller has observed, such fragmenting of landscape is generally characteristic of Arnold's descriptive verse, and plainly represents a radically un-Wordsworthian perception of nature: "Far from being, though apparently divided, actually one, a deep harmony in which man and nature share together in the inalienable presence of 'something far more deeply interfused,' Arnold's world has split apart. Nature is separated from man, and is a collection of unrelated fragments juxtaposed without order or form. Each rock, bird, tree, or cloud is self-enclosed and separate from all the others."[32] Such fragmenting of landscapes into discrete things, as Carol Christ has argued, often represents the alienation of the viewer, who in his "introspective morbidity" perceives no purposiveness, no sense of relation, no meaningful universal law in the natural world.[33] Even when Arnold attempted the romantic mode, the very movement of his descriptive verse betrayed his Victorian sense of isolation and estrangement from nature.

The full implications of Arnold's inability and unwillingness to embrace the Wordsworthian view are worked out in "Resignation," an ambitious programmatic poem about the post-Wordsworthian poetic character. "Resignation," a meditation addressed to the poet's sister on the occcasion of revisiting a remembered scene, is obviously and self-consciously modeled on "Tintern Abbey."[34] The description and interpretation of the landscape, however, are distinctly Arnold's own:

> The solemn wastes of heathy hill
> Sleep in the July sunshine still;
> The self-same shadows now, as then,
> Play through this grassy upland glen;
> The loose dark stones on the green way
> (ll. 96–107) Lie strewn, it seems, where then they lay;
> On this mild bank above the stream,
> (You crush them!) the blue gentians gleam.
> Still this wild brook, the rushes cool,
> The sailing foam, the shining pool!
> These are not changed; and we, you say,
> Are scarce more changed, in truth, than they.

The lines are the very antithesis of Wordsworthian. Instead of connecting the various elements in a complex organic harmony, the passage carefully separates them: hills, shadows, stones, gentians, and brook are isolated, each within its own couplet and have nothing to do with each other. Further, the assertion that nothing has changed is directly opposed to Wordsworth's sense in "Tintern Abbey" that the landscape has contributed to change the perceiving poet dramatically, with the result that the landscape at least *seems* to have changed.

Not surprisingly the un-Wordsworthian description of an eminently Wordsworthian situation leads Arnold eventually to a discussion of poets and poetry and to an implicit refutation of his predecessor. The Arnoldian poet, as described in "Resignation," is stoical, aloof, and detached from the vanity of "human cares" (l. 232). He has learned the lesson of quiet work from nature which, though "dumb" (as always in Arnold), reveals that her unromantic "secret is not joy but peace" (ll. 192–93). As a result of his quiet detachment, "His sad lucidity of soul" (l. 198), the poet sees life with uncommon clarity and scope. Such a notion seems a little cold-blooded to Fausta, the speaker's romantically disposed and romantically named sister, who evidently resents the poet's ability to escape the hardships of ordinary mortals. The poet may feel human misery more deeply than the apparently subhuman gipsies do, but he can also breathe

> when he will, immortal air,
> Where Orpheus and where Homer are.
> In the day's life, whose iron round
> Hems us all in, he is not bound;
> (ll. 207–14) He leaves his kind, o'erleaps their pen,
> And flees the common life of men.
> He escapes thence, but we abide—
> Not deep the poet sees, but wide.

The speaker disagrees with the views he attributes to his sister to the extent that he believes the poet's "rapt security" (l. 246) results not from "immortal air" but from a resigned acceptance of the transience of human life. He fully agrees, however, with the crucial concluding line: "Not deep the poet sees, but wide." The choice of a detached, serene, "classical" overview as opposed to the passionate, committed, deep empathy of romanticism is consistent with Arnold's thoughts about poetry in his letters to Clough. One should not be, like Clough, "a mere d——d depth hunter in poetry," for "wealth and depth of matter is merely a superfluity in the Poet *as such*." The "sole *necessary* of Poetry as such" is "an absolute propriety—of form," and the poet is likely to destroy the classical serenity of his surfaces if he thinks or feels too deeply. Thinking too deeply is especially dangerous to the poet in a "deeply *unpoetical* age":

> *I often think that even a slight gift of poetical expression which in a common person might have developed itself easily and naturally, is overlaid and crushed in a profound thinker so as to be of no use to help him to express himself. —The trying to go into and to the bottom of an object instead of grouping* objects *is as fatal to the sensuousness of poetry as the mere painting, (for,* in Poetry, *this is not* grouping*) is to its airy and rapidly moving life.*
>
> *"Not deep the Poet sees, but wide."*[35]

Such a notion exactly reverses the idea of the poet expressed in "Tintern Abbey":

> with an eye made quiet by the power
> (ll. 48–50) Of harmony, and the deep power of joy,
> We see into the life of things.

Arnold's conception of the poet, then, is closely linked to his postromantic view of nature, for harmony and joy are precisely the attributes he is at pains to deny to nature, and without them any attempt to "see into the life of things" is intolerable. His situation is analogous to Keats's in the "Epistle to John Hamilton Reynolds"—the wholesome, cheering aesthetic sense of the beautiful is destroyed if one looks too deeply into the nature of things,

> where every maw
> The greater on the less feeds evermore.—
> But I saw too distinct into the core
> (ll. 94–99) Of an eternal fierce destruction,
> And so from happiness I far was gone.
> Still am I sick of it.

As Arnold goes on to tell Clough, the role of the poet is to "attain the *beautiful*" and to make sure his "product gives PLEASURE,"[36] and in the postromantic world, depth of thought and feeling are necessarily at odds with beauty and pleasure.

Although Arnold defined "absolute propriety of form" as "naturalness," he was evidently using the word rather loosely—all of his early nature poems, and especially "Resignation," oppose the idea that nature is poetic or that poetry is natural. The closing section of "Resignation" is explicit about the impossibility of finding a cheering poetic voice in nature:

> the mute turf we tread,
> The solemn hills around us spread,
> This stream which falls incessantly,
> (ll. 265–70) The strange-scrawled rocks, the lonely sky,
> If I might lend their life a voice,
> Seem to bear rather than rejoice.

The lines, as Allott's annotations make clear, are drenched in Wordsworthian diction,[37] but only as a rebuttal of the romantic myth of Nature. The turf is mute, the hieroglyphs on the rocks are unintelligible—nature has no voice of her own and does not even *seem* to have a "deep power of joy." Arnold's divergence from Wordsworth is well summed up by U. C. Knoepflmacher: " 'The meadows and the woods and mountains' speak freely to Wordsworth in the 'language of sense.' Arnold, however, must scrupulously point out that the language he ascribes to the scene before him is really his own. . . . The poet thus is forced to superimpose his own order on the scene he sees before him. He can at best attribute an imagined 'voice' to the life he sees around him; he can only assume that the landscape would '*seem*' to teach him how to bear."[38] The inarticulateness of nature is especially significant since the poet has been described throughout the poem in terms of what he feels and sees—what he can know or say is never discussed. In his essay on "Language" Emerson argued the romantic position that nature is an open book, that it expresses the primal language, the "solid images" and "fit symbols and words" of the authentic poet's lexicon. But for Arnold the strange scrawl is a dead and lost language. Over and over again his poetry of nature leads to the same inevitable implication: in this "profoundly *unpoetical* age," the poet is alienated from nature and therefore separated from an unmediated, authentic language. Nature cannot offer him what it offered Emerson and the English romantics: "the spells of persuasion, the keys of power."[39]

"Natural Magic"

Arnold's skepticism drew him inevitably to the conclusion that language can only be lent to nature, not learned from her, but he nevertheless continued to seek a language with magical power—continued to seek what he eventually came to call "natural magic." In its romantic sense, as used by Coleridge, the term involves precisely the transcendental view of nature that Arnold rejected: "Natural Magic is the force above human reason which is the active principle in Nature."[40] And even as Arnold eventually defined it, the term referred to a kind of primal naming: "In Keats and Guérin, in whom the faculty of naturalistic interpretation is overpoweringly predominant, the natural magic is perfect; when they speak of the world they speak like Adam naming by divine inspiration the creatures; their expression corresponds with the thing's essential reality" (3:34). Of course Arnold's expression here in 1862 is figurative and hyperbolic, but it describes what he *wanted* language to be capable of. And in a number of the early poems he struggled to achieve at least the illusion of a magically potent language. In "The New Sirens," for example, he attempted to recapture the ancient magic of the Sirens by incantatory rhythms that, as W. S. Johnson has said, "have the sound of a charm; they echo some magical incantation rather than the Prayer Book."[41]

In other poems the "spells of persuasion" are less clearly associated with a demonic power, but generally the language that attempts magical potency is at best morally ambivalent. Both the incantatory rhythms and the moral ambivalence are evident in "The Forsaken Merman," Arnold's most successful attempt to achieve "natural magic." The story, from Hans Christian Andersen, is of a young woman who has been seduced by a Merman—a kind of male Siren, perhaps. She has five children by him, but eventually she is called back to an orthodox life on land by the sound of church bells and, apparently strengthened in her moral resolve by a sermon, she is ever after able to resist the imploring voice of the Merman. The woman, Margaret, is forced to choose between the magical voice and the Prayer Book, and she chooses the Prayer Book. Formally, however, the poem sides with magic, since it presents only the voice of the Merman as he acknowledges his failure to lure Margaret back. The Merman's description of his undersea home is perhaps the clearest example of "natural magic" in the poem:

Sand-strewn caverns, cool and deep,
Where the winds are all asleep;
Where the spent lights quiver and gleam,
(ll. 35–45) Where the salt weed sways in the stream,
Where the sea-beasts, ranged all round,
Feed in the ooze of their pasture-ground;
Where the sea-snakes coil and twine,

Dry their mail and bask in the brine;
Where great whales come sailing by,
Sail and sail, with unshut eye,
Round the world for ever and aye.

The description is in the form of a magical charm both in its attempt to be inclusive—to control everything by naming it—and in its heavily stressed trochaic and anapestic measure. Moreover, the lines are significantly imitative of Tennysonian attempts at magical, enchanted seascapes. Allott notes a debt to the coiled sea snakes of "The Mermaid,"[42] and a still more significant debt is to "The Hesperides": "Father Hesper, Father Hesper, watch, watch, ever and aye, / Looking under silver hair with a silver eye" (ll. 43–44). The influence is I think more pervasive and more important than this slight verbal echo might suggest—the association of a mythical, magical sea-kingdom with incantatory language may well have been inspired directly by Tennyson's poems. In any case, the mere fact that the poem is allusive at all is important: language never can express unmediated vision, or correspond with essential reality, but the use of allusion clearly demonstrates that the primary referent of the poem's language is not nature at all but other instances of language.

"The Forsaken Merman" is plainly concerned with the Tennysonian theme of a forced choice between beauty and duty, and by siding with the Merman and with the magical and threatened garden of the Hesperides it seems clearly to choose beauty. The choice is not quite so clear-cut, however, as is evident in the radical critical disagreement about whether Arnold sided with the Merman or with Margaret. The important point, I think, is not whether Margaret is redeemed from selfish immorality or returned to a life of slavery in a drab, gray society—indeed, as some of the poem's finest critics have pointed out, Arnold is ambivalent about the life of both the sea and the land.[43] For my purposes what is important is that for all its beauty and pathos, the voice from the depths no longer has the power to attract. If it is magical, it has lost much of its potency. In fact, it is not magical incantation but the Prayer Book (or the Bible), that has power over Margaret: "her eyes were sealed to the holy book" (l. 81). The voice, the essential instrument of power in primitive magic, has become less powerful than the written word. Both the Merman and Margaret continue to sing, but ineffectually. The Merman's song is merely a lament:

> There dwells a loved one,
> But cruel is she!
> She left lonely for ever
> The kings of the sea.
>
> (ll. 140–43)

And Margaret's song of joy cannot be sustained:

> She sits at her wheel in the humming town,
> Singing most joyfully.
> Hark what she sings: "O joy, O joy,
> For the humming street, and the child with its toy!
> For the priest, and the bell, and the holy well;
> For the wheel where I spun,
> And the blessed light of the sun!"
> And so she sings her fill,
> Singing most joyfully,
> Till the spindle drops from her hand,
> And the whizzing wheel stands still.
>
> (ll. 87–97)

The tone of her joyous song is perilously close to the agonized lament of Tennyson's "Break, Break, Break": "O, well for the fisherman's boy . . . O, well for the sailor lad . . . But O for the touch of a vanished hand / And the sound of a voice that is still!" (l. 5–12). Joy is for others—the song cannot suppress "a tear" and a "long, long sigh" (ll. 102–5).

"The Forsaken Merman" is not about the possibilities of song, or poetry, as a primary, explicit theme. Rather it is concerned with Arnold's usual and most pressing theme, human isolation and the impossibility of sustained joy. But the alienation of humanity from natural joy inevitably implies the inadequacy of "natural magic," and indeed the inadequacy of any song to inspire and sustain a sense of wholeness or joy. The submerged concern with poetry and song in "The Forsaken Merman" is brought to the surface in "The Strayed Reveller." The title poem of Arnold's first volume is explicitly about magic, enchantment, and poetic vocation. Indeed, the poem may well have been inspired, as Allott suggests, by "the 'natural magic' of Maurice de Guérin's 'Le Centaure,' which he read and was haunted by in 1847."[44] The poem is really a brief play with three characters: a youth with poetic ambitions, Circe, and Ulysses. It would seem perfectly designed to contrast the heroic life of Ulysses with the all too natural magic of Circe, but in fact Ulysses' strenuous life is barely alluded to, and Circe's magical wine only makes the youth giddy and puts him to sleep. It seems about as magical as port. This in itself, perhaps, constitutes a criticism of Circean enchantment. The reveller who drinks from the cup may well achieve harmony with nature, but only by brutalizing himself. The poem begins and ends with an invocation of the goddess and a magical incantation:

Faster, faster,
O Circe, Goddess,
(ll. 1–6, Let the wild, thronging train,
292–97) The bright procession
Of eddying forms,
Sweep through my soul!

As Andrew Hickman has said in a recent essay, the simple fact that "the last stanza is also the first . . . emphasizes that the Reveller is not getting anywhere, that he himself has not broken new ground in the creation of any theoretical poetic . . . but is firmly bound in Circe's spell."[45] In fact, the Reveller is awake only long enough to answer some questions and request more liquor before he falls asleep again, is again awakened to answer some more questions, and again requests more liquor—he is hardly the model of an earnest Victorian poet. He is so inert that Ulysses' questions about him seem to liken him to the figures on Keats's Grecian Urn:

Who is he,
That he sits, overweighed
By fumes of wine and sleep,
(ll. 90–95) So late, in thy portico?
What youth, Goddess, what guest
Of Gods or mortals?

Nevertheless, while he is awake he does manage to make some lucid distinctions, particularly between the serene vision of the gods and the painful song of wise bards. The gods see widely, but not deeply:

The Gods are happy.
They turn on all sides
(ll. 130–34) Their shining eyes,
And see below them
The earth and men.

But the gods only *see*—they do not sing or inspire poets to sing, and in any case their vision is not available to the poet, who might choose to write in a classical mode but can hardly choose to become a god. Ulysses' idea of a "divine bard" is, as Hickman says, "impossible . . . a contradiction."[46] In fact the gods are outright hostile to the idea of song. They grant vision to the "wise bards" but only on condition that the bards must suffer with those whom they see suffer:

such a price
(ll. 232–34) The Gods exact for song:
To become what we sing.

The "wise bards" are evidently romantic poets with a gift for "natural magic"—that is, the ability to seem to speak from within the very heart of nature. The poem therefore seems to reverse the idea of "Resignation" by insisting that the poet must see not wide but deep, yet its apparent romanticism is no more possible than Olympian detachment. Hickman is right, I think, in arguing that the poem is about the Reveller's disinclination to suffer the pain that goes with song, but in fact Arnold never offers him the possibility of doing so. The vision and the pains of song are given by the Gods (l. 214), and have not been given to him.

If the Reveller is in some sense a surrogate for his author, as is generally and reasonably assumed, his plight reflects Arnold's difficulty in finding a basis for poetry generally. The Reveller, in the end, is not a poet, but—like Mycerinus and perhaps from a similar frustration—a hedonist:

But I, Ulysses,
Sitting on the warm steps,
Looking over the valley,
All day long, have seen,
Without pain, without labour,
Sometimes a wild-haired Maenad—
Sometimes a Faun with torches—
And sometimes, for a moment,
Passing through the dark stems
Flowing-robed, the beloved,
The desired, the divine,
Beloved Iacchus.
(ll. 270–81)

The poem itself attempts the natural magic of romanticism by its invocation of Circean naturalism, but this, of course, is badly undercut by the Reveller's—and the poem's—inability to escape the charmed circle of enchantment, and by the Reveller's abundant lack of high seriousness. Moreover, the form of the poem is only halfheartedly given over to natural magic. In fact the dramatic structure seems designed to achieve a "grouping of objects" rather than "trying to go into and to the bottom of an object"—it seems, in other words, more classically detached than romantically involved.

The poem presents a series of tableaux, using the play as little more than a framing device to present detached descriptions of unrelated scenes: "Tiresias, / Sitting, staff in hand" (ll. 135–36), "the Centaurs / In the upper glens" (ll. 143–44), "the Indian / Drifting" (ll. 151–52) and so on. Allott suggests that the "pictorial vividness . . . may have been worked up partly to compensate for the lack of rhyme and conventional metre," and it is certainly true, as the earliest commentators lamented, that the poem's rhythms more closely resemble chopped prose than song.[47] In short, everything about the work suggests that its author has not poetically advanced beyond its protagonist—like the Reveller, he can *see* but he cannot *sing*. The distinction is important, for it is at the center of Arnold's difficulty in finding a usable language. To see clearly, to "see the object as in itself it really is," does not diminish, but emphasizes, the separation between thought and the object of thought, mind and nature. Detached vision only emphasizes the split between things and words, for words, as Newman said, express "not things, but thoughts." To see objects as they are is to see them divorced from human consciousness or concern, to see them without the order or coherence imposed by thought or feeling. It forces upon the viewer a sense of the absolute otherness of the object, and a sense of aloneness in a meaningless world of objects. When Rossetti's speaker sees a woodspurge as it really is, when the speaker of *Maud* sees a seashell as it really is, the effect is only to increase a sense of isolation, of entrapment within the mind. Sight alienates the beholder from the beheld, whereas a language of power ought somehow to take possession of the outer world, to integrate mind and other. But for an agnostic poet the gulf between self and other is unbridgeable by language because language corresponds only with the mind and is merely arbitrarily imposed on objects. Once again, the problem for Arnold is a split between a scientific epistemology that wants to *see* the object as it is and a desire to express the perception artistically. But as M. M. Bakhtin has made clear, the "object of the visible world of experience as it actually exists, independent of the possibilities and means of its representation, must be transferred into the system of the means of representation, the system of surface, line, shaping hand, and so forth." The object, that is, cannot be presented as in itself it really is, but must be perceived and expressed "from the point of view of [a] representational system, as a possible constructive aspect of it." In other words, the object perceived only as in itself it really is, independent of the presumably distorting representational system of a poetic structure, cannot be "sung"—it "has nothing to do with art."[48] The romantic phrase "visionary song" is, for Arnold, an oxymoron.

Harold Bloom has intriguingly said that "every Romantic has a tendency to drink unnecessarily from the Circean cup of illusion"—that is, to seek truths in "shamanistic, magical divination." And this is not only unnecessary but mistaken, for it wrongly assumes that man's place is in nature, whereas true romanticism always places man above nature, in the immortal Imagination.[49] Arnold was too tied to the material world to believe in any transcendental realm, but he saw clearly enough that Circean enchantment, a complete surrender to natural impulse, did not lead to wisdom or imaginative freedom:

Man must begin, know this, where Nature ends;
Nature and man can never be fast friends.
Fool, if thou canst not pass her, rest her slave!

("In Harmony with Nature," ll. 12–14)

Arnold, unlike his Reveller, was never willing to call Circe his goddess, but neither was he ready, like Blake, or Wordsworth, or Shelley, to place his faith in the inventions of the unaided imagination and so soar above nature into the intense inane. As always, he was caught in the middle, desperately in need of a language that could unite imaginative vision and natural image.

Arnold's diverse attempts to find an authoritative, oracular voice, a serene, classical poetic character, and a romantic natural magic all inevitably led him back to the same problem: his language had no power to integrate thought and the objects of thought, no power to alleviate the isolation of human beings estranged from God and nature. Much later, in an analysis of the poetic diction of another "profoundly unpoetical age," Arnold tried to describe a "language of genuine poetry": "The poetic language of our eighteenth century in general is the language of men composing *without their eye on the object,* as Wordsworth excellently said of Dryden; language merely recalling the object, as the common language of prose does. . . . This poetry is often eloquent . . . but it does not take us much below the surface of things, it does not give us the emotion of seeing things in their truth and beauty" (9:202). The poetic language of the eighteenth century is superficial because it remains detached from things, merely labels them. But this is, of course, also a description of the Reveller's language and of the language of Arnold's poetry generally. The alternative—"the language of genuine poetry"—is "the language of one composing with his eye on the object; its evolution is that of a thing which has been plunged in the poet's soul until it comes forth naturally and necessarily" (9:202). This is evidently the poetry of the wise bards, and it sounds admirable at first. But it is the language of Circean illusion—it may "give us the emotion of seeing things in their truth and beauty" (9:202), but it does not give the reality. Further, "genuine poetic language" can "come only from those who, as Emerson says, 'live from a great depth of being'" (9:202)—presumably those who "see deep, not wide." But even they can only have their eye *on* the object: they can see the surfaces of things, but cannot see into the nature of things. Further, even what the poet *can* see, he cannot *sing,* since he cannot entirely overcome the gap between the object and the verbal conceptualization. "Vision" is objective but is cut off from the possibility of expression, just as "voice," though expressive, has no objective validity. Vision is external and voice is internal, and never can the twain meet. Certainly, at least, they do not meet in the written characters of the poem, which can reproduce neither the act of vision nor the presence of voice. The poet may "live from a great depth of being," but his depths are nevertheless detached from the objects of sight, and Arnold never does explain how poetic identity and external reality are fused in "genuine poetic language." He cannot convincingly adopt Emersonian conclusions about the poetic character and poetic language because he has not accepted Emerson's first premise that a "radical correspondence between things and human thoughts" leads to a primal, authoritative language.

For Emerson a genuine poetic language was "a commanding certificate that he who employs it is a man in alliance with truth and God," but the very lack of such an alliance is the primary theme of Arnold's poetry. By Emersonian standards, Arnold's language verges on the "rotten diction" of writers in a decadent tradition: "Hundreds of writers may be found in every long-civilized nation, who for a short time believe, and make others believe, that they see and utter truths, who do not of themselves clothe one thought in its natural garment, but who feed unconsciously on the language created by the primary writers of the country, those, namely, who hold primarily on nature."[50] Arnold is saved from such a condemnation by his self-critical tough-mindedness—he did not claim to "see and utter truths," but continually sought for a way to do so. His poems cannot overcome the alienation of words from things that the agnostic, scientific spirit of the age had caused, but they represent a remarkable though failed attempt to find a way in which significant poetic achievement could still be possible in the latter ages.

II

Romantic Voices and Classic Form

In *The Strayed Reveller and Other Poems* insistent questions are left unanswered—no voices respond from the heavens, or from nature, or even from past poets. Consequently the volume, as contemporary critics lamented, was deeply pessimistic, almost despairing, about the possibility of finding any basis for human action or speech. But the pessimism seemed somewhat lightened in *Empedocles on Etna, and Other Poems,* published three years later. Part of the reason for this is that suddenly the air was full of voices. As Dorothy Mermin has observed, voices now are heard from the heavens, from nature, from past poets:

> *The volume reverberates with spectral voices that say what the poet already knows or wants to hear. In "Longing" the speaker imagines the words his beloved does not say; in "Meeting" "a God's tremendous voice" urges him away from love; in "Stanzas in Memory of the Author of 'Obermann'" and "Memorial Verses" he restates the words of dead poets; "Nature" speaks in "The Youth of Nature" and "Morality"; voices come from heaven in "Self-Dependence," "A Summer Night," and "Progress," from within in "Youth and Calm."*[1]

But the very multitudinousness of voices suggests that nothing has been solved, that no one, clear, authoritative voice is making itself heard. Indeed, as Mermin adds, the "metaphysical statements from without . . . are ventriloqual projections of the speaker's own voice."[2] In all of these poems the oracular, authoritative voice rings hollow as though the spectral reverberations were no more than echoes resonating in the void. The volume as a whole represents not the mediation of an authoritative voice through an ordinary speaker but the "dialogue of the mind with itself"—a dialogue in which no genuinely effective voice is ever heard.

Probably the most emphatically cheering of the various voices is also the clearest example of their hollowness. In "Self-Dependence" a voice "From the intense, clear, star-sown vault of heaven" gives the assurance that

> with joy the stars perform their shining,
> And the sea its long moon-silvered roll;
> (ll. 21–24) For self-poised they live, nor pine with noting
> All the fever of some differing soul.

The affirmation of a Wordsworthian "joy" in nature flatly contradicts the earlier "Resignation," but it is also at odds with much of the rest of "Self-Dependence." There is no harmony in nature here, but isolation, separation in "self-poised" indifference to anything outside. The various elements in nature are "Bounded by themselves, and unregardful / In what state God's other works may be" (ll. 25–26). In fact, the voice paradoxically describes a voiceless universe in which all is silent, unconnected, indifferent. The stars and waters are

> Unaffrighted by the silence round them,
> Undistracted by the sights they see,
> (ll. 17–20) These demand not that the things without them
> Yield them love, amusement, sympathy.

In a sense, the poem is about the speaker's failure to follow the advice to be like nature. He *does* demand sympathy, and finally, "Weary of [himself], and sick of asking" (l. 1), he gets it in the form of a disembodied voice. But the last stanza implies that the voice is only an echo of the speaker's "passionate desire" (l. 5):

> O air-born voice! long since, severely clear,
> A cry like thine in mine own heart I hear:
> (ll. 29–32) "Resolve to be thyself; and know that he,
> Who finds himself, loses his misery!"

Despite the apparent presence of an oracular voice from the heavens, the poem remains ambivalent about the sources of human wisdom, and unresolved about whether the heavens do actually speak, or are silent. And to a lesser or greater extent, the same is true of all the poems in which God or nature speaks—the seemingly authoritative voice seems never to represent more than the pious wish of the speaker. Mermin has said that "in the 1852 poems, more than in earlier or late ones, we feel that Arnold desperately wants his poetry to speak out and be heard," and so an authoritative speaking voice of nature is wished into existence, but without much conviction.[3]

God and nature never did speak in human language to Arnold, but earlier writers did, so his poems in response to Wordsworth, Goethe, Sénancour, Shelley, and Byron are of considerably more interest than such poems as "Self-Dependence." In "Stanzas from the Grande Chartreuse" he sadly dismisses the "voices [that] were in all men's ears" (l. 123) as unavailing to alleviate the pains of the modern world: Byron's "bleeding heart" (l. 136), Shelley's "lovely wail" (l. 141), and Obermann's "sad, stern page" (l. 146) can only, at best, add grace to the modern melancholy. Rather more enthusiastically, "Memorial Verses" celebrates "Goethe's sage mind and Byron's force" and especially "Wordsworth's healing power" (ll. 61, 63), but only to regret that all are now silenced:

> Goethe in Weimar sleeps, and Greece,
> Long since, saw Byron's struggle cease.
> But one such death remained to come;
> The last poetic voice is dumb—
> We stand to-day by Wordsworth's tomb.
> (ll. 1–5)

In a Bloomian sense such a mass murder of poetic fathers might be expected to clear the way for new poetry, but in fact the death of the romantic effort seems to represent the death, or permanent silencing, of poetry itself: "The last poetic voice is dumb." Arnold needed to keep these voices alive, to believe in a living and self-sustaining tradition, in order to see any point in his own continued writing.

Arnold needed to qualify and criticize his immediate predecessors, and at the same time to assert the continued vitality of their work. His dilemma is most evident in his treatment of Sénancour, whose melancholy so clearly anticipated Arnold's own that he seemed to have been robbed of his theme: "My melancholy, sciolists say, / Is a past mode, an outworn theme—" ("Stanzas from the Grande Chartreuse," ll. 99–100). The tension between Arnold's desire to redeem Sénancour and his desire to drive a stake through his heart is apparent in "Stanzas in Memory of the Author of 'Obermann.'" Like Arnold, Sénancour suffered in the modern world because he was unable to attain the serene Olympian detachment of Goethe or the naive natural magic of Wordsworth, whose "eyes avert their ken / From half of human fate" (ll. 53–54). He represents a strategy of withdrawal from the world's contagion—a year before writing the poem Arnold had written to Clough that rather than being "sucked for an hour even into the Time Stream in which [Clough and others at Oxford] plunge and bellow" he "took up Obermann, and refuged myself with him in his forest against your Zeit Geist."[4] Obermann is a figure like the Scholar-Gipsy, and both are told to "Fly hence" (l. 17; "The Scholar-Gipsy," l. 206), to avoid the feverish world, and he is like the monks of the Grande Chartreuse in his withdrawal to the high Alpine solitudes. He seems at first to be proof that a strategy of withdrawal may result in enduring works, for he seems to be a living presence in an articulate landscape:

The white mists rolling like a sea!
I hear the torrents roar.
(ll. 9–12) —Yes, Obermann, all speaks of thee;
I feel thee near once more!

Obermann's breath and heat, his living presence, are still found in his book:

I turn thy leaves! I feel their breath
Once more upon me roll;
That air of languor, cold, and death,
Which brooded o'er thy soul.
(ll. 13–16, 21–24) . . . . .
A fever in these pages burns
Beneath the calm they feign;
A wounded human spirit turns;
Here, on its bed of pain.

Even if Arnold's uncertainty about whether Obermann has the icy touch of death-in-life or a burning fever is ignored, there is an evident ambivalence about his continued vitality. The living presence is dying, and further, is infectious—unlike the Scholar-Gipsy or the monks, Obermann has seen deep, not wide, and his "strain" is obviously unlovely and unloved:

Some secrets may the poet tell,
For the world loves new ways;
(ll. 41–44) To tell too deep ones is not well—
It knows not what he says.

But this is defensive—the world is not too callow to understand the chilling counsel to despair:

Thy head is clear, thy feeling chill,
And icy thy despair.

(ll. 87–92) Yes, as the son of Thetis said,
I hear thee saying now:
Greater by far than thou are dead;
Strive not! die also thou!

The poem, in fact, seems less a eulogy of Obermann than a kind of exorcism, an attempt to face the dangers of his still potent voice, or "spell" (l. 82). Arnold has clearly identified with him, for like Obermann (somewhat anachronistically), and unlike Goethe and Wordsworth, Arnold did not pass his youth in a "tranquil world" (l. 67), but was born into the modern age:

brought forth and reared in hours
Of change, alarm, surprise—
(ll. 69–72)[5] What shelter to grow ripe is ours?
What leisure to grow wise?

Under such circumstances it is impossible to gain "Wordsworth's sweet calm," or Goethe's "wide / And luminous view" (ll. 79–80); it is impossible to withdraw from "The hopeless tangle of our age" (l. 83) except in depth. In short, Obermann's example will not serve, and his shade must be laid to rest. Consequently the last fifty lines of the poem constitute a long good-bye to Obermann, which obliterates his "hardly-heard-of grave" (l. 180) and stresses his "unstrung will" and "broken Heart" (l. 183). But it is, more than that, Arnold's farewell to melancholy romanticism generally and, apparently, an attempted farewell to many of his earlier themes and concerns:

> Away the dreams that but deceive
> And thou, sad guide, adieu!
> I go, fate drives me; but I leave
> Half of my life with you.
> (ll. 129–32)

The passage resembles such palinodes as Wordsworth's "Elegiac Stanzas," and seems more a farewell to his own earlier self than to Obermann. And the "sad guide" is left a "melancholy shade" (l. 138) whose spells are no longer obeyed. The end result of the poem, then, is to attribute a living power to the predecessor, to cast it as threatening and demonic, and to exorcise it, leaving the speaker free to return to the world where he "must live" (l. 137). Unfortunately, however, having eliminated the voices of his poetic predecessors, Arnold has only, in a sense, lobotomized himself—the half he has left behind is the half responsible for his best early poetry, and he is still left without an authoritative voice to write any other kind of poetry.

"Stanzas in Memory of the Author of 'Obermann'" is characteristic of the poems of the 1852 volume in its testing and final rejection of a possible poetic stance and voice. It is a self-canceling poem in a volume that Arnold effectively canceled with the Preface to *Poems* of 1853, and it suffers from precisely the problem Arnold described in the Preface: "The confusion of the present time is great, the multitude of voices counselling different things bewildering, the number of existing works capable of attracting a young writer's attention and of becoming his models, immense. What he wants is a hand to guide him through the confusion, a voice to prescribe to him the aim which he should keep in view" (1:8). The 1853 Preface, like many poems in the preceding volume, rejected all romantic poems and voices, including Arnold's own, as inadequate, but it was designed specifically to explain and justify the suppression of *Empedocles on Etna,* Arnold's most ambitious effort—and most conspicuous failure—to find a prescriptive voice.

Empedocles on Etna

Arnold's failure to find a firm basis for speech in *Empedocles on Etna* is arguably the cause of the poem's success. As Allott has said, "'Empedocles on Etna' is seen in a true perspective as Arnold's most comprehensive attempt to '*solve* the Universe' by bringing into unity the fragments of his thought, but paradoxically it is the failure of this intention that is responsible finally for the artistic success of the poem."[6] It is true that in 1847 he had chastised Clough for overambitiously trying to "*solve* the Universe," but in 1852, looking back on the composition of his *Empedocles* volume and presumably thinking of the title poem, he explained his motivation: "But woe was upon me if I analyzed not my situation: and Werter[,] Réné[,] and such like[,] none of them analyse the modern situation in its true *blankness* and *barrenness,* and *unpoetrylessness.*"[7] Arnold's problem, however, was to write poetry in what seemed to him an unpoetic age, and simply analyzing himself and his situation, it would seem, could only lead to a blank, barren, and poetryless poem—and ultimately Arnold concluded that exactly this had happened, and so suppressed *Empedocles on Etna.*

Very likely, as Allott has suggested, Arnold's initial purpose was to analyze his situation through the central vatic utterance of Empedocles, his long speech to Pausanias (1.2.77–426). This speech, standing alone, would certainly seem to match Arnold's initial idea of a poem about "Empedocles—refusal of limitation by the religious sentiment," and to reflect his early note on the title character. Like Obermann, Empedocles was conceived as sad, stern, and withdrawn to the mountain solitudes. But unlike Obermann, Empedocles possessed the unquestioned *truth,* a "great and severe" truth: "the truth of the truth." He undoubtedly saw the object as in itself it really is: "He sees things as they are—the world as it is—God as he is: in their stern simplicity."[8] He is in a position to speak as an oracle, to be a definitive and prescriptive voice. In 1849, according to the testimony of a friend, Arnold seemed to be at work on an oracular rather than a dramatic poem: "He was working at an 'Empedocles'—which seemed to be not much about the man who leapt in the crater—but his name and outward circumstances are used for the drapery of his own thoughts."[9] The speech itself, a kind of chant accompanied "in a solemn manner" (stage direction) on a harp, seems designed, as Walter Houghton has said, "to suppress the personality in order to emphasize the thought."[10]

Like the other oracular voices in the 1852 volume, this one was severely qualified, not to say completely undermined. It had to be, because Empedocles' thoughts, and his clumsy, stilted, and almost universally disliked verse are utterly inimical to poetry.[11] Refusal to limit the intellect by faith or feeling is the scientific way, the way of analysis, and the way, apparently, to truth, but it is barren, blank, and poetryless. Arnold lamented but could not overcome his conviction that "the service of reason is freezing to feeling, chilling to the religious mood. And feeling and the religious mood are eternally the deepest being of man, the ground of all joy and greatness for him."[12] Obviously Empedocles could not be an adequate oracle if he is cut off from the essential ground of joy and greatness in humanity, if his objective truths are inimical to the inner truth of mankind.

In the first place the speech is undercut—no doubt accidentally—by its sheer badness. It is repetitive, long-winded, often banal, and always derivative. It merges fragments of thought from Empedocles, Socrates, Marcus Aurelius, the Bhagavad Gita, Goethe, Sénancour, Byron, Wordsworth, and Carlyle to arrive at familiar Arnoldian sentiments: stoic resignation to an indifferent and godless world in conjunction with the Socratic injunction to "know thyself." Unlike most oracles, it insists most emphatically on what cannot be known and on the impossibility of an integrated vision:

> Hither and thither spins
> The wind-borne, mirroring soul,
> A thousand glimpses wins,
> (1.2.82–86) And never sees a whole;
> Looks once, and drives elsewhere, and leaves its
> last employ.

Many such passages in the speech recapitulate the concerns expressed in Arnold's earlier poems and in his letters to Clough, but without getting beyond them. The modern, multitudinous world cannot be seen whole, cannot provide joy, cannot offer grounds for faith or poetry. The aridity of Empedocles' language, moreover, represents a kind of apotheosis in Arnold's poetry of what results when language is forced to express no more than the conceptual "truth" of scientific reason. W. David Shaw puts the point extremely well: "The process of continuously paralleling metaphorical with conceptual language reaches a climax in the crabbed and tortured language of Empedocles' ode to Pausanias. There is a frightening spiritual slackness in this ode, an incredible flatness and despondency, which not even Empedocles' harp can quite turn into poetry. The banality and harshness match the transformation of Empedocles into a principle of pure, unbodied mind."[13] Almost any stanza would illustrate Shaw's point, but the following will do to express the bleak skepticism of the oracle:

> Fools! That in man's brief term
> He cannot all things view,
> (1.2.347–51) Affords no ground to affirm
> That there are Gods who do;
> Nor does being weary prove that he has where to rest.

Aside from the contemptuous epithet, the language is as flat—as blank and barren—as Arnold can make it. It is the language of pure logical reason, eschewing color and metaphor and only twisted into poetry by the contortions that provide the meter and rhymes. The only emotion expressed is contempt for the illogic of faith and hope. Like most of the rest of the speech, the stanza emphasizes in both form and content the sterile inhumanity of Empedocles' reason, and the poetrylessness of Empedocles and his age—or rather, of the modern age.

Even if Arnold had let Empedocles' ode stand on its own, as he may originally have planned, it would have demonstrated, whether deliberately or not, the inadequacy of the voice of reason as a voice of poetry. But Arnold's decision to cast the poem in dramatic form reveals his awareness of the limitations of Empedocles as an oracle—as soon as his speech became part of a play, it ceased to be oracular and became just another questionable voice. And to the extent that all the voices in the poem are seen as projections of Arnold's own diverse and unintegrated attitudes, it becomes just another role in the "dialogue of the mind with itself." Within the dramatic structure, Empedocles' speech is no more privileged as truth than other utterances—the other characters do not function, as in a Socratic dialogue, as a means to elicit the "wisdom of one master voice."[14] Because the poem does not resolve itself into one univocal utterance, it resembles the 1852 volume as a whole by presenting a din of contending voices, none of which can sway the others, or even fully communicate with them. At the beginning of the drama, for example, Callicles and Pausanias confront one another with radically different worldviews, but the confrontation results not in mutual edification, or reconciliation, or a dialectical movement toward truth, but only in genial invective. Callicles declares that Pausanias is "a learned man, / But credulous of fables as a girl," and Pausanias responds, "And thou, a boy whose tongue outruns his knowledge / And on whose lightness blame is thrown away" (1.1.159–62). The exchange, though trivial, demonstrates the general inconsequentiality of human speech, which may be too easily believed, too uninformed, or simply "thrown away," but seems never to have its intended effect. But the drama is designed to emphasize failed communications in more obvious ways as well. The two central characters, Callicles and Empedocles, never see each other, and at no point does Callicles even hear what Empedocles is saying. Empedocles, at the top of the mountain, does hear Callicles' songs and they seem at first to have the desired effect of soothing him (1.2.483), but in the end they vex him and help drive him to suicide. Indeed, Empedocles' consistent misunderstanding of Callicles' songs wonderfully epitomizes the problem of the modern poet who can never make himself properly understood, cannot communicate by poetry. Finally, Empedocles, as Mermin puts it, "speaks only half his mind to Pausanias."[15] After counseling him to resign himself, Empedocles dismisses the "good, learned, friendly, quiet man" (2.1.8) in terms akin to the faint praise with which

Tennyson's Ulysses damned Telemachus, and then declares that he cannot follow his own advice. And worse, despite Empedocles' self-congratulatory declaration that Pausanias "hath his lesson" (2.1.7), there is little reason to think that Pausanias could pass an exam on it. He had wanted to hear about miracles, after all, and he departs in regret that he cannot alter the sage's troubled and uneven state of mind: "I dare not urge him further—he must go; / But he is strangely wrought!" (1.2.479–80). Empedocles had given Pausanias only one specific injunction—to thank Callicles and ask him to stop playing (1.2.467–69)—but so little effect do his words have that the disciple leaves intent on disobeying them: "Callicles must wait here, and play to him" (1.2.484).

Not only do the principal speakers fail to communicate with one another in any effective way, but each speaker, and almost each speech, undercuts the preceding one. Even Empedocles' long monologue preceding his suicide consists of a series of tentative assertions, qualifications, and denials. The whole drama, from this perspective, seems an elaborate process of self-deconstruction in which no position (until Callicles' final song, at least) is allowed to stand unchallenged. The suicide of Empedocles is the logical end, for it is the only deconstruction thorough enough to put an end to the continuous vacillation. In fact, it is not even entirely clear that death will end the torments of mental uncertainty—death will deconstruct the body down to the very atoms, but the mind may be returned to earth to continue in baffling uncertainty:

> And we shall be unsatisfied as now;
> And we shall feel the agony of thirst,
> (2.355–58) The ineffable longing for the life of life
> Baffled for ever.

Even the suicide, which may or may not be final, must be done not on fixed conviction but on impulse, before Empedocles has a chance to change his mind again:

> And therefore, O ye elements! I know—
> (2.404–16) Ye know it too—it hath been granted me
> Not to die wholly, not to be all enslaved.

I feel it in this hour. The numbing cloud
Mounts off my soul; I feel it, I breathe free.
Is it but for a moment?
—Ah, boil up, ye vapours!
Leap and roar, thou sea of fire!
My soul glows to meet you.
Ere it flag, ere the mists
Of despondency and gloom
Rush over it again,
Receive me, save me!

Though Empedocles' speech and suicide have been regarded as a kind of triumph,[16] they effectively undo everything he has claimed to believe. Not only does his speech to the elements put him among those he had condemned for "peopling the void air" (1.2.278), but his act is based not on intellect but on feeling: "I feel it in this hour. . . . I feel it." The suicide does indeed eradicate his mind—or at least his doctrines—as well as his body.

Very obviously Empedocles does not represent an unquestioned, authoritative voice in this poem, but what, then, of Callicles? There is good reason to think that in rejecting the Empedoclean vision both in its rational mode of stoical resignation (the speech to Pausanias) and in its romantic mode of tortured Byronic inwardness (the Manfred-like soliloquy on the mountaintop), Arnold was opting instead for the serene classical vision of Callicles. Paul Zietlow has recently and rightly said that as Arnold's "life progressed, the way of Callicles increasingly came to be his way."[17] The 1853 Preface rejects Empedocles, but not Callicles—classical serenity like that of Callicles is held up as a model of what art ought to achieve, and in fact Arnold excerpted Callicles' songs from their objectionable context and reprinted them separately. And of course Callicles does get the last word, as he serenely sings a hymn to Apollo and the Muses after Empedocles has flung himself into the volcano. But though Arnold evidently came to endorse the way of Callicles by 1853, within *Empedocles on Etna* the young poet's voice, as Zietlow notes, "is merely one of several" and has no special authority.[18] The point of the poem, in fact, can not be made with any one voice, because no adequate univocal utterance is possible to "*solve* the Universe" and reduce multitudinousness to unity. The point is in the dramatic structure, which juxtaposes two powerful but incompatible voices and demonstrates their incapacity to complement or complete each other—instead, as I have suggested, they tend to negate each other.

It is difficult to be precise about what each of the two voices represents. The issue is not simply of romanticism against classicism, since Empedocles owes as much to Marcus Aurelius as to Byron, and Callicles is associated as much with the romantic "natural magic" of Keats, Guérin, and Wordsworth as with classical, Olympian calm.[19] Nor is the distinction simply between Apollonian and Dionysian, as has sometimes been suggested, since Empedocles and Callicles are both followers of Apollo, and are both in some sense associated with the Dionysian: Empedocles ends up identifying with the primitive world of the titans, and Callicles, with his "head full of wine, and [his] hair crowned" (1.1.32) is akin to the earlier Strayed Reveller, a wanderer from a Bacchic or Dionysian rout. But the Nietzschean terms help to define the world of *Empedocles on Etna.* What is missing in both characters is the genuine Dionysiac identification with natural, primal, mysterious forces—it had been possible in Empedocles' youth, but is possible no more (2.235–75). For Arnold and Nietzsche both, the loss of primal harmony with the natural world dates back to the fifth century B.C., when the "dialogue of the mind with itself has commenced" (Preface, 1:1), but for Nietzsche the dialogue is precisely the Socratic one that—like Arnold's Empedocles—elevated the scientific, reasoning mind over feeling, wonder, and awe. The resultant extermination of myth, according to Nietzsche, led to precisely the multitudinousness and the impossibility of finding an authoritative voice that troubled Arnold: "Let us consider abstract man stripped of myth, abstract education, abstract mores, abstract law, abstract government; the random vagaries of the artistic imagination unchanneled by any native myth; a culture without any fixed and consecrated place of origin, condemned to exhaust all possibilities and feed miserably and parasitically on every culture under the sun. Here we have our present age, the result of a Socratism that is bent on the extermination of myth."[20] Nietzsche was far more aware than Arnold that the scientific spirit of analysis and abstraction is antithetical to poetry, that it led to fragmentation of consciousness and isolation of the individual from the general life of nature and of mankind—that it led to the "individuated world which is the essence of Apollonian art."[21] Still, Arnold was working toward some such conception with his portrayal of Empedocles, who was Apollo's votary until he became so oppressed by the burden of individuation that he revolted from the "young" but "intolerably severe" God:

> Thou keepest aloof the profane,
> But the solitude oppresses thy votary!
> The jars of men reach him not in thy valley—
> But can life reach him?
> Thou fencest him from the multitude—
> (2.207–17) Who will fence him from himself?
> He hears nothing but the cry of the torrents,
> And the beating of his own heart.
> The air is thin, the veins swell,
> The temples tighten and throb there—
> Air! Air!

The modern problem is the sense of stifling, claustrophobic entrapment within the isolated self, cut off from the general life by relentlessly analytic thought. As Arnold wrote to Clough, "*Congestion of the brain* is what we suffer from—I always feel it and say it—and cry for air like my own Empedocles."[22]

For Nietzsche the solution was to recognize that the modern scientific faith in the attainability of *truth* by abstract reason is illusory,[23] but Arnold's persistent desire to see things as they really are kept him loyal to the idea of scientific reason as an absolute—a staple of his later criticism is the notion that "the prescriptions of reason are absolute, unchanging, of universal validity" (3:264). Still, his use of Callicles seems to have been an attempt to achieve a Nietzschean solution by returning to myth. Critics have often pointed out that Callicles represents the artist of "natural magic"—or, in Nietzschean terms, he represents the "Dionysiac magic," the "powerful esthetic magic" that transports an audience instead of simply "arousing moral and religious responses."[24] Though I have already suggested that Callicles is not genuinely Dionysian, his songs, all concerned with the triumph of Apollonian calm over primitive turbulence, seem at first to embody the fusion of Dionysian and Apollonian that Nietzsche regarded as the highest art of classical serenity, "the ripest fruit of Apollonian culture—which must always triumph first over titans, kill monsters, and overcome the somber contemplation of actuality, the intense susceptibility to suffering, by means of illusions strenuously and zestfully entertained."[25] But a closer look at the songs, and at their failure to overcome Empedocles' "somber contemplation of actuality," reveals that they represent, at best, what Nietzsche called the modern misinterpretation of classical serenity as "a condition of undisturbed complacence."[26] Instead of embodying two opposite poles of a dialectic, such as romantic versus classical or Dionysian versus Apollonian, Empedocles and Callicles end up embodying two parts of the fragmented modern self, both incapable of retrieving the lost wholeness of an earlier world.

The first of Callicles' songs is unarguably one of the finest examples of Arnoldian natural magic. It beautifully describes the streams, the woods, the flowers of the lower slopes of Etna, but it conspicuously fails to incorporate the part of the landscape that involves a less than comfortable prospect:

> but glade,
> And stream, and sward, and chestnut-trees,
> End here; Etna beyond, in the broad glare
> Of the hot noon, without a shade,
> Slope behind slope, up to the peak, lies bare;
> The peak, round which the white clouds play.
>
> (1.2.51–56)

The second part of the song, which describes the centaur Chiron's teaching Peleus and Achilles "all the wisdom of his race" (1.2.76), takes place "In such a glen" (1.2.57), but the wisdom that may be found on the higher slopes is not taught here. Callicles' eyes, like Wordsworth's, "avert their ken / From half of human fate" (ll. 53–54). It may be possible to learn all the wisdom of Chiron's race in such a way, but Chiron is only half human—Empedocles' speech to

Pausanias, which immediately follows, only points the implicit moral that the serenity of the glen comes from ignoring, not transcending, the actual conditions of human existence. The inadequacy of Callicles' complacent vision is even more obvious in his second song, in which he celebrates the metamorphoses of Cadmus and Harmonia from a suffering and "grey old man and woman" (1.2.449) to "two bright and aged snakes" (1.2.435). Once again serenity can be achieved, but only at the expense of one's humanity. In fact, Arnold deliberately altered his source to emphasize the point. In Ovid's account Cadmus and Harmonia remember "what they once were," but in Arnold's version they achieve calm only by utterly forgetting their humanity:

Placed safely in changed forms, the pair
(1.2.457–60) Wholly forget their first sad life, and home,
And all that Theban woe, and stray
For ever through the glens, placid and dumb.

According to Allott, the song provides "lyrical relief after the philosopher's instruction of Pausanias,"[27] but more than that, it provides a kind of ironic coda. Empedocles had been preaching resignation, had been insisting on the danger (to which he himself succumbed) of trying to know too much—Cadmus and Harmonia parody the achieved calm of a resigned existence. Callicles, evidently, finds the story merely gratifying, but Arnold plainly undercuts him by stressing the brutalizing complacency of the old snakes in his closing phrase. Surely serene beauty is not to be desired for the sake of a dehumanized, "placid and dumb" existence.

Callicles' third song is certainly more than lyrical relief, since it directly affects the action. Empedocles, like Manfred on the Jungfrau, has just resolved to pitch himself into the intense inane when he is plucked back—not, like Manfred, by the grasp of a chamois hunter, but by the "lyre's voice," which, sings Callicles,

is lovely everywhere;
In the court of Gods, in the city of men,
(2.37–41) And in the lonely rock-strewn mountain-glen,
In the still mountain air.
Only to Typho it sounds hatefully.

The real subject of the song is the lyre's voice itself, the power and charm of lyric, but the "sub-subject," as Buckler puts it, is the defeat of titanic energy by Olympian cunning.[28] Callicles sympathizes with the rebel giant Typho to an extent, but it is clear that he sees the subduing of fierce, rebellious energy as essential to Olympian serenity—his lyric concludes with a description of the "awful pleasure bland" (1.67) of Jove and the other "soothed Gods" (2.81) in an Olympus anesthetized from all distress:

the loved Hebe bears
(2.84–86) The cup about, whose draughts beguile
Pain and care.

As in all of Callicles' songs, Olympian calm is celebrated, but with an undercurrent sense that it is "bland," or "placid and dumb," and that it is achieved by suppressing and forgetting the primitive passions. The gods beguiled by Hebe's cup are not unlike dumb beasts beguiled by Circe's. Classical calm is not here a transcendence of human misery but a drugged oblivion. Callicles himself, who is rather damningly associated with the Strayed Reveller, is not distressed by this, but his cruel indifference to the pain of Typho certainly undermines his role as a model for the modern artist. Further, as Zietlow has said, the poem is susceptible to a "romantic misreading" by the Byronic Empedocles,[29] though his interpretation of the story can only be regarded as a "misreading" if authorial intention is taken as the sole basis of a correct critical interpretation. Rather like the later Arnold who deconstructed the myths of the Bible, Empedocles demythologizes the tale to arrive at its "real" meaning:

He fables, yet speaks truth!
The brave, impetuous heart yields everywhere
To the subtle, contriving head;
(2.89–94) Great qualities are trodden down,
And littleness united
Is become invincible.

Empedocles interprets the story of Typho precisely as Byron interpreted the story of Prometheus. It is a case of "plainness oppressed by cunning," of great passions and energies repressed by petty tyranny. Of course this is the "real" meaning only from a certain perspective, but the point of juxtaposing Callicles' "classical" sense of the myth with Empedocles' "romantic" interpretation would seem to be that in a multitudinous world the same events have different meanings when seen from different angles. Once again, no one lyrical or interpretive voice is adequate, and once again communication or harmony among different views and voices is impossible—they are simply incompatible, contradictory.

Callicles' lyric about the "lyre's voice" and the triumph of Olympian serenity provides a particularly clear case of the difficulties of using authorial intention as the grounds for critical interpretation. It is difficult to say definitively what Callicles meant, whether he intended a subtle disparagement of the Olympians with such words as "bland" and "beguile"—is Empedocles' interpretation simply a "close reading," or is it a postromantic deconstruction? It is equally difficult to determine what Arnold intended—is Callicles' song meant to be a compelling model of classical calm, or is it deliberately undercut with subtle irony? If the latter, is Callicles the ironist, or is Arnold? The biographical evidence can be read either way. The critic might point to Arnold's appreciation of classical calm in the 1853 Preface, or he might point to the 1849 complaint that "these are damned times—everything is against one—the height to which knowledge is come, the spread of luxury, our physical enervation, the absence of great *natures,* the unavoidable contact with millions of small ones."[30] Arnold could, plainly, speak with either the voice of Callicles or that of Empedocles. I do not, of course, plan to solve the dilemma, but rather to point out that the dramatic conflict of voices thematically and formally illustrates the extreme difficulty of communication from one mind to another. It is impossible to say exactly what one means, and to be precisely understood. Indeed, in the oral rather than written song that Empedocles hears, the "lyre's voice" may as easily be the "liar's voice" that pleases everywhere by beguiling the hearer from pain and care. In fact, Empedocles responds to the song as though this were its intended meaning: he refuses to be associated any longer with the Olympian Apollo and disparages those who seek not wisdom, but illusion, those who seek

not wisdom,
But drugs to charm with,
(2.115–18) But spells to mutter—
All the fool's-armoury of magic!

The problems inherent in attempting to establish the complacent Apollonian song by the suppression of anything that ruffles its surface are especially clear in Callicles' next song, which celebrates Apollo's victory over the faun Marsyas in a singing contest. Apollo's calm, scornful (and as Empedocles sees it, "intolerably severe" [2.206]) flaying alive of his vanquished Dionysian opponent clearly represents, to Callicles, the final triumph of the Apollonian arts of beguiling pain and sorrow:

The music of the lyre blows away
The clouds which wrap the soul.
(2.123–26) Oh! that Fate had let me see
That triumph of the sweet persuasive lyre.

For many readers Callicles' song is a recognition that "Apollo's victory was not only just but necessary for the sake of the preservation of the awful truth of the highest beauty,"[31] and it thus "may symbolize [Arnold's] decision to reject the Dionysiac element in Greek poetic tradition, looking instead for inspiration to . . . Apolline serenity and control."[32] This seems to be borne out by the 1853 Preface, and it may very possibly have been Arnold's intention, but it is difficult at best to accept the serenity based on indifference to suffering as "the highest beauty," and it is impossible to see the sweeping away of melancholy knowledge as the way to the "awful truth." Once again the "persuasive lyre" may seem a persuasive liar. It may be argued that the young poet's serene songs of the Olympian victories over Typho and Marsyas set forth the Nietzschean "ripest fruit of Apollonian culture" as they "triumph first over titans, kill monsters, and overcome the somber contemplation of actuality," but within the dramatic structure they simply do not have this effect. Empedocles' contempt for the "young, implacable God" (2.232) only increases. To him—and consequently, I think, to the reader—this serene classicism is only "a condition of undisturbed complacence." Callicles' celebration of Apollo's cruelty seems not an acceptance of "the awful truth of the highest beauty" but merely acquiescence in tyranny. Empedocles' response is to jump into the volcano.

Still, Callicles gets the last word. After Empedocles, like Typho and Marsyas, has been vanquished, Callicles sings a final song—its very presence as the last word representing, apparently, "That triumph of the sweet persuasive lyre, / That famous, final victory." But from another perspective it represents not a victory but a defeat, since Callicles, after all, had been trying to soothe the philosopher, not to drive him to suicide. Nevertheless, some of Arnold's most influential critics have seen the final hymn to Apollo as a definitive statement of the author's shift from the tortured romanticism and intellectualism of Empedocles to an aesthetic of calm classicism. E. D. H. Johnson observes that "Callicles has the final word in his hymn to Apollo, which voices a serene and joyous acceptance of things as they are. Although Callicles has previously sung that 'the lyre's voice is lovely everywhere,' he now concludes that the scene of Empedocles' suicide is wanting in poetic inspiration."[33] And Culler makes explicit the point about Arnold's intention: "In the final lyric the process whereby Callicles becomes a kind of chorus or disembodied voice is carried to the point where his voice is indistinguishable from that of the author. For in the last lyric there is nothing said that is not also said in the Preface of 1853."[34] But Callicles' final words are not so definitive. Their serenity may seem rather callous after Empedocles' suicide—the philosopher's torment has been too tellingly rendered to be forgotten as readily as Cadmus and Harmonia forget their humanity, or dismissed as easily as scornful Apollo dismisses the pain of Marsyas. His song, however "serene and joyous," does not describe "things as they are." Instead, it dismisses the actual scene on Etna and wishes itself upon Mt. Helicon, rapt away from mortal care into the presence of the gods:

(2.441–46) What sweet-breathing presence
Out-perfumes the thyme?

What voices enrapture
The night's balmy prime?

'Tis Apollo comes leading
His choir, the Nine.

Shortly before, Empedocles had congratulated himself because he had "Sophisticated no truth, / Nursed no delusion" (2.401–2), but surely Callicles could not say the same—he has merely wished himself away from the troubling scene. To the extent that Culler is right in identifying the "disembodied voice" with "that of the author," *Empedocles on Etna* resembles other poems of the 1852 volume by wishing a definitive, authoritative voice into being. Very possibly Arnold was here attempting, as apRoberts has said, to make "the case for art" as opposed to "discursive logic" or "science,"[35] but he could only do so by boldly declaring a faith in what he had persistently failed to hear—an authoritative voice of God, a "sweet-breathing presence." Finally, the simple fact that Arnold withdrew the poem in 1853 indicates that he himself did not regard Callicles' song as definitive, did not regard the "dialogue of the mind with itself" as closed.

Everything about *Empedocles on Etna* epitomizes Arnold's poetic plight in 1852. The philosopher's sense that his great nature is oppressed by multitudes of small ones echoes Arnold's own sense that "a great career is hardly possible any longer" in a world that is becoming "more comfortable for the mass, and more uncomfortable for those of any natural gift or distinction."[36] The awfulness of Empedocles' sermon to Pausanias demonstrates the incompatibility of modern, scientific modes of thought with poetry, and the self-deluding calm of Callicles' lyre demonstrates the inadequacy of a poetry without depth of thought.[37] Further, the inability of the contending voices to make themselves heard, or understood when heard, and the ineffectuality of Callicles' songs to sooth Empedocles' modern concerns, all imply grave doubts about the possibility of poetry in the modern, increasingly scientific world. And finally, the closing implication that the poet's own voice echoing in the void is the voice of God indicates only that Arnold was still seeking and still not finding the authoritative voice he needed. Under the circumstances it is not surprising that Empedocles abandoned his poetic vocation, that Arnold rejected *Empedocles on Etna* in 1853, and that he eventually all but abandoned poetry for critical prose. And yet *Empedocles on Etna* remains, as it has often been called, one of the finest and most important utterances of the nineteenth century, and it does so because the sum of its failures adds up to a success. The excitement of the poem comes not from the individual speeches and lyrics—all of which, as we have seen, fail of their immediate purpose—but from the juxtaposition of views, the subtle ironies, the internalized literary criticism of Empedocles' "readings" of the songs, and from the devastating stripping away of illusions as the text relentlessly deconstructs itself. In this sense, at least, the work does become a kind of Nietzschean endeavor, as it takes "down the elaborate edifice of Apollonian culture stone by stone until we discover its foundations."[38]

The Neoclassical Manifesto of 1853

The Preface of 1853, with its withdrawal of *Empedocles on Etna,* represents, it is generally agreed, a definitive shift in Arnold's poetics. Certainly it would seem to represent his true last word on the situation of Empedocles, the definitive rebuttal in the dialogue of the mind with itself. The purposes of the Preface are obvious. Arnold was, to begin with, intent on rejecting the romantic excesses of inwardness and formlessness—the morbid introspection of Empedocles and the consequent neglect of the external form of works of art. He withdrew *Empedocles on Etna* not because he had failed with it but because he had succeeded too well in exhibiting the plight of the poet and of poetry in the modern age, in which "the last poetic voice is dumb," and in which the divine, authoritative, healing song of Orpheus and Musaeus was no longer possible. He had succeeded too well in his intention to "delineate the feelings of one of the last of the Greek religious philosophers, one of the family of Orpheus and Musaeus, having survived his fellows, living on into a time when the habits of Greek thought and feeling had begun fast to change, character to dwindle, the influence of the Sophists to prevail. Into the feelings of a man so situated there entered much that we are accustomed to consider as exclusively modern" (1.1).

The modern world, however, was not engendered so much by the Sophists as by Socrates, whose dialogic search for truth, Nietzsche would argue, issued in the modern intellectual sterility and exhaustion described by Arnold: "The dialogue of the mind with itself has commenced; modern problems have presented themselves; we hear already the doubts, we witness the discouragement, of Hamlet and of Faust" (1.1). Arnold's purpose in sacrificing *Empedocles on Etna* is profoundly backward-looking: it is to restore what he sees as "the calm, the cheerfulness, the disinterested objectivity" of the "early Greek genius" (1.1). But it is absolutely consistent with the buried desire in his earlier poetry, for in seeking to hear once again the mythical, oracular, and divine songs of Orpheus and Musaeus, he is once again listening for a voice of God to order the chaos of modern life. Of course he cannot recommend imitation of mythical poets, but his actual recommendation—here and for the rest of his career—is to imitate the Greek classics in order to find "the only sure guidance, the only solid footing" through the "bewildering confusion of our times" (1.14).

Invoking Aristotle, Hesiod, and (somewhat less congruously) Schiller, Arnold insists that the purpose of art is to inspirit and rejoice, and the modern, romantic emphasis on the individual, isolated, and eccentric mind cannot do this. The poet, therefore, must emphasize plot rather than curious thoughts and feelings, must emphasize "actions; human actions; possessing an inherent interest in themselves, and which are to be communicated in an interesting manner by the art of the poet." The poet must, like the ancients, subordinate all such "attractive accessories" as "profoundness of single thoughts," "richness of imagery," and "abundance of illustration" to the architectonic whole in which the action is presented (1.9). And this austere style Arnold calls the "grand style": "With [the ancients], the action predominated over the expression of it; with us, the expression predominates over the action. Not that they failed in expression, or were inattentive to it; on the contrary, they are the highest models of expression, the unapproached masters of the *grand style*. But their expression is so excellent because it is so admirably kept in its right degree of prominence; because it is so simple and so well subordinated; because it draws its force directly from the pregnancy of the matter which it conveys" (1.5). In the Preface, Arnold is not entirely clear about how the grand style affects us, but he implies the point made explicit in the later essays *On Translating Homer*: "The grand style . . . is something more than touching or stirring; it can form the character, it is edifying" (1.138). Evidently it gets this power by presenting *things* with the minimal amount of mediation by *words*, by drawing "its force directly from the pregnancy of the matter," not from the words of the poet. It is a style that attempts sheer transparency, that attempts to efface the poet from the work. He declares that the poet is "most fortunate, when he most entirely succeeds in effacing himself, and in enabling a noble action to subsist as it did in nature" (1.8). Arnold was quite explicit on the point in a letter to Clough written several months before the Preface: "More and more I feel that the difference between a mature and a youthful age of the world compels the poetry of the former to use great plainness of speech as compared with that of the latter: and that Keats and Shelley were on a false track when they set themselves to reproduce the exuberance of expression, the charm, the richness of images, and the felicity of the Elizabethan poets." Modern poetry, he argues, must once again be a guide to life, must serve a religious function, and to perform this "immense task" its "language, style, and general proceedings . . . must be very plain direct and severe: and it must not lose itself in parts and episodes and ornamental work, but must press forwards to the whole."[39] Arnold's ideal, as always, was "to see the object as in itself it really is," and he was evidently becoming increasingly convinced that poetic language could only get in the way. He obviously meant to "reck his own rede"—the bulk of his poetry after 1853 consists of three long pieces meant to demonstrate his neoclassical aesthetic. *Sohrab and Rustum* (1853), *Balder Dead* (1855) and *Merope* (1857) were all conceived to demonstrate the importance of a great action, of attention to the architectonic whole, and of the grand style.

But despite Arnold's confident tone and his willingness to act on his own principles, the Preface is, at best, problematic. Its urbane self-confidence is a fitting prelude to Arnold's later critical work partly because it so well illustrates T. S. Eliot's famous remark that "he had no real serenity, only an impeccable demeanour."[40] In fact, he was probably ruffled by unfavorable comparisons of his early work with the spasmodic poetry of Alexander Smith, whose inchoate spasms of outlandish imagery must have struck him as a parody of the confused multitudinousness of Keats, Browning, and Tennyson.[41] As Manfred Dietrich has well said, the somewhat pedantic Preface, the repudiation of *Empedocles,* the "arbitrary, and confused selection of early poems" for the 1853 volume all seem an "effort to mask his uncertainty with decisive gestures."[42] In order to make his case for a return to the classics convincing, Arnold misrepresents the ancients with a naive assertion of their calm and cheerfulness, misrepresents his own *Empedocles on Etna* by declaring that the topic rather than the handling was at fault, and by stating—quite contrary to the obvious climactic action of his protagonist—that it could "find no vent in action." Further, in order to establish his own divergence from the critical climate of his day, he misrepresents that climate. He takes to task a "modern critic," who "not only permits a false practice; he absolutely prescribes false aims.—'A true allegory of the state of one's own mind in a representative history,' the poet is told, 'is perhaps the highest thing that one can attempt in the way of poetry.' And accordingly he attempts it. An allegory of the state of one's own mind, the highest problem of an art which imitates actions! No assuredly, it is not, it never can be so: no great poetical work has ever been produced with such an aim" (1.8). But the critic under attack (since identified as David Masson) was, in fact, explicating the theory of Arnold's critical idol, Goethe, and was, moreover, not "prescribing" a kind of poetry but discussing the limitations a poet faces—what he *can* attempt, not what he should attempt.[43] Masson was, in fact, in the process of attacking Alexander Smith for excessive imagery, and his essay is in large part a more moderate statement of many of Arnold's views—Arnold's unfair use of him as a whipping boy seems to imply more an Empedoclean need to set himself above the common throng than a desire to see his age unified in a correct view of things.

But the real problems of the Preface result simply from the impracticality of Arnold's positions. Most clearly, he advises the poets of his age how to write poetry and so attempts to set up a program for poetry in the nineteenth century, and yet he also clearly anticipates his later, more explicit statements that poetry is all but impossible in the present age. Just as he concludes "The Function of Criticism at the Present Time" with the sentiment that criticism only, and not poetry, is worth pursuing in this age, so he concludes the Preface with the sense that great poetry may well be impossible "under the circumstances amidst which we live." If so, he says, "let us not bewilder our successors; let us transmit to them the practice of poetry, with its boundaries and wholesome regulative laws, under which excellent works may again, perhaps, at some future time, be produced, not yet fallen into oblivion through our neglect, not yet condemned and cancelled by the influence of their eternal enemy, caprice" (1.15). He is not far from advising young poets to give up writing poetry and turn to neoclassical criticism instead.

Other, less obvious, implications of the Preface are still more disturbing. Arnold's ideal of a transparent language is, of course, simply impossible to attain or even approach, and its real bent, paradoxically, is to eliminate language from poetry. Great poetry, Arnold argues, consists somehow "in the action itself" rather than in "the language about the action" (1.7). He faults not only the romantics but even Shakespeare for excessive ornamentation, excessive richness, and abundance of language, and he seems to praise Menander for telling "a man who enquired as to the progress of his comedy that he had finished it, not having yet written a single line, because he had constructed the action of it in his mind" (1.7). In effect, he praises the work that has not found its way into language at the expense of those that have. (As an additional irony, Menander's play, if ever written, was subsequently lost—thanks, Arnold later declares, to the "instinct of humanity" to dispense with the "sceptical, frivolous, and dissolute" [1.30]. Menander's saving merit seems to be that none of his works survives, that his language is completely transparent!). Arnold is in more control of the implications of his argument when he declares that those who have carefully studied the ancients "are more truly than others under the empire of facts, and more independent of the language current among those with whom they live" (1.13), but his desire is even more clearly to wish away language as something that obstructs rather than clarifies one's sense of the "facts." In the lectures *On Translating Homer* Arnold repeatedly insisted that whereas Homer "sees his object and conveys it to us immediately," his translator "cannot forbear to interpose a play of thought between his object and its expression. Chapman translates his object into Elizabethan, as Pope translates it into the Augustan of Queen Anne; both convey it to us through a medium" (1.116). Of course Arnold is arguing for "perfect plainness and directness" (1.116) as opposed to elaborate ornamentation, but once again the ideal is to eliminate language and the "play of thought" altogether, to see the object unmediated by language. His description of the ideal work of art, perfectly perceived by its audience, manages to transform classical drama into a nonlinguistic event, and for that matter, to transform its "action" into stasis:

(1.6) *The terrible old mythic story on which the drama was founded stood, before he entered the theatre, traced in its bare outlines upon the spectator's mind; it stood in his memory, as a group of statuary, faintly seen, at the end of a long and dark vista: then came the poet, embodying outlines, developing situations, not a word wasted, not a sentiment capriciously thrown in: stroke upon stroke, the drama proceeded: the light deepened upon the group; more and more it revealed itself to the riveted gaze of the spectator: until at last, when the final words were spoken, it stood before him in broad sunlight, a model of immortal beauty.*

This crucial passage—referred to by Mermin as the "imaginative center" of the Preface—inspired J. Hillis Miller's remark that "nothing in Arnold's criticism is more striking than the way he forgets that poetry is written with words, and wants it to become solid and sculptured, as detached from the mind and its 'devouring flame of thought,' as a group of Greek statues."[44] For the same reason his favorite word for the ancient masterpieces was "monuments"—objects, not words.

Arnold's antiromanticism in the Preface almost compelled him to take a stand against language itself, for language corresponds to the inner and individual world of thought, not to the outer world of objects and "facts." As Shelley put it, "Language is arbitrarily produced by the Imagination and has relation to thoughts alone,"[45] but this arbitrariness of the Imagination is just the "eternal enemy, caprice" that Arnold was combating. Obviously one could not have a poetry without words, but the ideal would be a poetry in which the words have as little potential as possible for capricious individuality. The ideal would be, and is for Arnold, poetry written in a dead language. Admiration of the ancient classics is, to be sure, laudable, but Arnold's extreme privileging of the productions of a dead language over those of a living language has disheartening implications. In the first place, it makes the greatest art an exclusively academic concern. Although Arnold, in his social writings and in his insistence on middle-class education became the greatest of all champions of culture to leaven the masses, his neoclassicism nevertheless tended to appropriate culture for the privileged few. As J. D. Coleridge spitefully but not unreasonably argued at the time, "If the best poetry is not to be understood without a profound acquaintance with, and relish for the classics, the best poetry is to be written for a hundred or two of the male sex only out of the population of a great country."[46] Once again the buried tendency of Arnold's argument is not to bring about a national consensus but to preserve art and culture from the national hurly-burly.

Another problem with Arnold's exclusive emphasis on the ancients is both more subtle and more deeply rooted. He wanted an art that would appeal to primary human feelings, that would bring pleasure, joy, edification, that would be a guide to life, and he realized that to have this effect literature must have a powerful immediacy. But he also sensed that one way—perhaps the only way—for literature to have this effect is to produce the illusion of a present, living voice. His contemporary David Masson had argued that the "literature of moral stimulation" is "oratorical literature" and in the same article had suggested that postclassical literature had become less oratorical: "It seems probable that the tendency to excess of imagery is natural to the Gothic or Romantic, as distinct from the Hellenic or Classical imagination; but it is not unlikely that the fact that poetry is now read instead of being merely heard, as it once was, has something to do with it."[47] Arnold, more strongly than Masson, saw the ornamentation of romantic art as interfering with the immediacy of literature, and therefore championed what he called the "true oratorical flow of ancient tragedy" (1.62). But of course his desire for an immediate and moving presence is totally at odds with his desire to efface the poet and to avoid the eccentricities and "play of thought" that can scarcely be avoided in a too lively language. So his emphasis on the strict rules of a dead language paradoxically moves him away from the immediacy he seeks. As Walter Ong has argued at length, the culture that cuts itself off from its "mother tongue" necessarily alienates itself from the immediacy of human experience. The languages of academic culture are "languages learned by males from other males, always as second languages acquired by those who already have other mother tongues. . . . they depend on writing rather than oral speech for their existence. Writing establishes them at a distance from the immediate interpersonal human lifeworld where the word unites one human being with another."[48] Even Arnold, in his Preface to *Merope,* acknowledged that the dead languages could not speak to many, and could perhaps not speak intimately to anyone: "Not only is it vain to expect that the vast majority of mankind will ever undertake the toil of mastering a dead language, above all, a dead language so difficult as the Greek; but it may be doubted whether even those, whose enthusiasm shrinks from no toil, can ever so thoroughly press into the intimate feeling of works composed in a dead language as their enthusiasm would desire" (1.39). And this, of course, is precisely why Arnold wanted to reproduce the effects of the Greek "monuments" in the English language, but it is also precisely why his goal was unattainable. The primary problem is implicit in Arnold's decision not simply to translate "one of the great works of Aeschylus or Sophocles": "No man can do his best with a subject which does not penetrate him: no man can be penetrated by a subject which he does not conceive independently" (1.39–40). But he has just said that no one can "press into" or "be penetrated by" the works of a dead language, so presumably he cannot do his best with the forms of a dead culture. It is difficult to avoid the sense that the curiously erotic denials of Arnold's language make the generation of new life in art impossible. Or, to put it another way, the application of exclusively male learning to what had become an exclusively male language was likely to end in sterile academicism. Or, to put it still less fancifully, Arnold would have had to agree with Nietzsche's assertion that modern men (women do not enter into the matter) are "able to approach the once-living reality of myth only by means of intellectual constructs. Yet every culture that has lost myth has lost, by the same token, its natural, healthy creativity."[49] Nietzsche wonderfully describes the Arnoldian sense of a hopeless modern alienation in multitudinousness, in which "the random vagaries of the artistic imagination" are unchanneled by any native myth and in which "a culture without any fixed and consecrated place of origin" is "condemned to exhaust all possibilities and feed miserably and parasitically on every culture under the sun."[50] The analysis alarmingly summons Arnold's feeding on Persian legend for *Sohrab and Rustum,* on Norse mythology for *Balder Dead,* on Greek mythology for *Merope*. Modern art based on the classics becomes mere imitation, a reproduction of the dead letter and not of the living spirit—and indeed the all but universal response to Arnold's poems in this manner is that insofar as they succeed in reproducing ancient actions without modern "play of thought" they are dry, sterile, dead. His recognition of this difficulty no doubt discouraged Arnold as a poet and encouraged him to write critical prose—which he evidently felt free to write in a living language. Ironically, as he was initiating his professorship at Oxford with the dead language of *Merope,* he was also determining to abandon the standard practice of lecturing in Latin because, as he wrote to his brother Tom, "the Latin has so died out, even among scholars, that it seems idle to entomb in a dead language a lecture which, in English, might be stimulating and interesting."[51]

Arnold's efforts to reproduce the moving effect of the ancients were doomed to failure for a still more fundamental reason. As soon as he moved from the dead letter of a dead language into living English, and as soon as he chose a subject that "penetrated" him, he could not keep his own modern thoughts and feelings out of the poems. And this, as Arnold's critics have always felt, is the only saving grace of these poems. Once again, the submerged sexuality of the language is oddly suggestive. For Nietzsche, as for Arnold, the not so latent subtext is sexually charged, as the frustrated desires of the sterile academic search are attributed to "the loss of myth, of a mythic home, the mythic womb."[52] Seen in this light, Arnold is the very model of the orphaned apostle of culture who has cut himself off from the immediacy of experience and, in a sense, from his own infancy, his own mother culture and mother tongue, to seek a more purely masculine bond with the father, and to find only death. One does not need to enter into elaborate psychoanalytic readings of the works in the "grand style" to see the point. Critics have frequently seen *Sohrab and Rustum* as the allegory of Arnold's own mind, in which the youthful Matthew/Sohrab leaves behind the tender world of his mother to seek his father, but only to be slain by a father whose greatness he refuses to overcome. And *Balder Dead,* not too dissimilarly, is about a God/Poet who cannot survive in the world of the living but finds the shadowy world of the dead rather more comfortable. Even *Merope,* the most purely academic of the works, begins at the tomb of a slain father, presents a youth literally obscured by his father's tomb, and ends with the slaying of a false father. In short the poems do not unambiguously reflect Arnold's "definitive" aesthetic creed as set forth in the 1853 Preface, and could not possibly do so. All they can accomplish is an uneasy juxtaposition of archaic form with a modern content and a modern language that refuses, apparently, to be buried alive in monuments of antiquarianism.

The Grand Style

Arnold's attempt at a "grand style" in *Sohrab and Rustum, Balder Dead,* and *Merope* deserves more than immediate dismissal on the grounds that the works are based on an unworkable theory of poetry and that they are susceptible to the mockeries of a too simple psychoanalytic criticism. *Sohrab and Rustum* is not only, by general consensus, the best of these works, but is also the one most clearly related to the aims of the Preface. It was, in effect, the replacement for the withdrawn *Empedocles on Etna,* and was plainly meant to be a model of the grand style. The poem is concerned with a great human action, so Arnold's praise of it to his mother not surprisingly stressed the "noble and excellent" story rather than the execution, and it was designed, as Arnold told Clough, to be animating.[53] And of course it was very explicitly an effort to imitate the manner of Homer. But insofar as it succeeds in these aims, it fails as a poem.

The language, for example, is certainly "severe," but it is stilted and exaggeratedly artificial. Despite one critic's sense that Arnold did in fact achieve something like the "simplicity, directness, rapidity, and nobility" that seemed to the critic the "defining qualities of Homer's grandeur,"[54] these are not quite the characteristics that most readers have seen even in some of the poem's best passages:

> And the first grey of morning filled the east,
> And the fog rose out of the Oxus stream.
> (ll. 1–5) But all the Tartar camp along the stream
> Was hushed, and still the men were plunged in sleep;
> Sohrab alone, he slept not.

The diction, to be sure, is simple, but the passage is nevertheless self-consciously "literary"—as an imitation of another poet's manner, after all, *has* to be, since it refers first to other texts and only afterwards to the "action." And it is not direct and rapid: the echoing rhyme of "stream / stream" in lines two and three, especially when combined with the assonantal resonance of "east" and "sleep" in lines one and four gives the whole a circular, self-reflexive quality—a quality that is emphasized still further by the stilted inversion in line five: "Sohrab alone, he slept not." I am by no means faulting the lines for being artificial—quite the reverse, since I believe it is the modern, Tennysonian (though Arnold denied it) cadences and assonance that give the lines what melancholy power they possess and redeem them from the bathos of syntax that is simple to the point of simple-mindedness: "And . . . And . . . But . . . And . . ." Nevertheless, the overall effect of 892 lines of this studied style on most readers is reflected in Culler's witty characterization of the work:

> *It was his poetic Crystal Palace for the English people, a kind of showy pageant which he, as the Prince Albert of the literary world, would put on to distract the thoughts of the middle classes from the meager quality of their lives. This showy, self-conscious quality of*

> *the poem is its most unfortunate aspect. The similes preen themselves before the mirror of their style; the great, primary human affections pulsate audibly; and the river Oxus gurgles as it flows. Admirably as everything is done, one feels that it is all a little false.*[55]

Far from being transparent, the language is showy and calls attention to its own Homeric postures. The poem is less an Aristotelian imitation of nature than an imitation of other poetry, with the result that the style actually distances the reader from the story.

The epic similes provide perhaps the clearest example of how Arnold's grand style works. The similes are, of course, self-consciously Homeric, and their purposes are to compare great things with small and so show the magnitude of the action, and to provide a large social and natural context for the events. But even Culler, who argues that "in the context they do function organically by completing the symbolic typology of the poem," concedes that they are, "in a sense," "inorganic and merely decorative."[56] Other critics, less kindly, have said that the similes are so merely ornamental, in precisely the sense Arnold deplored in the Preface, that they seem "a kind of patchwork brocade, tricking out the substance of Firdawsi's tale," and that, occurring so frequently and unnecessarily, they "seem a parody, not an imitation of the epic manner."[57] The most famous of the similes reveals that they are indeed distracting rather than illustrative. At the crucial recognition scene, Sohrab bares his arm to show

> a sign in faint vermilion points
> Pricked; as a cunning workman, in Pekin,
> Pricks with vermilion some clear porcelain vase,
> An emperor's gift—at early morn he paints,
> (ll. 671–78) And all day long, and, when night comes, the lamp
> Lights up his studious forehead and thin hands—
> So delicately pricked the sign appeared
> On Sohrab's arm, the sign of Rustum's seal.

The simile quite clearly draws attention away from the climactic action and to the patient diligence of the craftsman or artist. The stamp of Rustum's paternity and Sohrab's identity is obscured by a kind of signature or self-portrait of the cunning artist who devised the whole and claims paternity. Other similes, such as those comparing the horse Ruksh to a wounded lion, and that comparing Sohrab, at great length, to a wounded eagle, are full of Victorian rather than Homeric pathos and, as Gabriel Pearson has noticed, the famous simile comparing Rustum to "some rich woman" eyeing "a poor drudge" (ll. 302–8) is full of Victorian class-consciousness that is totally alien to the poem. Pearson makes the excellent general point that the similes "instance a seepage of contemporary reality into what should be monuments of timeless order." The result of juxtaposing Victorian sentiments and ornamental bric-a-brac with the Persian tale and the Homeric simplicity is, Pearson has well said, a poem that "is about gaps and distances: between cultures, generations, classes, sexes; between, indeed, medieval Persia (or any spacial or temporal remoteness) and the contemporary world whose onrush consumes the past as exotica."[58] A poem written hundreds of years after the event cannot help but register these gaps. Like Borges's Pierre Menard, who becomes so penetrated with the spirit of Cervantes that he writes *Don Quixote* word for word, the modern writer could theoretically produce absolutely convincing pastiche, but the simple fact of modern consciousness would still ensure that the meaning would not be in the events portrayed, but in the cultural gap. Arnold does not even come close to such fidelity to Homer's style, and his lapses emphasize the cultural discontinuity and fragmentation that he is trying to overcome.

Trying to efface himself and his age from the poem, Arnold could not help insisting on his own contemporary presence. Similarly, trying to produce a transparent medium for the action, he could not help insisting on words, on the language itself. William Buckler, who aptly describes the source of the story as an opportunity "to make literature out of literature out of literature—something English out of something Persian via something Greek," adds that it was also an opportunity "to efface authorial imposition at almost an ideal level."[59] But from another perspective it produced a situation in which every level draws attention to the gaps between levels and the various overlays of language. The insistence on language itself is evident not only in the style but in the story itself. Sohrab is able to hold his own in the battle against Rustum as long as physical action alone is involved, but he is defeated by the word, by Rustum's shouting of his own name: "Sohrab heard that shout, / And shrank amazed" (ll. 516–17) and was run through with the spear. It is not Rustum's merely human voice that has such power, however, but as elsewhere in Arnold, it is a transcendent decree. Arnold could feel that *Sohrab and Rustum,* unlike *Empedocles on Etna,* was genuinely tragic because it depicted not the unending dialogue of the mind with itself but the struggles of humanity under the authoritative decree of fate. He makes the point, far too explicitly, through Sohrab:

> I but meet to-day
> The doom which at my birth was written down
> In Heaven, and thou art Heaven's unconscious hand.
> Surely my heart cried out that it was thou,
> When first I saw thee; and thy heart spoke too,
> I know it! but fate trod those promptings down
> Under its iron heel; fate, fate engaged
> The strife, and hurled me on my father's spear.
> But let us speak no more of this! I find
> My father; let me feel that I have found!
> (ll. 708–17)

The point seems to be that human utterances are vain, that a higher authority generates the great human actions of epic and tragedy—though one might argue that a greater faith in romantic inwardness could have averted the catastrophe. Interestingly, Empedocles too had said, "I know it," and had acted on the basis of that inner knowledge, but presumably because his end is the result of an inner voice rather than the decree of fate, his death is not tragic. The authoritative decree in *Sohrab and Rustum* is once again the voice of God that makes the world comprehensible and so makes human utterance in poetry meaningful. Unfortunately, however, the decree is utterly unconvincing—it has no more real authority than the voices of God and nature that echo in the void elsewhere in the volumes of 1852 and 1853. Sohrab protests too much, and his assertion about fate's decree is only a conjectural ex post facto explanation that reflects a desire for order rather than a conviction of it. "Fate" and "Heaven" are mere words, empty signifiers that can only gesture at the inscrutability of events. When Sohrab concludes, "But it was writ in Heaven that this should be" (l. 725), one is tempted to respond that it was not writ in Heaven by Fate, but was writ in Persia by Firdawsi. The authority is words, but the words of a previous human author, not of a transcendent force.

One other way in which Arnold tries to de-emphasize language in the poem is to turn verbal description of experience into monuments or sculptures. The end result of the epic battle is that Sohrab, transfixed by the word of Rustum, and Rustum, transfixed by the sign on Sohrab, are utterly stilled. Both are monumentalized in a simile:

> As those black granite pillars, once high-reared
> By Jemshid in Persepolis, to bear
> His house, now 'mid their broken flights of steps (ll. 860–64)
> Lie prone, enormous, down the mountain side—
> So in the sand lay Rustum by his son.

The simile is perhaps more fitting than Arnold intended in its implications that such monumental language cannot house living forms, but can only memorialize the fragments of a past culture. In fact, Sohrab explicitly asks for a monument over his dead body:

> And heap a stately mound above my bones
> And plant a far-seen pillar over all.
> That so the passing horseman on the waste
> May see my tomb a great way off, and cry: (ll. 788–94)
> *Sohrab, the mighty Rustum's son, lies there,*
> *Whom his great father did in ignorance kill!*
> And I be not forgotten in my grave.

As Culler rightly notes, the tomb is a work of art, and "of course, the true work of art erected over Sohrab's grave is the poem itself, a poem which Arnold originally entitled *The Death of Sohrab*."[60] Arnold's poem becomes, in one sense, the utterance of the horseman, but in its epic proportion and stateliness it becomes also a tomb, a monument or memorial that can house only what is dead. Moreover, by petrifying his language in the grand style, Arnold comes as close as he can to reproducing the effects of a dead language.

It is precisely this that makes appropriate the famous and beautiful closing passage, which describes the indifference of the Oxus river as it flows past the scene and onward under the night sky and into the timeless sea. The passage has seemed irrelevant to some, and positively outrageous to Charles Kingsley: "Who cares whither the Oxus goes, or what becomes of it, while Rustum is lying in the sand by his dead son, like one of 'Giamschid's fallen pillars in Persepolis?' The Oxus, and all the rivers on earth, yea all nature, and the sun and moon, if they intrude themselves at such a moment, are simply impertinences. Rustum and his son are greater than they: nearer to us than they." There is some justification for Kingsley's bellicose tone as he wonders whether Arnold can really have meant to suggest that "it is somewhat beneath a wise man to make himself unhappy about the puny little human beings who fight and love, and do right and do wrong upon its banks."[61] Insofar as Arnold wanted to show a great human action, to bring the warriors back to life, to bring them "nearer to us," the end symbol would seem to be self-defeating. But as we have seen, everything about the poem is designed, sometimes deliberately and sometimes not, to distance author and reader from the immediacy of human experience. The language and style of the poem memorialize or mummify experience. The grand style is the very antithesis of transparent—it is not a window to human experience but a buffer against it. Arnold, in fact, is using language to disengage himself from things, not to see them as they really are. The poem that produces "literature out of literature out of literature" disengages itself from actuality and creates an autonomous, isolated, protected realm for poetry and culture. Arnold's Preface and the letter to Clough in which he declared that modern poetry must be a *magister vitae* indicate that he intended just the reverse, but his attempt to create a truly objective poetry buffered from modern problems could only result, to the extent that it could succeed, in an inert and lifeless objet d'art.

But of course *Sohrab and Rustum* does not succeed in becoming entirely bloodless. Despite Buckler's observation that reading Arnold's relations with his father into the poem smacks of "mental tackiness," critics as eminent as Lionel Trilling and Kenneth Burke have not been able to resist such an analysis.[62] Virtually all readers have agreed that the poem achieves a limited success "precisely because it does not take Arnold out of himself but is that very thing which he deplores, 'a true allegory of the state of one's own mind.' "[63] Generally the poem is said to draw on the same concerns as Arnold's other poems—it is likened to *Empedocles on Etna,* with Rustum akin to Empedocles and Sohrab to Callicles, or to the Prize poems and the sonnet in praise of Wellington in its tribute to great natures, or to "Mycerinus" and "The Sick King in Bokhara" as a work "in which the individual's estrangement from his fellow human beings suggests a wider, cosmic divorce."[64] I do not think one needs to choose among these readings—clearly the poem is steeped in many of Arnold's most deeply felt concerns, including also his concern to find some kind of definitive, authoritative voice. My point has been that the poem is peculiarly divided against itself, as though the imposition of a marmoreal form on living ideas could be a way of stilling, entombing, memorializing them. The poem only lives because the modern ideas, and especially the pathos of modern alienation from the integrated past, have been—apparently accidentally—breathed into it.

To a much lesser extent the same dynamic is at work in *Balder Dead,* which may have been written in response to critical complaints that Arnold should turn to native legends if he meant to restore a national feeling for myth.[65] In *Balder Dead* Arnold used fewer similes and a still sparser diction than in *Sohrab and Rustum,* with the result that the work seems even more stiff and academic than its predecessor—an impression that is encouraged by frequent and extraneous disquisitions from the *Prose Edda* and by obvious and direct imitations of the *Iliad* and the *Aeneid.* But to the very limited extent that *Balder Dead* is effective, it is so by invoking familiar but less than joy-inspiring Arnoldian themes. It begins where *Sohrab and Rustum* left off, with the mourning of a noble father for a promising son, the mourning of Odin for Balder:

If any here might weep for Balder's death,
(1.20–22) I most might weep, his father; such a son
I lose to-day, so bright, so loved a God.

The poem is about the loss of youth, the loss of mythic wholeness, the loss of joy. Balder had been, among other things, a kind of Wordsworthian poet of natural joy:

But when thou sangest, Balder, thou didst strike
Another note, and, like a bird in spring,
(3.141–44) Thy voice of joyance minded us, and youth,
And wife, and children, and our ancient home.

Balder's death is the death of romantic poetry, but here it is lamented, not celebrated as a way to make room for classicism. In general the poem formally imitates the classical epic, but without energy, or passion, or joy it seems an empty shell. It has been praised for its Virgilian melancholy, and indeed it is only melancholy that invigorates the poem—but the sadness is Arnold's, not Virgil's, and is modern, not ancient. It is most apparent at the end, when Balder resigns himself to the half-life of Hades in terms that suggest the withdrawals from modern society of the Scholar-Gipsy, or Obermann, or the monks of the Grande Chartreuse:

Mine ears are stunned with blows, and sick for calm.
(3.508–10) Inactive therefore let me lie, in gloom,
Unarmed, inglorious.

Quintessentially Arnoldian, Balder is caught between a vanished past and a wished-for future. He predicts a "happier day" (3.513) and a redeemed heaven and earth, in what seems a prophecy of the Christian dispensation, but the emphasis in the bulk of the poem on the impossibility of resurrecting a dead god seems to deny any real hope in the redemptive power of Christianity. The closing simile emphasizes the desirability of withdrawal from life, even if only into death:

And as a stork which idle boys have trapped,
(3.559–65) And tied him in a yard, at autumn sees
Flocks of his kind pass flying o'er his head

To warmer lands, and coasts that keep the sun;
He strains to join their flight, and from his shed
Follows them with a long complaining cry—
So Hermod gazed, and yearned to join his kin.

The form of *Balder Dead,* its epic structure and diction, plainly follows the prescriptions of the Preface, but it is very difficult to see how the despair and yearning for death represent a greater *action* than Empedocles' leap into Etna, and it is impossible to see how it can inspirit or rejoice. Yet the most melancholy passages are by far the best in the poem, since they are the only ones that do not merely present the dead bones of antiquarian research. But then the lifeless language of most of the poem represents an end to the melancholy yearning of Balder and of Hermod—it epitomizes peace, calm, the end of the dialogue of the mind with itself. It exhibits all too well the logical culmination of an aesthetic that seeks to remove modern thought and feeling from verse—an entombing or enshrining of legend and myth rather than a regeneration of it, a protection from suffering and grief rather than an overcoming of them.

The closing simile, however, reveals that the poem turns upon its own form, seeming to undermine the sense of grandeur and monumentality of the impersonal epic form. As in *Sohrab and Rustum* the similes represent a "seepage of modern thought and feeling," but even more clearly here they have an insidious effect. The comparison of Hermod to a stork captured by idle boys is indeed a comparison of great things with small, but another way to put it would be to say that it is simply degrading. In fact, the epic similes in this poem are generally degrading, as when the warder of the bridge to Hell is compared to a herd of cows (2.90–99). Appropriately, two of the most ambitious similes are given to the demonic Lok, who insultingly compares Hermod to a "farmer, who hath lost his dog" (3.6–19) and mockingly compares all of the gods to a squeamish cow (3.340–44). It is impossible to know what Arnold had in mind here, but the effect of using poetic ornamentation to degrade his own action, and then of casting the demeaning similes into the demonic mouth of Lok is to heighten the contrast between classic and romantic form. Romantic form is suppressed, reduced to ornamentation as simile, but it continues to seep back. In the slight dramatic tension generated by this dialogue of the poem with itself lies most of the work's scant attraction.

Arnold eliminated romantic elements even more successfully in *Merope,* a play that no one has ever read with pleasure. Perhaps the finest tribute the work has ever received is Pearson's: "*Merope* deserves applause as an act of intrepid, grandiose bloody-mindedness."[66] Arnold was resolute in producing a large work on the principles of his Preface, but even he seemed to realize that the result was of merely academic interest. He wrote to a friend that "you are not the least bound to like her, as she is calculated rather to inaugurate my Professorship with dignity than to move deeply the present race of *humans.*"[67] Others have doubted that the forbidding work, preceded by the scholarly apparatus of a lengthy preface and a "Story of the Drama" is of even academic interest.

Even though Arnold took pains to eliminate anything personal or contemporary, he was unable to do so. He needed, for example, to find a plausible story for Aepytus to tell as he fabricated his own suicide, but he avoided simply making one up. Instead he found a story in Pausanias that would serve his turn, and used that, on the grounds that "the tradition is a great matter to a poet; it is an unspeakable support; it gives him the feeling that he is treading on solid ground" (1:53). But the story he chose, of a young hunter swept into a chasm and drowned, is, as Culler has said, reminiscent of "A Dream" and other poems—the fall into a chasm is reminiscent too, perhaps, of Empedocles. Culler is surely right in saying that the passage in which Aepytus describes his own death "almost alone in the drama, is vital and alive because in it Arnold is returning to the source of his own feeling."[68] Arnold evidently could not totally empty his classic form of all feeling or personal meaning—the very choice of materials from the tradition must, after all, be a subjective one. Indeed, even the two long passages he chose to translate from Homer in *On Translating Homer* demonstrate the inescapability of his personal concerns—and both resemble Aepytus' description of his own death. The first is Hector's speech to Andromache in which he imagines his own death in battle, and the second is the dialogue of Achilles with his divinely inspired horse, in which he too foresees his death (1:164, 166–67). Both, in other words, are about the Arnoldian theme of the death of youth and valor in the pursuit of duty. And all of these pieces obliquely suggest the self-burial of Arnold's romantic individualism in the dead language of culture for the greater good.

Arnold chose the subject of *Merope,* he said, because Aristotle had recommended it and because no ancient plays on the subject survive. But the story would have appealed to him on more subjective grounds as well. It is about the moral duty of a young man to take the place of a noble father who has met a tragically early death, and it begins at the tomb of the father—at one point the young Aepytus even hides behind the tomb. Further, it takes place, like *Empedocles on Etna,* in an age of transition very much like the present age, an age when myth and heroism were fast giving way to confused multitudinousness. The events, Arnold said, "belong to the period of transition from the heroic and fabulous to the human and historic age of Greece."[69] Not surprisingly, the only real interest in *Merope* results from the clash of old beliefs, represented by Aepytus, with the new, thoughtful, introspective relativism of Polyphontes, the usurper of the throne. The clash is, in fact, not entirely different from the clash of values between Callicles and Empedocles. Arnold significantly chose to "set aside" the tradition in his treatment of Polyphontes (1.54), because he was of little modern interest in his traditional, totally villainous character. In Arnold's version he becomes not villainous but Arnoldian—a man perplexed by the difficulties of moral choice and the necessities of moral action. He dominates the play and is, in fact, the only character ever really to come to life at all, but the plot demands that he be killed by Aepytus with a sacrificial ax. Perhaps he must be killed because his modern vitality destroys the statuesque serenity of classical form. Rather like the similes in *Balder Dead,* he is an intrusive and abrasive modern voice that must be silenced. If the play is regarded as an Arnoldian psychodrama, the slaying of Polyphontes is quite remarkable, for it suggests that the emphasis on plot and action is simply a way of lopping off modern complexity. The attempt to return to a "heroic and fabulous age," however, involves a genuine sacrifice of the "human and historical," of the world we recognize as our own, the only world that means anything to us now. But even with the death of Polyphontes the play cannot produce any real serenity, though Aepytus behaves with impeccable demeanor over the dead body of his antagonist. Instead of arriving at transcendent wisdom or heroism, Aepytus only learns that he should exercise "the moderation of a man" (l. 2013), and so he goes off to offer "grateful sacrifice" to the gods (l. 2019). The play ends with a rather stiff chorus:

> Son of Cresphontes, past what perils
> (ll. 2021–24) Com'st thou, guided safe, to thy home!
> What things daring! What enduring!
> And all this by the will of the Gods.

The function of the chorus in Greek tragedy, Arnold said in the Preface to *Merope,* was to be an "ideal spectator" and so lead the "actual spectator" to feel more deeply the "*profound moral impression*" of the action (1.60). But his *Merope* makes no unified moral impression—the conflict of Aepytus and Polyphontes is a morally ambiguous dialogue of the mind with itself. All the closing chorus can do is declare—without any support from the rest of the play—that the ending must be morally right because it represents the "will of the Gods." In other words, Arnold still was finding a unifying moral statement in a wished for and projected voice of God—classic form, alone, could not provide it.

The only profound impression *Merope* has generally made on readers is that of profound boredom with its sterile academicism, but the play nevertheless contributes importantly to an understanding of Arnold's developing thought. In "Stanzas in Memory of the Author of 'Obermann' " he had wistfully buried the romantic voice of Sénancour under a damning weight of faint praise; in *Empedocles* he had buried the troubling modern voice beneath a mountain; in *Balder Dead* he relegated it to Hell; in *Merope* he buries the modern Polyphontes beneath the petrifaction of a dead form and the mimicry of a dead language. As in *Sohrab and Rustum* the poem becomes a tomb and a monument to lost youth, so in *Merope* the form becomes a tomb or monument to a dead tradition. Or perhaps, given the academicism of the piece, and Arnold's sense that it was a fitting introduction to an academic career, the metaphor should be changed—the drama represents the withdrawal of the tradition into the stifling atmosphere of the ivory tower, preserved from the real problems of modern life and reserved for the edification of educated males. In this sense Pearson is surely right in saying that "*Merope* must be regarded as a monumental tomb with the word Culture inscribed upon it."[70]

Empedocles on Etna, Sohrab and Rustum, Balder Dead, Merope—all of Arnold's major efforts with classical subjects or classical form reveal an effort to crush merely modern thought and its uncertain language under the weight (or "solidity," one of Arnold's favorite words for classicism) of monumental form. The efforts were never entirely successful, since even in *Balder Dead* the melancholy of modernism speaks in the similes, and even in *Merope* Polyphontes retains a kind of demonic life in death—a "buried life" in the tomb of ancient form. But the tendency toward petrifaction nevertheless indicates the significance of Arnold's shift from poetry to criticism, a shift that in its zealous efforts to preserve literature ends by embalming it. The poetry of *Empedocles on Etna* did not fully silence Empedocles, but the criticism of the Preface did. In fact Arnold's example is a cautionary tale for modern academics about the dangers of too zealous preservation. Pearson's description of Arnold's aesthetic is very much to the point: "Aesthetic is the detached cultural repository of achieved (almost wholly verbal) artifacts, which, by their persistence, have acquired hierophantic significance. Literature, we know, was to replace religion, but it was also to replace literature as imaginative activity. Such activity requires constant renovation of experience; but the aesthetic exists precisely to order, not enter experience."[71] Paradoxically, Arnold's distrust of language led him to place his trust in "almost wholly verbal" artifacts, but as artifacts, as *things* handed down from a better, more inspired past.

Once again, Arnold's situation can be better understood by reference to Nietzsche's profound analysis of Greek art and his devastating critique of nineteenth-century classicism. As Arnold saw it, modern Socratic man, like Empedocles, has trusted too much in the thinking power alone, has arrived at a scientific understanding that has cut him off from the possibilities of feeling, of faith and hope. Modern man, guided by scientific principles, can admit no new fables or myths, and so he sets himself to preserve old ones: "Our art is a clear example of this universal misery: in vain do we imitate all the great creative periods and masters; in vain do we surround modern man with all of world literature and expect him to name its periods and styles as Adam did the beasts. He remains eternally hungry, the critic without strength or joy, the Alexandrian man who is at bottom a librarian and scholiast, blinding himself miserably over dusty books and typographical errors."[72] Arnold, to be sure, never became the pedant Dryasdust, but his increasing scholasticism tended to transform the natural magic of Adamic naming to a naming of texts, just as his imitation and preservation of past literature tended to reduce the living word to the dead letter.

The Poetry of the Wilderness

In the famous conclusion to "The Function of Criticism at the Present Time," Matthew Arnold slyly surrendered his place as a poet in the great tradition in order to sneak back in as a critic: "The epochs of Aeschylus and Shakespeare make us feel their pre-eminence. In an epoch like those is, no doubt, the true life of literature; there is the promised land, towards which criticism can only beckon. That promised land it will not be ours to enter, and we shall die in the wilderness: but to have desired to enter it, to have saluted it from afar, is already, perhaps, the best distinction among contemporaries; it will certainly be the best title to esteem with posterity" (3:285). Arnold, abandoning the role of Joshua to settle for that of Moses, or the role of Christ for that of John the Baptist, not only established his own uneasy relationship with the central literary tradition that he could neither avoid nor fully join, but also established himself as a model for the modern critic aware of his own belatedness. Later critics aware of their debt to Arnold, like Geoffrey Hartmann, who salutes his predecessor in the title of his *Criticism in the Wilderness,* and critics like Harold Bloom, who would like to deny Arnold's paternity, still follow him through the critical desert. Bloom, for example, concerned with the "functions of criticism," is driven throughout his works by what he describes as "the particular inescapability of literary tradition for the teacher who must go out to find himself as a voice in the wilderness."[1] But Arnold's inescapable placing of the postromantic—and indeed postmodern—critic in the wilderness came only after repeated encounters with the same wilderness in his poetry. His most concise description of the modern dilemma, of course, is the much quoted passage from "Stanzas from the Grande Chartreuse":

Wandering between two worlds, one dead,
The other powerless to be born,
With nowhere yet to rest my head,
Like these, on earth I wait forlorn.
(ll. 85–88)

Arnold's frequent response to encountering this sense of homelessness and alienation was, even within his poetry, to turn to a kind of criticism. In "Stanzas from the Grande Chartreuse," he engages in a critique of Byron, Shelley, and Sénancour, and more typically, in "The Scholar-Gipsy," he confronts the wasteland of modern life in mid-poem and shifts to a mode critical of his own poeticizing. But not yet content in the early 1850s to lapse into criticism, Arnold also struggled to find a poetics of the wilderness, a mode within which he could exploit his own alienation, his sense of purposeless drifting.

A likely poetic mode, and one that Arnold did indeed explore, was that of romance, for romance, as Fredric Jameson has argued, is a mode particularly suited to express the sense of being caught between two worlds, in an age of transition. Jameson describes "romance as a form [that] expresses a transitional moment, yet one of a very special type: its contemporaries must feel their society torn between past and future in such a way that the alternatives are grasped as hostile but somehow unrelated worlds." Jameson almost seems to be describing Arnold's own sense of being caught in the middle, and his further comment seems almost a gloss on the situation of "Stanzas from the Grande Chartreuse": "This genre expresses a nostalgia for a social order in the process of being undermined and destroyed by nascent capitalism."[2] Moreover, as Northrop Frye has argued, the wilderness is the appropriate setting for romance, and further, the structure of romance is perfectly embodied in the story of Exodus, of the wanderings in the wilderness between a past world and one yet unborn.[3] Frye's biblical model of romance would give its language the plenitude of biblical typology and would suggest an inevitably successful quest, since the promise of the promised land will not be broken—language originating from God's word is truth. But Arnold, who could not foresee any very consoling future, was more truly a wanderer, and his secular language is without plenitude or "truth." A more accurate description of Arnold's poetic situation can be found in Patricia Parker's splendid study of the mode of romance, in which she echoes Arnold to describe the conditions of the postromantic poet: "In poetry from the Romantics forward, the poet himself approaches the condition of the wanderer between two worlds. . . . The figure of the poet as vagabond or exile becomes virtually inseparable from the differentiated, exiled nature of poetic language. Jacques Derrida . . . conflates the historical situation of the 'Wandering Jew' with the situation of the poet caught within the 'error' of language, 'le Désert de la Promesse.'"[4] Arnold, who struggled all his life to assert the saving powers of literature, would have been appalled to see his name in such company, yet analysis of many of his most famous poems indicates that they can be best appreciated as a form of romance thus broadly understood. Arnold's exploration of the possibilities of romance is, of course, most clear in his handling of actual romance materials, as in *Tristram and Iseult* and *The Church of Brou,* where he explores and exploits the conventions of naive romance in a postromantic world. But the errantry of romance also underlies such poems of wandering and quest as "The Scholar-Gipsy" and "Thyrsis," which seek a simpler world but become entangled in the encoiling errors of language, and in "Rugby Chapel," where the poet seeks reassurance in his quest by invoking (unsuccessfully) the linguistic plenitude of the typology of Exodus.

Romance in the Wilderness

The poem that in many ways provides the clearest paradigm for Arnold's poems of wandering is "Stanzas from the Grande Chartreuse." Though not, strictly speaking, a romance, the poem obviously represents a kind of quest for something, but for precisely what is unclear—for the monastery, of course, but will the monastery "mean" anything clearer than, say, the Dark Tower at the end of Childe Roland's quest? The quest evidently is not for revelation, not for "Truth," but is explicitly a respite from that far more demanding quest. The speaker even expresses a sense of guilt that he has wandered astray:

—And what am I, that I am here?

For rigorous teachers seized my youth,
And purged its faith, and trimmed its fire,
(ll. 66–72) Showed me the high, white star of Truth,
There bade me gaze, and there aspire.
Even now their whispers pierce the gloom:
What dost thou in this living tomb?

Or perhaps he is searching for a truth that his evidently too rigorous teachers have neglected—certainly the sense of loss expressed in the lines reveals less certainty about the "high, white star of Truth" than the capitalization would seem to imply. And in fact only six lines later the "Truth" has been sadly reduced to a relative and uncertain proposition: "your truth" (l. 78). The crucial point is that in such uncertainty the speaker cannot proceed in a straight line to a certain goal, but is condemned to wander aimlessly. The poem's deepest concerns and enforced wanderings are completely at odds with the apparently purposeful march to the mountaintop, described in the first four stanzas and culminating in the assertion "Approach, for what we seek is here" (l. 25). Indeed, the speaker explicitly laments his own purposelessness and confusion and acknowledges that he seeks only escape:

Oh, hide me in your gloom profound,
Ye solemn seats of holy pain!
Take me, cowled forms, and fence me round,
(ll. 91–96) Till I possess my soul again;
Till free my thoughts before me roll,
Not chafed by hourly false control!

Evidently what the speaker desires is the freedom to wander in his thoughts, the freedom to escape the false control, imposed, presumably, by the "rigorous teachers," the "masters of the mind" (l. 73).

These teachers no doubt include Thomas Arnold as well as "Carlyle, Goethe, Sénancour, and Spinoza . . . perhaps also Epictetus and Lucretius,"[5] but they also presumably include *all* of the great voices of the Western tradition, *all* that Arnold was later, more cheerfully, to call "the best that is known and thought in the world." His desire to seek an earlier world even though its "faith is now / But a dead time's exploded dream" (ll. 97–98) is evidently a desire to retreat to a time when the contending voices were not so confining, when the tradition had not become too great a burden. It is for this reason that his seemingly anomalous refutation of his "fathers" (l. 121), Byron, Shelley, and Sénancour, makes poetic sense. Byron bore "The pageant of his bleeding heart" (l. 136) across Europe, Shelley lifted his "lovely wail" (l. 140) through Italian trees, and Sénancour's "sad, stern, page" (l. 146) described a gloomy seclusion. These "fathers" not only anticipated Arnold's lament but also showed that it was pointless.[6] Any poetic utterance on Arnold's part would be both futile and redundant:

> Our fathers watered with their tears
> This sea of time whereon we sail,
> Their voices were in all men's ears
> Who passed within their puissant hail.
> (ll. 121–28) Still the same ocean round us raves,
> But we stand mute, and watch the waves.
>
> For what availed it, all the noise
> And outcry of the former men?

Apparently the response to finding himself wandering in a wilderness here, as in "The Function of Criticism at the Present Time," is to be poetically silent, to "stand mute"—he insists on the need for silence: "Silent, while years engrave the brow; / Silent—the best are silent now" (ll. 113–14). Yet he is not mute, not silent, but writing a poem in which he has become utterly enmeshed in the errors of language that he wants to repudiate. Even as he insists that silence is best, even as he prepares to reject the modern tradition and the "lovely wail" of Shelley in particular, he echoes it. Even, that is, as he states that "The kings of modern thought are dumb" (l. 116), he perpetuates Shelley's voice by echoing lines from "Adonais": "the kings of thought / Who waged contention with their time's decay." And more, the whole passage, with its rejection of Byron and Shelley and its praise of silence echoes another king of modern thought,

Carlyle. In "Characteristics" Carlyle described nineteenth-century life as a faithless wandering in the wilderness where, "for Contemplation and love of Wisdom, no Cloister now opens its religious shades; the Thinker must, in all senses, wander homeless, too often aimless." Carlyle even blamed Byron for "cursing his day" and Shelley for "filling the earth with inarticulate wail."[7] In general, he recommended stoic silence.

As is well known, Arnold made some factual errors in describing the Carthusians, but these errors of fact only reflect a more pervasive erring, or wandering, within literary conventions. He was wrong, for example, about the rites of the monks, but wrong within an interesting context:

The humid corridors behold!
Where, ghostlike in the deepening night,
Cowled forms brush by in gleaming white.

The chapel, where no organ's peal
(ll. 34–42) Invests the stern and naked prayer—
With penitential cries they kneel
And wrestle; rising then, with bare
And white uplifted faces stand,
Passing the Host from hand to hand.

The monks did not, of course, pass "the Host from hand to hand"—Arnold apparently confused the sacrament of the Eucharist with the ritual circulation of the Pax. But the important point, I think, is that he was not especially rigorous about getting his facts straight because he was seeing—and describing—the monks within a purely literary context. These cowled, ghostlike forms brushing by in humid corridors are straight out of Radcliffe, Lewis, and Maturin—Arnold was not objectively describing a real monastery ("the object as in itself it really is") but a literary monastery from the tradition of Gothic novels. His false assertion in the next stanza that the monks' beds would be used as their coffins shows the same elevation of Gothic sensationalism above scrupulous fact.[8] In short, the poet not only cannot escape from his age, but he also cannot escape from the maze of literary language. Wander where he will, he remains within its confines, painfully aware that even his innermost feelings, his grief and melancholy, are belated in the literary tradition. Because he has been beaten to it by Byron, Shelley, and Sénancour, his melancholy is, "sciolists say," and they are right, "a past mode, an outworn theme" (ll. 99–100). The poem demonstrates, then, that neither the externalized romance of the quest or pilgrimage nor the errantry of language can bring about any true escape, that the externalized quest, indeed, only leads back into outmoded fantasy ("a dead time's exploded dream") and into the jaded language of literary convention. There is no escape from the insistent voices that have formed—and entrapped—his consciousness: "Even now their whispers pierce the gloom."

The first three-fourths of the poem clearly establish the poet's dilemma, but the last fourth plaintively defies it. The closing section introduces a simile that compares the Arnoldian speaker and his like with children raised in the shadow of a monastery, ultimately identifies the children with the monks themselves, and asks simply to be left alone—asks only for the peace and silence that have so far been denied. Significantly, the desire for escape is closely associated with the enchanted ground of romance:

> We are like children reared in shade
> Beneath some old-world abbey wall,
> Forgotten in a forest-glade,
> And secret from the eyes of all.
> Deep, deep the greenwood round them waves,
> Their abbey, and its close of graves!
>
> (ll. 169–74)

The world of romance suggested by the "forest-glade" and especially by the self-consciously literary "greenwood" (used elsewhere by Arnold only in *Tristram and Iseult,* and there four times) is also, as the "close of graves" makes clear, a "living tomb" like the Carthusian monastery. The reference to children, similarly, is hopeful at first, yet these children, associated with what is old rather than young, are curiously belated. And, of course, the very use of a simile indicates the poet's withdrawal from actuality into an alternate world of art—explicitly of romance, though self-consciously belated romance. The following stanzas make it abundantly clear that the late romance is mediated by consciousness of the modern tradition:

> But, where the road runs near the stream,
> Oft through the trees they catch a glance
> Of passing troops in the sun's beam—
> Pennon, and plume, and flashing lance!
> Forth to the world those soldiers fare,
> To life, to cities, and to war!
>
> (ll. 175–80)

Behind this stanza, clearly, is Tennyson's "Lady of Shalott" (also strongly echoed in *The Church of Brou*) and its analogous situation of withdrawal from life into an alternative, but terribly confining, world of art. In "The Lady of Shalott," however, as Lancelot, dazzlingly flashing in the "sun's beam," goes riding by "To life, to cities, and to war," the Lady is drawn by the cheery "Tirra lirra" of his song to leave her enchanted tower, to enter the world of action. The moment is a characteristic one in Tennyson, akin to the departure of the soul from the Palace of Art, and perhaps more closely still to the withdrawal of the melancholy speaker from Locksley Hall as his "merry comrades call [him], sounding on the bugle-horn" (l. 145). Indeed, the moment is a characteristically Victorian one, perhaps most insistently set forth by Carlyle, whose "Characteristics" insisted on a turn from romantic melancholy to Victorian action. The speaker of "Locksley Hall" economically sums up the underlying issue: "I myself must mix with action, lest I wither by despair" (l. 98). Yet the children—associated with both Arnold and the monks—explicitly refuse to follow when wooed by the flashing banners and the "bugle-music on the breeze" (l. 189). One reason for this is clear enough: the Lady of Shalott, who does follow the "Tirra lirra" (Lancelot sings, but is also associated with a silver bugle), follows it only to die. Arnold, too, characteristically saw the alternative to the paradoxically *living* tomb of romance as the "gradual furnace of the world" (*Tristram and Iseult,* 3:119) or the "strange disease of modern life" ("The Scholar-Gipsy," l. 203)—that is, as dying life. In *The Church of Brou,* for example, the Duke who follows as "Hunters gather, bugles ring" (l. 16) is almost immediately killed. And in "Thyrsis" the speaker runs the other way when he hears the bugles of hunters. There was, in Arnold's mind, something fatal about the Victorian call to action, so the world of romance, however delusive and confining, remained preferable to "actuality." But there is also a subtler reason why leaving the enchanted ground of romance at this bugle-summons is pointless. The "Tirra-lirra" of Lancelot on his way to Camelot and the "Pennon, and plume, and flashing lance" of the passing world are hardly images of actuality anyway—they are images of a somewhat busier but equally delusive romance. They do not represent "Truth," or even a clear and purposeful quest, but only a gaudier and less thoughtful form of wandering. Once again the plight of the poet in the wilderness is that he is "caught within the 'error' of language," and cannot escape from one literary convention except into another. When Arnold first published "Stanzas from the Grande Chartreuse" in 1855, he was apparently determined to insist upon the legitimacy and desirability of escape into the world of art, and so he ended the poem with a plea that the greenwood of romance be left in peace: "Pass, banners, pass, and bugles, cease; / And leave our forest to its peace" (ll. 209–10). But by the time he republished the poem in 1867, after he had come to see the enchanted landscape of postromantic art as a wilderness, he altered one word in the final line and so fully brought out the fearful implications latent in the poem's struggle for a free ground to wander in: "And leave our desert to its peace."

But in the very early 1850s, before facing this melancholy realization, Arnold made his most ambitious attempt to write a full-scale traditional romance, *Tristram and Iseult*. In the sense that Arnold was the first modern poet to use the legend, anticipating Tennyson, Swinburne, and Wagner, he for once seems to be at the beginning of a tradition. Yet the material itself is, obviously, old, and Arnold came to it in the latter ages and self-consciously as an heir of the romantics. From Tristram's opening speech Arnold echoes his romantic predecessors:

> Is she not come? The messenger was sure.
> Prop me upon the pillows once again—
> Raise me, my page! This cannot long endure.
> —Christ, what a night! how the sleet whips the pane!

The echo, significantly, is of Keats's "Eve of St. Agnes," another self-consciously modern romance and, more significantly still, it recalls the storm ("the sharp sleet / Against the window-pane" [ll. 323–24]) and its suggestion of a harsh world outside of the artfully protected romance within Madeline's chamber. Arnold's poem not only alludes several more times to Keats, and specifically to "The Eve of St. Agnes" and "La Belle Dame Sans Merci," but also to romances of Coleridge, Byron, and Tennyson.

The poem, struggling both with the limitations of romance as a modern genre and with the burden of the postromantic tradition is, like "Stanzas from the Grande Chartreuse," necessarily very much concerned with the relation of romance to real life—or, as Buckler has put it, "with the deadly soul distress that certain kinds of poems must suffer when caught in a naive but violent discrepancy between the world of reality and the world of fantasy."[9] Tristram, at the end of his life, can only relive the romance of the past in dreams, hallucinations, delusions. Like the haggard and woebegone Knight at arms of Keats's "La Belle Dame," this knight is "weak and pale," as though once removed from the dream of romance he must necessarily, like Porphyro, grow "pallid, chill, and drear" ("The Eve of St. Agnes," l. 311). Consequently, he avoids reality, "wanders" back to his youth in a passage that once again juxtaposes the Keatsian storm with the dream of the past:

> Loud howls the wind, sharp patters the rain,
> And the knight sinks back on his pillows again.
> He is weak with fever and pain,
> And his spirit is not clear.
> Hark! he mutters in his sleep,
> As he wanders far from here.
>
> (1.83–88)

As in "Stanzas from the Grande Chartreuse," the speaker realizes that the dream of romance is delusory, but hopes nevertheless that it will be restorative, and so seeks peace for the dreamer: "let him dream!" of youth, love, beauty, valor. The plea is insistent—the word *let* (for permit) is repeated an even dozen times in the fifty-six lines of verse that try to induce Tristram's dream of youth. But the crucial point is that Tristram is already a belated figure for whom the age of romance is over, for whom the only hope of solace is in dreams: "Let a dream like this restore / What his eye must see no more!" (1.159–60). And the poem's ambivalence about wandering in dreams, and therefore about its own mode, romance, becomes even clearer when Tristram's dreams are seen to do no good. As in "The Lady of Shalott," the world of romance seems to offer two possibilities—solitary dreaming ("musing fits in the green wood" [1.247]) or the clarion call to action:

The march, the leaguer, Heaven's blithe air,
(1.258–60) The neighing steeds, the ringing blows—
Sick pining comes not where these are.

But sick pining does come there—neither alternative of romance, the speaker sorrowfully acknowledges, can provide solace or escape from misery:

Ah, poor soul! if this be so,
Only death can balm thy woe.
The solitudes of the green wood
(1.288–93) Had no medicine for thy mood;
The rushing battle cleared thy blood
As little as did solitude.

As in "The Lady of Shalott," once into the world of romance there is no way out but death, and if wandering in dreams has any beneficent purpose, it is only the mournful one of hastening death. As Tristram himself says, such dreams are killing: "I have had dreams, I have had dreams, my page, / Would take a score years from a strong man's age" (1.304–5). Tristram's dreams, of course, represent a view of romance within the context of the larger romance, *Tristram and Iseult.* Within that context, also, Arnold seems to be presenting the alternative of "nonromance" in the character of the usually forgotten member of the triangle, Iseult of Brittany. She has drunk no love potion, responded to no bugles—she has, on the contrary, been a good and meek wife, a gentle and loving mother, a very model of Victorian domesticity and, in fact, the main character of Arnold's romance.[10] Yet even Iseult of Brittany provides no real escape from the willful delusions of romance. And this is so not only for the obvious reason that she is herself a character in a medieval legend, but also because even to the extent that she represents a model of Victorian domesticity she becomes, like Patmore's Angel in the House, the dream-heroine of the Victorian romance of the family:

> I know her by her mildness rare,
> Her snow-white hands, her golden hair;
> (1.50–55) I know her by her rich silk dress,
> And her fragile loveliness
> The sweetest Christian soul alive,
> Iseult of Brittany.

Such a woman lives primarily as a Victorian literary convention: her kin are Amelia Sedley and Esther Summerson. Her children are similarly sentimentalized within the most traditional metaphor for the safe Victorian home: "they sleep in sheltered rest, / Like helpless birds in the warm nest" (1.327–28). Further, they are deliberately located in a fairy world—were they awake they could look out on "the fairy sight / Of [their] illumined haunts by night" (1.353–54). The children, doubly within the sentimental romance of the Victorian home and the traditional romance of fairyland, escape further still into a deeper and perhaps more potentially lonely and dangerous romance: "But you see fairer in your dreams" (1.371). Similarly, Iseult, also idealized in a double romance, still finds no happiness but only a living death: "She seems one dying in a mask of youth" (3.75). She, too, seeks escape, not by facing reality, but by immersing herself more deeply into fantasy, into old tales:

> the tales
> With which this day the children she beguiled
> (3.106–11) She gleaned from Breton grandames, when a child,
> In every hut along this sea-coast wild.
> She herself loves them still, and, when they are told,
> Can forget all to hear them, as of old.

Once again the function of romance is escape, forgetfulness, enchantment—the old tales may beguile or deceive us, however temporarily, into contentment, or at least peace.[11]

But the tale that Iseult tells the children, the romance within the romance, perfectly illustrates Arnold's troubled ambivalence about the uses of art, and of romance in particular. Her story describes a perfect "green wood," a "fairy-haunted land," of "deep forest-glades," "green boughs," "golden sunshine," and "enchanted" trees (3.153–58), but the setting of the romance is also, very significantly, a "tangled wilderness" for the tale's protagonists, Merlin and Vivian, to wander in: "they had travelled far and not stopped yet" (3.172–73). Further, the tale suggests no particular destination, no apparent quest, but only a wandering in the romantic wilderness, an escape from the ordinary wilderness of daily life. It is not the wandering that brings respite, however, but the rest in the peaceful forest:

> white anemones
> Starred the cool turf, and clumps of primroses
> (3.207–10) Ran out from the dark underwood behind.
> No fairer resting-place a man could find.

But as in "Stanzas from the Grande Chartreuse," such complete withdrawal into the greenwood, such profound rest, is more than sleep, is "more like death" (3.214). The point is blatantly emphasized as Vivian casts a spell to entrap Merlin in the forest-glade forever:

> Nine times she waved the fluttering wimple round,
> And made a little plot of magic ground.
> (3.219–22) And in that daisied circle, as men say,
> Is Merlin prisoner till the judgment-day.

The forest-glade of romance, the respite from the wilderness, becomes precisely what the monastery of the Grande Chartreuse was for Arnold, a "living tomb." The clear implication is that the desire for escape into the dead past of romance is a desire for the tomb, a kind of death wish. But just as clearly, the tomb, the daisied circle, is beautiful and paradoxically life-preserving. Further, the allusion to the dangerous poet of "Kubla Khan," ("Weave a circle round him thrice") suggests both the power of poetry and its sterility—Arnold's language refers ultimately to Coleridge's and so remains entrapped within the enchanted circle of poetry.[12] Nevertheless, though art cannot escape its own conventions and extend its enchantment to the humdrum of everyday life, it can paint over the fact of death and make it beautiful.[13]

The image of Merlin entrapped in the daisied circle epitomizes Arnold's conception of romance in the early 1850s. In *The Church of Brou* (1852) the historical figures of a duke and duchess become figures of romance only when they are dead and turned to paradoxically living art as sculptures on a tomb—like Merlin's, their condition is somewhere between death and sleep:

> So sleep, for ever sleep, O marble Pair!
> Or, if ye wake, let it be then, when fair
> On the carved western front a flood of light
> Streams from the setting sun, and colours bright
> (3.16–25) Prophets, transfigured Saints, and Martyrs brave,
> In the vast western window of the nave;
> And on the pavement round the Tomb there glints
> A chequer-work of glowing sapphire-tints,
> And amethyst, and ruby—then unclose
> Your eyelids on the stone where ye repose.

The echoes of the most beautiful passages of "The Eve of St. Agnes" underscore the point that the enchantments of romance cannot only make death beautiful but can even bestow a kind of life—even if only in the imagination of the poet. The power of art to bestow life is still more abundantly evident as other works of art in the church, those that had never known life, are brought to consciousness: "Only the blessed saints are smiling dumb, / From the rich painted windows of the nave" (3.4–5). But this insistence on the beautifying tendency of romance is also an implicit admission that the saving power of poetic art is only saving *within* the "error of language," the lies of poetic conventions such as metaphor and personification.

An extremely similar tableau is at the center of *Tristram and Iseult,* where the two great lovers fail to revive the romance of their own past but are restored to beauty and nobility by the artifice of the poet. Against all expectation Iseult of Ireland has come to the dying Tristram, but the romance is over, and the best that can be achieved is a reminiscence of a falsified past as Tristram asks Iseult to "Sit—sit by me! I will think, we've lived so / In the green wood, all our lives, alone" (2.35–36). But he soon dies and Iseult, swearing she will never leave him, falls by his side. The narrator describes the scene:

> You see them clear—the moon shines bright.
> Slow, slow and softly, where she stood,
> She sinks upon the ground; her hood
> (2.101–6) Has fallen back; her arms outspread
> Still hold her lover's hand; her head
> Is bowed, half-buried, on the bed.

The description continues at considerable length, bathing the tableau in the beautifying moonlight of romance. The scene is so beautiful, in fact, that it is difficult at first to realize that Iseult has died, and that the lovely spectacle is of two cold corpses, "lifeless lovers" (2.149). But they have also become, like the marble effigies at Brou, immortal in art. The somewhat surprising "You" at the start of the description is the modern reader, who can "see" the lovers that cannot pass away—like the figures on Keats's urn. Iseult's "arms outspread / *Still* hold her lover's hand" (my emphasis). The sleep of the lovers is restorative, healing, since it is an end to the hopeless longings in the "gradual furnace of the world," the desert wasteland that "Consumed her beauty like a flame, / And dimmed it like the desert-blast" (2.134–35). If Iseult could lift her face, it

> Would charm the gazer till his thought
> Erased the ravages of time,
> (2.139–43) Filled up the hollow cheek, and brought
> A freshness back as of her prime—
> So healing is her quiet now.

But very obviously it is the gazer ("You") who is affected by the charm of romance, who is beguiled to believe that time can stop, that there is a beauty even in death. Hidden beneath the spell of poetry are the unalterable "ravages of time," the "hollow cheeks"—

the function of romance is to hide the skull, the ultimate reminder of mortality.

As in *The Church of Brou,* Arnold made a point of emphasizing the withdrawal into art by introducing, and bringing to life, a work of art within his work of art. Comparable to the stained glass saints at Brou is the Huntsman on an arras that overlooks the dead lovers:

The air of the December-night
Steals coldly around the chamber bright,
Where those lifeless lovers be;
(2.147–54) Swinging with it, in the light
Flaps the ghostlike tapestry.
And on the arras wrought you see
A stately Huntsman, clad in green,
And round him a fresh forest-scene.

I quote the passage at length because it is important to note both that the Huntsman is described as a figure from the greenwood, and that the passage echoes Byron, Keats, and Tennyson—that it insists upon its own literariness to make its point.[14] To emphasize that art can only give "life" within the autonomous world of art, Arnold gives the Huntsman more life than the lovers, even heats him up a bit in the world's furnace:

He gazes down into the room
With heated cheeks and flurried air,
And to himself he seems to say:
(2.161–67) "*What place is this, and who are they?*
Who is that kneeling Lady fair?
And on his pillows that pale Knight
Who seems of marble on a tomb?"

But by far the most remarkable characteristic of the Huntsman is that once brought to life he self-consciously ponders his state and wonders if some enchantment has removed him from the greenwood of romance and made him the agent who will call others from their sleep of death:

(ll. 175–82) —What, has some glamour made me sleep,
And sent me with my dogs to sweep,

By night, with boisterous bugle-peal,
Through some old sea-side, knightly hall,
Not in the free green wood at all?
That Knight's asleep, and at her prayer
That Lady by the bed doth kneel—
Then hush, thou boisterous bugle-peal!

Not only will there not be, for once, the Victorian call to action, but more clearly than anywhere else in Arnold's poems, more clearly even than in the "Tirra lirra" of Lancelot, such a call is seen to be only to another world of illusion. There is no possibility of movement from the artificial world of romance back to the "real" world, no way in which its enchantments can be effectual as anything but escape. To make the point even clearer, Arnold closes Part 2 of *Tristram and Iseult* with yet another allusion to "The Eve of St. Agnes." Keats ends his romance with the reminder that his characters "lived" "ages long ago" and that their ashes are long since cold. Arnold concludes by advising his Huntsman to blow his bugle without fear,

For thou wilt rouse no sleepers here!
For these thou seest are unmoved;
(2.190–93) Cold, cold as those who lived and loved
A thousand years ago.

Yet for all its self-conscious irony about romance, Arnold's poem strongly implies that even though the work of art offers no outlet, is a tomb, it may yet have a beauty and a consoling pathos. It can still enchant, still bring magic to the wasteland. It is not that the limbo of "between two worlds" is susceptible to regeneration, or that roses can be made to bloom in the desert, but at least the enchantment of art can preserve the beauty of the dead past. Perhaps this appears most tellingly near the end of the poem when, following his description of how Iseult of Brittany is beguiled by old tales, Arnold suddenly breaks out into a jarringly modern digression about what can only be viewed as Victorian angst:

'tis the gradual furnace of the world,
(3.119–24) In whose hot air our spirits are upcurled
Until they crumble, or else grow like steel—

Which kills in us the bloom, the youth, the spring—
Which leaves the fierce necessity to feel,
But takes away the power.

This is the theme and tone of Arnold's poems about the modern wilderness of Victorian society, and seems strikingly out of place in a medieval romance. Yet emerging here, at the end of the poem, it starkly shows what has been displaced. Still, the emergence of what should have been entirely sublimated reveals that the romance has not fully succeeded, and perhaps for that reason Arnold suddenly switches to a ludicrously archaic diction—as if to conceal that he has ever departed from his medieval setting. Unfortunately there is a kind of desperation to such absurd lines as "And yet, I swear, it angers me to see / How this fool passion gulls men potently" (3.133–34) and such clumsy references as one to "that bald Caesar, the famed Roman wight" (3.143). The lack of control, I think, is an index of the poet's anxiety to return to the relatively safe past. Arnold apparently realized that he needed a better way to bring the poem back to its proper key, to the beautiful and enduring realm of enchantment, and so he "brought in" the story of Merlin and Vivian, he said, "on purpose to relieve the poem, which would else I thought have ended too sadly."[15]

Romance, for Arnold, seems to have involved a continual straining against modern despair—it involves an escape, but into the greenwood or a daisied circle that achieves calm only in a kind of living death. Arnold wrote no more romances after *Tristram and Iseult* and *The Church of Brou,* but his pastorals and pastoral elegy approximate the mode of romance by exploring the possibilities of wandering and quest, and by exploiting a pastoral landscape akin to the greenwood. The landscape of shepherds and swains is also an alternative to modern urban life, but Arnold's attempts to exploit it show an even greater ambivalence about the possibility and desirability of poetic escape than do his romances.

Pastoral and Elegy

In the pastoral elegy, the form of "The Scholar-Gipsy" and "Thyrsis," Arnold seems to have found a perfect vehicle for the poetry of the wilderness. The highly conventional genre, inherited from the

Greek of "The Lament for Bion" and Theocritus' *Idylls* and from the Latin of Virgil's *Eclogues,* would satisfy his need for classical form, and the pastoral landscape would enable him to bring beauty to the wilderness with "natural magic." The setting he chose for the poems, the countryside around Oxford, was perfectly suited for his own version of the quest romance, since Oxford, as one of his most famous and poetic prose passages makes clear, was associated for him with the quest of medieval romance. He associated the idea that "we are all seekers still!" with Oxford as "this queen of romance," and he memorably apostrophized the city:

> *Beautiful city! so venerable, so lovely, so unravaged by the fierce intellectual life of our century, so serene!*
>
> *"There are our young barbarians, all at play!"*
>
> *And yet, steeped in sentiment as she lies, spreading her gardens to the moonlight, and whispering from her towers the last enchantments of the Middle Age, who will deny that Oxford, by her ineffable charm, keeps ever calling us nearer to the true goal of all of us, to the ideal, to perfection,—to beauty, in a word, which is only truth seen from another side?—nearer, perhaps, than all the science of Tübingen. Adorable dreamer, whose heart has been so romantic!* (3.289–90)

The passage, written in 1865, plainly shares the sense of questing for faith in a dream that animates "Thyrsis," but it corresponds also with the impulse in the earlier "Scholar-Gipsy" to "again begin the quest" (l. 10).[16] Unlike the poems, however, the prose speaks with certainty about the "true goal"—both "The Scholar-Gipsy" and "Thyrsis" are about quests, but precisely what is sought remains unclear. In consequence they become poems not about purposeful seeking but about wandering—the Scholar-Gipsy is himself a "wanderer" (l. 63), the speaker of "Thyrsis" is "wandering" (l. 23), and Thyrsis' life gains value because he (supposedly) "*wandered till* [*he*] *died*" (l. 237).

The poems themselves epitomize the condition of wandering and, moreover, of wandering in a confined space. Because the Gipsy, the signal-elm of "Thyrsis," and the landscapes themselves are, as is generally agreed, symbolic projections of the speaker's thoughts and feelings, the poems are in the tradition of what Bloom calls internalized quest romance.[17] Despite their adoption of classical form and tradition, the poems are emphatically romantic, are emphatically allegories of the state of the poet's mind. Still, the classical conventions seem a deliberate effort to avoid entrapment in an internalized dialogue of the mind with itself. Even though "The Scholar-Gipsy" was written after the 1853 Preface, and after *Sohrab and Rustum,* and despite such obvious differences that it seems "a conclusive refutation of nearly everything that Preface stands for,"[18] it has certain affinities. As Arnold said, "It was meant to fix the remembrance of . . . delightful wanderings . . . in the Cumner Hills"[19]—that is, to stabilize, memorialize, the flux of experience in the stilled form of art. And of course "Thyrsis" was intended as a monument to Clough. It is, I think, only slightly farfetched to hint that Arnold's elegies for the Oxford countryside, for Clough, and for his own lost youth are related to the tableaux of *Tristram and Iseult* and *The Church of Brou,* and even more to the monument-building of *Sohrab and Rustum, Balder Dead,* and *Merope.* In this context the association with Oxford is disconcerting, since the poems, like the university, become monuments to lost causes, beautiful but ineffectual in the modern world, associated more with the past than the present, more with death than with life.

By using an extremely conventional form, Arnold could exploit universal rather than personal associations. He could, for example, exploit the traditional juxtaposition of an idealized pastoral landscape with a harsher actuality in order to demonstrate the inadequacies of modern life and the extent of the fall from a better, simpler world. The use of convention allows an escape from isolation within the self in another way as well. It involves a self-conscious calling upon the thoughts of great poets of the past, an invocation of the "best that is known and thought in the world"—Arnold's conventions invoke not only Theocritus and Virgil, but Milton's "Lycidas" and Gray's "Elegy" as well. In fact, as Paul Alpers has recently pointed out, convention in pastoral elegy must be understood in part as a "convening" of poetic predecessors. In Virgil's fifth eclogue, for example, "the idea of convention . . . involves . . . a usage that implicitly convenes an absent predecessor—the poet who instituted the rhetorical practices exemplified here."[20] Such a usage, related to the singing contests characteristic of pastoral, enables the surviving poet to inherit from and triumph over his predecessors, to profit from and build on the poetic tradition. But by the nineteenth century, when originality and spontaneity have been exalted by romanticism, convention has become problematic and such benign inheritance is no longer possible.[21] In "Thyrsis" the assertion that there is "for Corydon no rival now" (l. 81) is not enabling but discouraging—"Time, not Corydon, hath conquered" Thyrsis (l. 80), and by implication, will conquer Corydon too. The convening of past poetic voices does not, in fact, readily permit Arnold to achieve a classical objectivity or classical purity of form, or even to exploit an enabling poetic tradition. Rather, it confines him within the autonomous language of literature, within the historical errors of language. Very obviously the conventions of literature point to *words,* not *things,* to venerable fictions, not facts. Nietzsche aphoristically said that "the idyllic shepherd of modern man is but a replica of the sum of cultural illusions which he mistakes for nature,"[22] but of course Arnold's use of conventions borrowed from Theocritus and Virgil involves deliberate, not mistaken, reference to culture rather than nature. He is less in control, however, of the numerous allusions to poets in the English tradition—Milton, Gray, Tennyson and, especially, Keats. Bloom, in fact, complains that Arnold is driven out of his own poem by a language that is imitative of Keats's odes to the point of plagiarism.[23] Though unfair, Bloom's comment does suggest the extreme difficulty Arnold had in controlling alien voices within his poems. When he tried to contrast the deliberately artificial pastoral ideal with actuality, poetic predecessors, poetic language, and romantic assumptions interfered, so that he actually contrasted not the ideal and the real but rather two equally limited ideologies, both products of an inescapable and partially disabling literary tradition—"the sum of cultural illusions."

"The Scholar-Gipsy" has been interpreted in many, and wildly divergent, ways, but it has generally been understood as belonging to Arnold's romantic side, the side he rejected in the 1853 Preface, probably just before writing the poem. Arnold's own comments to Clough indicate that he did not see the work as accomplishing the proper aims of poetry: "I am glad you like the Gipsy Scholar—but what does it *do* for you? Homer *animates*—Shakespeare *animates*—in its poor way I think Sohrab and Rustum *animates*—the Gipsy Scholar at best awakens a pleasing melancholy."[24] The poem, as Arnold saw it, is akin to "Obermann" and "Stanzas from the Grande Chartreuse"—its melancholy is an outworn theme. But Arnold resisted the melancholy even within the poem, partly by his adoption of a quasi-classical form and partly by insistently contrasting the romantic isolation of the wandering Gipsy and the idle quester with the real business of the world. It is clear from the outset, when the speaker dismisses his companion to perform his duties as a shepherd, that the poem is concerned with the conflicting claims of duty and beauty, and it is clear also that the poem wants to see both duty and reverie as legitimate activities, one moral and social, the other poetic and private. But what is particularly interesting is that both are described and justified with literary allusions. The shepherd is not merely dismissed to his rustic duties, but to his Miltonic pastoral duties:

> Go, for they call you, shepherd, from the hill;
> Go, shepherd, and untie the wattled cotes!
> (ll. 1–5) No longer leave thy wistful flock unfed,
> Nor let thy bawling fellows rack their throats
> Nor the cropped herbage shoot another head.

The pastoral convention itself idealizes and spiritualizes the shepherd's duty, and the famous prior use of it in "Lycidas," especially, establishes it as a moral imperative. But the speaker, apparently idling in a working world, must also be justified in his conduct:

> Here, where the reaper was at work of late—
> In this high field's dark corner, where he leaves
> His coat, his basket, and his earthen cruse,
> (ll. 11–16) And in the sun all morning binds the sheaves,
> Then here, at noon, comes back his stores to use—
> Here will I sit and wait.

Again, it is Milton who justifies the activity (or inactivity)—most people must work hard and purposefully, but "They also serve who only stand and wait." Yet Arnold's line betrays a certain spiritual slackness that is, perhaps, inevitable when an agnostic adopts the spiritual language of a zealous Puritan—Milton stood, waiting for God; Arnold's speaker sits, waiting "till sun-down" (l. 22) for the shepherd. The situation betrays, I think, Arnold's radical ambivalence about the moral utility of poetic reverie—he tries to invoke Milton as a powerful ally to justify the speaker's passivity, but in these latter days, as the later part of the poem makes clear, waiting for a "spark from heaven" (l. 171) is an exercise in futility and despair. The language that pointed, for Milton, to ultimate truth can only point, for Arnold, to Milton. For the agnostic, language is no longer sacramental, only self-referential. The important point is that the first two stanzas of "The Scholar-Gipsy" anticipate the central thematic contrast of purposeful work with wise passivity, but they do so by enacting the poem's crucial and largely unconscious central drama, a wandering or erring in the closed confines of literary language.

The next section of the poem (ll. 20–130) presents the idyllic world of the Gipsy in the most lush descriptive verse Arnold ever wrote:

> Through the thick corn the scarlet poppies peep,
> And round green roots and yellowing stalks I see
> (ll. 23–27) Pale pink convolvulus in tendrils creep;
> And air-swept lindens yield
> Their scent.

Here, if anywhere, is Arnoldian "natural magic," and the situation is perfect for it. The ability to "make magically near and real the life of Nature," Arnold later said, requires "a peculiar temperament, an extraordinary delicacy of organization and susceptibility to impression; in exercising it the poet is in a great degree passive (Wordsworth thus speaks of a *wise passiveness*); he aspires to be a sort of human Aeolian harp, catching and rendering every rustle of Nature" (3:30). The object of such "natural magic" is, of course, to transcend literary convention, to see the thing in itself and to match it with the word—poets of natural magic "speak like Adam naming by divine inspiration the creatures; their expression corresponds with the thing's essential reality" (3:34). But how far Arnold was from such an ideal is evident in his uncertainty about whether the convolvulus was pink (as in the 1885 edition) or blue (as in all editions from 1853–1881), but far more importantly it is evident in the necessary exigencies of alliteration and rhyme, and in the probable allusions, noted by Allott, to Keats's "To Autumn" and Tennyson's "The Lotos-Eaters." Once again, the poetry refers to poetry, not to nature—and to the extent that it refers to "The Lotos-Eaters" in its lazy rhymes, it underscores the sense that this is not "wise passiveness" but merely idleness.

Given the speaker's reliance on texts rather than nature for inspiration, it is fitting that he should now consult "Glanvill's book" to inspire his vision of the Gipsy. The subsequent descriptions of the Gipsy and his haunts present the ideal of the pastoral idyll. The Gipsy is, as has often been noted, a kind of genius loci who animates the landscape and embodies the dream of a timeless world that is still available in reverie if not in actuality. It is, of course, only belaboring the obvious to stress that the ideal is a literary one, a conventional one made up from hints in Gray and Keats as well as Glanvill, but the pastoral description concludes, incongruously, with reference to personal experience. After describing the various rural folk who have seen the Gipsy, always on the outskirts of society, the speaker apparently claims personally to have seen him:

> And once, in winter, on the causeway chill
> Where home through flooded fields foot-travellers go,
> (ll. 121–25) Have I not passed thee on the wooden bridge,
> Wrapped in thy cloak and battling with the snow,
> Thy face tow'rd Hinksey and its wintry ridge?

Unlike most rhetorical questions, this one seems to require an answer—and of course it gets one in the next stanza: "But what—I dream!" (l. 131). But even within the description of the dubious vision, the language is tentative, unsure, turned against itself. The modifying phrases and clauses suspend and delay any arrival at meaning, as do the grammatical inversion and periodic structure, and the rhetorical form of the question leaves the whole suspended in uncertainty. Indeed, until the closing question mark one could conceivably read the passage as a denial of the vision—"Have I not passed thee" is an inverted form of "I have not passed thee." The point is that as soon as the language attempts to delineate experience, rather than to embellish tradition and sustain cultural illusions, it becomes grammatically strained and uncertain—it becomes skeptical, agnostic.

With the loss of the naive, unexamined dream, the poem abruptly shifts to an analysis of the

strange disease of modern life
(ll. 203–5) With its sick hurry, its divided aims,
Its heads o'ertaxed, its palsied hearts.

The language becomes harsh, abstract, "unpoetical." The diction comes almost to resemble that of Empedocles' ode to Pausanias in contrast with the fresher, Calliclean lyricism of the pastoral sections—the dialogue of the mind has recommenced. The language strives for a kind of absolute, bleak honesty in presenting the poetrylessness of modern, multitudinous experience in order to show that even in the arid wasteland of modern life, the visionary gleam embodied in the Gipsy can be kept alive in the imagination:

The generations of thy peers are fled,
And we ourselves shall go;
(ll. 155–59) But thou possessest an immortal lot,
And we imagine thee exempt from age
And living as thou liv'st on Glanvil's page.

Like the Gipsy himself, the speaker in these dark times is "Still nursing the unconquerable hope, / Still clutching the inviolable shade" (ll. 211–12). The need and the possibility of clinging to a pastoral dream in an industrial age is, according to Alan Roper's admirable commentary, the essential argument of the poem: "As often as it is read, the poem confirms the possibility of good dreams in bad times; and if the poem also questions the validity of such dreams, it never quite commits itself against them: that, after all, is what the Gipsy Scholar does for you."[25] This is well put, and concisely sums up the precariousness of Arnold's vision of an ideal outside the hurly-burly of modern life. Nevertheless, I would like to suggest that in addition to Arnold's deliberate and explicit questioning of the dream, the poem's language and ideological assumptions undercut the vision still further, relegating it to a literary never-never land where it can have no real contact with modern life.

In the first place, the values represented by the Gipsy can be preserved only by banishing them. He is told to "Fly hence, our contact fear!" (l. 206)—removed from the "gradual furnace of the world" he may live forever. The notion may anticipate Arnold's later critical strategy of disinterestedness, of removing oneself from the fray to preserve a sense of the ideal, but it also anticipates the problem of that strategy—anyone so distanced from society cannot be effective or meaningful within it.[26] By corporealizing his ideal in such a tangible form as the Gipsy, Arnold cut off the possibility of absorbing it. The Gipsy and the ideal are preserved, but only on the outskirts of society. Poetic reverie is, in a sense, banished or outlawed, or at the very least rendered irrelevant. It can have no practical influence on life. Somewhat less obviously, the force of the contrast Arnold established between the Gipsy's life and modern reality depends upon a falsification of both terms. The Gipsy is an attractive figure in the first half of the poem precisely because he is a happy wanderer, drifting through the countryside with the nonchalance of nature herself, but when Arnold wanted to contrast him with the aimlessness of modern life, he suddenly turned him into a zealous quester: "Thou hadst *one* aim, *one* business, *one* desire" (l. 152), as opposed to modern people, "Who fluctuate idly without term or scope, / Of whom each strives, nor knows for what he strives" (ll. 167–68). The second half of the poem, in effect, "misreads" the first half for dramatic contrast—as Empedocles "misread" Callicles' songs. The misreading not only implies the difficulty of seeing the object as it really is, and suggests the deceptive force of words, but it also accidentally demonstrates the inapplicability of the Gipsy's wanderings as an alternative to modern life. Also, as always, Arnold cannot specify a goal, the object of the Gipsy's aim, business, and desire. Consequently, despite the increasing bravado of the language in its insistence on purpose, the Gipsy remains purposeless, a wanderer. He is, in fact, too much like modern man to provide naturally the kind of contrast the poem brings about by rhetorical shifts.

The falsification of the Gipsy in the second half of the poem reveals that the abstract, sincere, straightforward language does not, in fact, adequately represent actuality. This section inevitably misrepresents the modern world by measuring it against not just a fictional construct but a falsification of a fictional construct. William Buckler has made the point that the modern world set forth is as much a "mythic construct" as is the pastoral, and is brought about in response to it: "The very delight of the image of the created world of the scholar-gipsy motivates [the speaker], in the second half of the poem, to create the image of the modern world, not exactly as it is, but as a coherent counter-image."[27] For Buckler the poem is a kind of dramatic monologue in which a detached Arnold can ponder the perplexities of his speaker, but it seems at least as likely that Arnold was himself trapped in a Victorian, but still romantic, ideology that led him to judge the present against a romanticized ideal of the past. It was, after all, the habitual strategy of his age, the strategy of Scott, Pugin, Ruskin, Carlyle, Tennyson, Morris, and others. In this respect the literary, poetic ideal of the Scholar-Gipsy is not merely irrelevant but pernicious, for it leads to an overharsh condemnation of the present and an unnecessary despair. The poem thus enacts the myth of a fall, in which a pastoral landscape is blighted and wandering has clearly become erring, but what has really occurred is a shift in ideological perspective—as Blake said, "The eye altering alters all." But the most important point is that even in the starkest, most unpoetic sections of the poem, the language does not refer to actuality but to other texts, literary representations of a past that never was and of a contemporary ideological perspective.

The language of this section, in fact, enacts the dilemma it describes, the condition of aimless wandering and incapacity to escape from the errors of language to nonlinguistic truth. "Mortal men" (l. 142—the redundancy is significant in its implication that the poet, trying to force the words to *mean* what they mean, only ends up returning to where he has started) wear themselves out in pointless activity

Till having used our nerves with bliss and teen,
(ll. 147–50) And tired upon a thousand schemes our wit,
To the just-pausing Genius we remit
Our worn-out life, and are—what we have been.

The passage wears itself out, but finally ends up getting precisely nowhere. Rhymes, of course, inevitably suggest a kind of back-tracking, but the rhyme scheme of Arnold's stanza emphasizes this quality. The stanza consists of a sestet (*a b c b c a*) and a quatrain (*d e e d*), both of which begin and end with the same rhyme, thus returning upon themselves and enclosing what is within. For that matter, the ten-line stanzas are, with only one real exception, self-enclosed tableaux, which do not push the narrative in a direct, questing line.[28] But the most significant wandering is through the terrain of past poetical works. In the first half of the poem Arnold attempts a "magical" poetry, and in the second half he attempts a "scientific" diction, but the second is no more an unmediated language than the first. In fact, the second half is packed even more densely with allusions than is the first. The turning point is a response to the open-ended rhetoric of the first part in the exclamation "But what—I dream!" (l. 131). According to Allott, this is an allusion to Keats's "Ode to a Nightingale": "Was it a vision, or a waking dream?"[29] Allott is probably right, since Keats's odes resonate throughout the poem, but its syntax more closely echoes "Lycidas": "Ay me, I fondly dream." The doubly allusive line suggests not a straightforward "return to everyday reality," as Allott says, but a turning again in the byways of literature. Fittingly the stanza moves on to an account of the Gipsy legend *as* a legend, and then buries him in the shadow of Gray's elegy:

And thou from earth art gone
Long since, and in some quiet churchyard laid—
(ll. 136–40) Some country-nook, where o'er thy unknown grave
Tall grasses and white flowering nettles wave,
Under a dark, red-fruited yew-tree's shade.

The actuality is that the "real" Gipsy-Scholar is dead, but the poem's allusive reference keeps the ideal alive by assimilating it to the ideologically similar sentimentalizations of Gray. Fifteen lines later, reality is again kept at bay by literary allusion:

> The generations of thy peers are fled,
> And we ourselves shall go;
> (ll. 155–60) But thou possessest an immortal lot,
> And we imagine thee exempt from age
> And living as thou liv'st on Glanvil's page.

As I said earlier, the passage declares that the visionary gleam can be kept alive even in the face of death, but it is kept alive within the autonomous realm of art, with the language and ideology of Keats's "Ode to a Nightingale": "Thou wast not born for death, immortal Bird! / No hungry generations tread thee down." And of course he is kept alive only as he lived "on Glanvil's page"—in literature. The remainder of Arnold's criticism of modern life moves through indirect reference to Tennyson and explicit allusion to Virgil's Dido in Hades to a final Keatsian consummation as the Gipsy is urged to "fly our paths, our feverish contact fly" (l. 221) or else his "glad perennial youth would fade, / Fade, and grow old at last, and die like ours" (ll. 229–30). The double "fade," I think, echoes Keats's desire in the "Ode to a Nightingale" to "fade away into the forest dim: / Fade far away" and so escape "The weariness, the fever, and the fret" of actual life where "youth grows pale, and spectre-thin, and dies." The apparently crucial difference is that the Gipsy is being told to avoid death, and the Keatsian speaker comes increasingly to realize that the escape he desires *is* death ("Now more than ever seems it rich to die"). Arnold's Gipsy continues to seek the kind of immortality Keats grants only to the nightingale. But arguably the real meaning of Arnold's poem lies in the intertextual implication that the escape from death is also a flight from life, a flight in fact into the autonomous realm of art. I do not mean, of course, that there is anything wrong with this, any more than there is anything wrong with Keats's immortal Grecian urn, or Yeats's golden bird upon a golden bough, but Arnold's poem gains its poetic force as a poem of wandering strictly within the confines of the poetic tradition.

The end symbol, the description of the Tyrian trader fleeing from the Greeks, certainly does not tie up the poem's loose ends, despite Culler's assertion that it represents the resolution of the poem's dialectic. In this reading, the poem "is essentially three-fold because its main movement is the vision, the loss of the vision, and its recreation in a different mode. It is the product, first, of the heart and imagination, then, of the senses and understanding, and finally, of the imaginative reason."[30] Such an interpretation, of course, shows the poem dramatizing the teleological optimism of purposeful quest, but it depends upon a peculiar interpretation of Arnold's Greeks as representatives of "a debased, modern civilization, whose sailors timidly hug the shore," and a correspondent exaltation of the Tyrian: "By contrast, the Tyrian trader is the grave representative of an ancient civilization which, finding itself superseded by low cunning, refuses to compete, but indignantly strikes out to a new world, harder, but more pure."[31] But this bears scant resemblance to Arnold's brief description of the "merry Grecian coaster" that the Tyrian saw

> Freighted with amber grapes, and Chian wine,
> Green, bursting figs, and tunnies steeped
> in brine—
> And knew the intruders on his ancient home,
>
> The young light-hearted masters of the waves.
>
> (ll. 237–41)

Whether deliberately or not, the end symbol undercuts the ideal of the gipsy by associating his flight from society with the flight of the grave and indignant Tyrian from civilization.[32] The Tyrian's mode of trade with the "dark Iberians" (l. 249), in which no human contact is ever made, is nothing if not antisocial—and this too suggests a negative response to the Gipsy. The end symbol has been a source of critical controversy because it can as easily be seen to undermine the vision of the Gipsy as to reinforce it, and because critics have generally assumed that if the poem is to be successful the closure must unify it by resolving its dialectic. Consequently, Culler praises the poem on these grounds, while Buckler, who sees the conflicts as unresolved, faults it. But such judgments are based on a romantic aesthetic that assumes all great works must achieve a complex organic unity, must achieve, in Coleridge's phrase, "multeity in unity." However, Arnold's multitudinous world could not be contained in a neat aesthetic unity, and his poem may reasonably be judged a success precisely because it fails to resolve itself into a cheering but false dialectical vision. Its end symbol, presenting a wandering and homeless Tyrian, perpetuates the poem's thematic concern with alienation but does not resolve it, and more, its extraordinary allusiveness perpetuates the enactment of wandering in texts. As Culler points out, in the end symbol "Arnold has distilled a good bit of cultural history which he picked up from passages in Herodotus, Thucydides, Diodorus Siculus, and his father's *History of Rome*."[33] The conventions of pastoral have been left behind by this time, but the poet continues to "convene" the literature and legends of the past; the poem continues to wander in the tradition, and to wander among its various modes. In all of these respects the real significance of "The Scholar-Gipsy" as a modern poem is that it displays the purposeless multitudinousness of modern life. Its inability to resolve a dialectic is a proper and inevitable reflection of a godless society in which no goal can be posited and no quest is possible, and in which literature cannot point to "Truth" but can only engage in a certain errantry of language.

The difficulty of finding ways to make the quest meaningful is still more obvious in the companion poem to "The Scholar-Gipsy" written fifteen years later. "Thyrsis," Arnold's elegy for Clough, was not finished until 1866, fifteen years after "The Scholar-Gipsy," and long after Arnold had stopped writing poetry regularly, and it shows a far greater urgency to retain some kind of faith. The form of the pastoral elegy, the setting in the Oxford countryside, the stanza form, the "natural magic" of description, all, of course, assimilate "Thyrsis" to "The Scholar-Gipsy," even to the extent that one critic has chosen to regard the two poems as "two parts of the same poem."[34] But despite the evident similarities, the poems are very different, and comparison of them must inevitably focus on the passage of time between them. As Culler has said, "With Arnold fifteen years—especially when they extend from the early 'fifties to the mid 'sixties—is a long time. Much has happened in that time, and indeed, this 'much' is essentially what the poem is about."[35] Very obviously the poem is about the death of a friend, the loss of youth, the ravages of time. The first line is concerned with the passage of time: "How changed is here each spot man makes or fills!" And the motto that originally preceded the poem is even more emphatic:

> Thus yesterday, to-day, to-morrow come,
> They hustle one another and they pass;
> But all our hustling morrows only make
> The smooth to-day of God.

The thematic preoccupation with time is self-evident, but I will be more concerned with the effect of time's passage on Arnold's poetic aspirations and language. The motto is significant in this respect also, because it hints that Arnold is more dependent upon, entrapped by, and anxious about the poetic tradition than ever. In the first place the motto obviously gains its force from the allusion to Macbeth's famous nihilistic speech:

> Tomorrow, and tomorrow, and tomorrow,
> Creeps in this petty pace from day to day,
> (5.5.19–23) To the last syllable of recorded time;
> And all our yesterdays have lighted fools
> The way to dusty death.

Whether Macbeth's nihilism is seen as a corrosive subtext undermining the apparent religious serenity of the motto, or the motto is seen as a deliberate corrective to nihilism, the effect is to suggest how much must be overcome to achieve serenity. Further, the motto is attributed to "*Lucretius,* an unpublished Tragedy," and may have been used, Allott speculates, because Arnold had heard that Tennyson was working on a *Lucretius* and he wanted to assert his priority[36]—in other words, the motto may be the direct result of Arnold's anxiety about his own place in the tradition. Also, of course, the unfinished—and never finished—*Lucretius* was to be a poem about a poet. And finally, the likely context of the motto would probably undercut its evident serenity—for Lucretius "The smooth to-day of God" would be merely a measure of God's indifference to mankind. Perhaps it is unfair to make so much of a motto that Arnold eventually canceled, but the pressures exerted on its placidity seem perfectly to epitomize the pressures exerted from within on the eventual serenity of "Thyrsis" as Arnold tried to resist the idea that life

is a tale
Told by an idiot, full of sound and fury,
Signifying nothing.
(*Macbeth* 5.5.26–28)

Arnold's evident desire to strengthen his poem with the great tradition is, of course, clear not only in the choice of form, the conventional title, and the various convenings of pastoral elegy, but in the subtitle as well, a recollection of the heading of "Lycidas": "A MONODY, to commemorate the author's friend, ARTHUR HUGH CLOUGH, who died at Florence, 1861." "Lycidas" is famous for its omission of Edward King and its formal use of pastoral elegy for more general concerns, so Arnold's invocation of it is particularly appropriate—he felt that "not enough is said about Clough" in the elegy, but he "was carried irresistibly into this form."[37] The poetic form, not the occasion or the meaning of the event, dictates what Arnold will say—Clough, in himself as he really was, is effaced even as he is memorialized. Still, enough is said about Clough to misrepresent and insult him. In the first half of the poem he is unfairly blamed for his failure to retain the ideals of Oxford and of the Scholar-Gipsy, for rushing prematurely into the world. Clough is even associated with the cuckoo, another "Too quick despairer" (l. 61) who leaves before he must. Arnold is, in fact, wrong about the reasons for Clough's departure, and wrong even about the cuckoo's migration, but the real issue is his own loss of youth and song:

Ah me! this many a year
My pipe is lost, my shepherd's holiday!
Needs must I lose them, needs with heavy heart
Into the world and wave of men depart;
But Thyrsis of his own will went away.
(ll. 36–40)

The implied censure of Thyrsis is hardly fair, since the poem acknowledges the *need* to leave the pastoral world behind, but

Arnold is determined to establish the value of that world—to insist that one should not sacrifice it willingly.

Indeed, it soon becomes apparent that "Time, not Corydon, hath conquered" Thyrsis (l. 80), and has conquered Corydon as well. The elegy modulates into a generalized lament about living in a poetryless time and place, far from the mythic landscape of Sicily. In fact, for twenty lines (ll. 81–100) the modern Corydon invokes the ancient names and echoes the earlier poets to lament the inefficacy of the modern poem that Proserpine will not hear:

She loved the Dorian pipe, the Dorian strain.
But ah, of our poor Thames she never heard!
Her foot the Cumner cowslips never stirred;
(ll. 97–102) And we should tease her with our plaint in vain!

Well! wind-dispersed and vain the words will be,
Yet, Thyrsis, let me give my grief its hour.

The shift in tone, signaled by the conversational "Well!" and the low-key matter-of-factness of what follows is analogous to the shift from "natural magic" to an abstract, "unpoetic" language in "The Scholar-Gipsy." But once again the apparent shift from literary tradition to personal experience leads to a loss of hope and, in this case, a desire for death:

strange and vain the earthly turmoil grows,
(ll. 148–50) And near and real the charm of thy repose,
And night as welcome as a friend would fall.

The real source of despair in this part of the poem is the loss of poetic power, despite the speaker's attempt to prove his authority to speak out:

Who, if not I, for questing here hath power?
I know the wood which hides the daffodil,
I know the Fyfield tree,
I know what white, what purple fritillaries
(ll. 104–11) The grassy harvest of the river-fields,
Above by Ensham, down by Sandford, yields,
And what sedged brooks are Thames's tributaries;

I know these slopes; who knows them if not I?

The rhetorical questions betray a certain anxiety, but beyond this, the appeal to personal experience is, as Allott's notes reveal, a continued appeal to literary tradition, an echo of lines from *Comus* and *A Midsummer Night's Dream*.[38] The irony is that, having denied the continuing validity of the pastoral tradition and turned to supposedly personal experience, the speaker finds himself defining personal experience in the terms of that tradition. What follows is a reprise of the ubi sunt formula: "Where is the girl . . . ? Where are the mowers . . . ? They all are gone, and thou art gone as well!" (ll. 121–30). And this is followed by the most apparently personal section of the poem, a despairing account of the speaker's own loss of youth:

> Yes, thou art gone! and round me too the night
> In ever-nearing circle weaves her shade.
> I see her veil draw soft across the day,
> I feel her slowly chilling breath invade
> The cheek grown thin, the brown hair sprent
> with grey.
> (ll. 131–35)

Even here the language draws on pastoral tradition. Allott notes the use of Collins's "Ode to Evening" ("Thy dewy fingers draw / The dusky veil") and the lines also echo Thomson's "Summer," in which the shadows of "sober Evening" "In circle following circle, gather round, / To close the face of things" (ll. 1648–53). And finally the poem moves toward its deepest despair, a death-wish reminiscent of Keats's "Ode to a Nightingale," via further echoes of Pope and Johnson, and perhaps of Hesiod and Donne.[39] I am far from disparaging Arnold's poem as derivative—he makes, it seems to me, brilliant use of the tradition, and his allusive style is no more blamable than that of Pound or Eliot. In fact, Eliot's description of how we ought to read poetry would lead us to a high estimate of "Thyrsis." Eliot argued that we tend to praise too highly what is unique in a poet, what seems to give "the peculiar essence of the man," but "if we approach a poet without this prejudice we shall often find that not only the best, but the most individual parts of his work may be those in which the dead poets, his ancestors, assert their immortality most vigorously." Arnold's own views about the saving power of the tradition are akin to Eliot's, and he was, to be sure, most often at his best as a poet when he was most freely allusive. But my point is that the more apparently personal Arnold's language gets, the more it is in fact related to texts, not experience. This phenomenon, too, is explained by Eliot: "The poet has, not a 'personality' to express, but a particular medium, which is only a medium and not a personality."[40] But Arnold could never easily accept the idea of a self-enclosed world of art as an autonomous medium cut off from life, and as texts begin, in effect, to take over and crowd out personal experience, the poem becomes increasingly despairing.

It is altogether fitting that the elegiac turn of "Thyrsis," its movement away from despair, should be signaled by the word "hush!" (l. 151). Yet it is a peculiar word—the poem is being "spoken" to Thyrsis, who surely does not need to be hushed any further. According to Culler, this "elegiac reversal . . . is accomplished by the poet's 'hushing' his false poetic voice and assuming his true." I will not dispute whether Arnold finds a "truer" voice, but Culler is right, I think, in describing the speaker's attempt to turn from poeticizing to actuality, his attempt to hush the many voices of the poetic tradition and to look outward, at the here and now. But once again, the attempt to speak *sincerely* leads Arnold into trouble. Hearing the sound of hunters, the speaker—like the Gipsy—flees their contact and so comes upon what Culler calls his "poetic vision":[41]

> Quick! let me fly, and cross
> Into yon farther field!—'Tis done; and see,
> (ll. 156–60) Backed by the sunset, which doth glorify
> The orange and pale violet evening-sky,
> Bare on its lonely ridge, the Tree! the Tree!

This is indeed the elegiac reversal, and from this point on the poem will defiantly combat despair, will desperately seek to sustain a saving vision. But Arnold was an agnostic, and the strain of trying to sustain a vision shows in his language and in his logic.

Too much of the burden is borne by "the Tree! the Tree!" as a "happy omen" (l. 166). As Roper has pointed out, the tree itself is a vegetable, long-lived, but not immortal—and it is not being too literal-minded to note this in a pastoral poem that emphasizes "the vegetable indices of impermanence."[42] The argument that the tree is not a tree but a symbol probably gets close to what Arnold wanted, but it does not solve the problem of putting "an allegorical object in a literal landscape."[43] The objection to the tree as a symbol of the permanence of the Scholar-Gipsy as an ideal is that it is arbitrary; it depends entirely on a youthful fancy, wishful thinking, and a stipulative definition:

while it stood, we said,
(ll. 28–30) Our friend, the Gipsy-Scholar, was not dead;
While the tree lived, he in these fields lived on.

It is so because I say it is so. But this is the logic and language of Wonderland—the tree stands for the immortal ideal in the same way that a word of Humpty Dumpty's "means just what I choose it to mean—neither more nor less." Arnold's arbitrary attachment of significance to the tree summons up Alice's perplexity with Humpty Dumpty:

> *"That's a great deal to make one word mean," Alice said in a thoughtful tone.*
>
> *"When I make a word do a lot of work like that," said Humpty Dumpty, "I always pay it extra."*
>
> *"Oh!" said Alice. She was much too puzzled to make any other remark.*[44]

According to Philip Drew, the "epiphany," the vision of the tree, grants Arnold "the assurance that the tree was not imaginary, that the vigour, certainty and happiness of youth are realities, even though he can no longer recover them."[45] Evidently the tree was not imaginary—but as for the rest, can Arnold mean so many things with his words, no matter how much he pays for them?

The remainder of the poem totters over this shaky vision. The speaker calls upon Thyrsis to hear his cheering news, but immediately realizes the impossibility of this:

Hear it, O Thyrsis, still our tree is there!
(ll. 171–81) Ah, vain! These English fields, this upland dim,
These brambles pale with mist engarlanded,

That lone, sky-pointing tree, are not for him;
To a boon southern country he is fled,
And now in happier air,
Wandering with the great Mother's train divine
(And purer or more subtle soul than thee,
I trow, the mighty Mother doth not see)
Within a folding of the Appennine,

Thou hearest the immortal chants of old!

But of course this eludes the more fundamental point that Thyrsis cannot hear these reassurances because he is dead—and so eludes the crippling sense that elegiac language addressed to the dead is a casting of words into the void. Still, the speaker recognizes the vanity of his words and can only regain his composure by leaping back into an otherwise irrelevant description of the ancient pastoral song that once had power to be heard beyond the grave. Yet the realization that Thyrsis cannot hear his song sends the speaker again to the brink of despair, to a more tortured language than ever, and to a desperate attempt to save, not Thyrsis, but himself:

There thou art gone, and me thou leavest here
Sole in these fields! yet will I not despair.
Despair I will not, while I yet descry
'Neath the mild canopy of English air
(ll. 191–200) That lonely tree against the western sky.
Still, still these slopes, 'tis clear,
Our Gipsy-Scholar haunts, outliving thee!
Fields where soft sheep from cages pull the hay,
Woods with anemones in flower till May,
Know him a wanderer still; then why not me?

The stanza protests too much, especially in the awkward Miltonic inversion of the second and third lines, the repetition in the sixth, and the reliance on the arbitrary symbolism of the tree. Even more striking is the implicit dismissal of Thyrsis, who has been outlived by the Gipsy and the speaker, and the extraordinary self-concern as the stanza leans heavily on its final clause and final word: "then why not me?"

A certain emphasis on the speaker's own hopes for salvation is not unusual in pastoral elegy, but denigration of the subject indicates an evident straining against the form. And Thyrsis is denigrated with a vengeance just before the poem's conclusion:

What though the music of thy rustic flute
Kept not for long its happy, country tone;
Lost it too soon, and learnt a stormy note
(ll. 221–26) Of men contention-tossed, of men who groan,
Which tasked thy pipe too sore, and tired thy throat—
It failed, and thou wast mute!

The abuse of Thyrsis is perhaps necessary in order to establish a saving distance from him, but the poem must not conclude on such a harsh note. Instead it ends on a discordant note, as Thyrsis is suddenly and incongruously praised for wandering in the ways of the Scholar-Gipsy. Still more incongruously, the poem concludes with the voice of Thyrsis communicating the sentiments of the Gipsy:

—Then through the great town's harsh, heart-wearying roar,
Let in thy voice a whisper often come,
To chase fatigue and fear:
(ll. 234–40) *Why faintest thou? I wandered till I died.*
Roam on! The light we sought is shining still.
Dost thou ask proof? Our tree yet crowns the hill,
Our Scholar travels yet the loved hill-side.

But the poem has blamed Thyrsis precisely for *not* wandering till he died and has further declared that Thyrsis cannot hear the good news that the tree yet crowns the hill. And of course if Thyrsis cannot hear, he is still more unlikely to be heard. The projected voice of Thyrsis is another of the echoes in the void that Arnold claims to hear when he most needs reassurance, but in this case it is a phantom voice speaking in blatantly bad faith.

Partly because it was written fifteen years after "The Scholar-Gipsy," and partly, perhaps, because it was an elegy that had to face the ultimate consequences of agnosticism, "Thyrsis" shows a far greater anxiety than the earlier poem to arrive at fixed conclusions, to find *proof* for the possibility of vision. Ironically, the poem enacts a quest ("Who, if not I, for questing here hath power?") at the same time that it declares questing for the "throne of Truth" (l. 144) to be fruitless, a path to despair. Thyrsis himself is blamed, in effect, for questing—for seeking answers rather than wandering in the ways of the Gipsy. Wandering, in fact, is presented as the ideal. The speaker is "wandering through this upland dim" (l. 23) at the outset, while Thyrsis is "Wandering with the great Mother's train divine" (l. 177) in Sicily and the Gipsy-Scholar is "a wanderer still" (l. 200). To redeem Thyrsis, the speaker declares that "Thou wanderedst with me for a little hour" (l. 212) and that "thy foot resumed its wandering way" (l. 229).[46] And finally, Thyrsis is asked to state, quite falsely, that "*I wandered till I died.*" But the tension between the ideal of wandering and the poetic enactment of purposeful seeking pulls the poem apart into contradictions, bad faith, and an unworkable Humpty Dumpty language of wish fulfillment. Arnold's best poetry comes about from an acceptance of the wilderness as wilderness, and of wandering as the inevitable existential condition of modern humanity. But in "Thyrsis" he wants *proof* that "The light . . . is shining still" and he turns the wilderness into a sanctified landscape and the poetic wandering into a forced march. His language and logic show the strain, and "Thyrsis" becomes a moving poem more for its poignant failure to do what poetry in an agnostic age cannot do than for its forced and false success in achieving a redemptive vision.

In "Rugby Chapel" the pressure to achieve a saving vision of truth is even greater, if only because the subject of the elegy is the poet's own father—and here the forced march is the explicit subject of the poem, not a critical interpretation of what the poem enacts. In fact, the entire poem resembles the opening imagery of "Stanzas from the Grande Chartreuse" by portraying a just and purposeful life as an arduous mountain journey toward the Truth. In "Stanzas from the Grande Chartreuse," however, it soon becomes clear that the speaker prefers wandering to a too eager seeking, just as in "Thyrsis" he turns away from "The mountain-tops where is the throne of Truth" (l. 144). The problem, as we have seen, is that the object of the quest is difficult to define, and the point of the quest is difficult to justify, so the poetry vacillates between wandering and questing, between strolling and striding. When questing is privileged, the language, seeking to define real purpose and real values, is generally strident. In "Rugby Chapel" the moral issues are resolved forcefully—wandering is wrong and questing is right—so the poem avoids ambivalence and uncertainty. Even the poetic form, with its short three-stressed lines and narrative verse paragraphs, drives forward purposefully. But the attitudes of striving and moral certainty are undercut by the poet's uneasiness with a language of affirmation:

> And there are some, whom a thirst
> Ardent, unquenchable, fires,
> Not with the crowd to be spent,
> Not without aim to go round
> In an eddy of purposeless dust,
> Effort unmeaning and vain.
> (ll. 73–86) Ah yes! some of us strive
> Not without action to die
> Fruitless, but something to snatch
> From dull oblivion, nor all
> Glut the devouring grave!
> We, we have chosen our path—
> Path to a clear-purposed goal,
> Path of advance!

The verse finally arrives at its statement of a "clear-purposed goal," but only by itself wandering in double negatives, bold assertion ("Ah yes!"), more double negatives, and a general vagueness. "Something to snatch" is reminiscent of Clough's agnostic substitution of the vague "somebody" for God, and the passage only snatches its resolution from Tennyson's resolute Ulysses: "Death closes all; but something ere the end, / Some work of noble note, may yet be done."[47] When the goal is finally announced, it is with the emphatic repetition of rhetorical overkill, and it is nevertheless left hopelessly vague—and even ungrammatical. What is the goal? And shouldn't the seeker, rather than the goal, be "clear-purposed"?

The remainder of the poem will seek, as its goal, the definition of a goal in life.[48] The "Path of advance" is described as an arduous journey through stormy mountain gorges. Travelers struggle on through adversity, lose their companions along the way, but finally arrive at the goal:

We, we only are left!
With frowning foreheads, with lips
Sternly compressed, we strain on,
On—and at nightfall at last
Come to the end of our way,
To the lonely inn 'mid the rocks;
(ll. 104–16) Where the gaunt and taciturn host
Stands on the threshold, the wind,
Shaking his thin white hairs—
Holds his lantern to scan
Our storm-beat figures, and asks:
Whom in our party we bring?
Whom we have left in the snow?

Presumably, if the "end of our way" is not utterly trivial, the gaunt host must be an allegorical figure—but what can the allegory possibly mean? The host seems, in fact, to be an empty signifier, far more arbitrary than even the tree in "Thyrsis"—he can hardly serve as an adequate symbolic goal. Indeed, he provides no solace or answers at the end of life's journey, only censure and questions.

Part of the poem's point, however, is to contrast this inadequate journey with the allegorized life of Thomas Arnold, who saved not only himself, but others as well. He is presented, interestingly, as the good shepherd of pastoral Christian tradition:

Therefore to thee it was given
Many to save with thyself;
(ll. 140–44) And, at the end of thy day,
O faithful shepherd! to come,
Bringing thy sheep in thy hand.

The passive construction enables Arnold to evade the crucial question—"given" by whom? What is the ultimate source of authority? What does it mean to be "saved," unless the word is being used in conventional Christian sense? The pastoral imagery suggests that the poem *is* modulating into acceptance of Christian faith, and in fact the next section becomes an act of faith, a creed:

> And through thee I believe
> In the noble and great who are gone. . . .
>
> Yes! I believe that there lived
> Others like thee in the past.
>
> (ll. 145–46, 153–54)

Still, this is at best a secular creed—the protestations of faith amount to very little. Substituting Thomas Arnold for Christ and heroic men for God empties the language of faith of any transcendental meaning.[49] Consequently the poem is still without any real sense of what the goal is, where salvation lies.

But passing from the gaunt host to the good shepherd to the utterance of even a limited and secular creed has involved a steady heightening of rhetoric, an increasing readiness to accept words as things. This movement culminates in the final sections, which pick up the pastoral language of Matthew's gospel and then the imagery of Exodus to introduce biblical plenitude into the previously profane words.[50] And now the ultimate source of authority becomes blatantly clear: "A God / Marshalled them, gave them their goal" (ll. 174–75). Great men, Victorian heroes like Thomas Arnold, come like pillars of fire and smoke, "like angels" (l. 190), to shepherd mankind to Paradise:

> Ye fill up the gaps in our files,
> Strengthen the wavering line,
> Stablish, continue our march,
> On, to the bound of the waste,
> On, to the City of God.
>
> (ll. 204–8)

The lack of real conviction in all of this rhetoric is perhaps clearest in the statement that it is not God who provides the goal but "*A* God." This is either polytheism or empty language, and of course it is the latter. The "City of God" is no more definite in its meaning than is the inn with the taciturn host. For Arnold, after all, "God" is the stream of tendency that maketh for righteousness and the "City of God" is language "thrown out" at a vast object of consciousness. But even if Arnold's slightly later definitions are ignored, it is evident that the poem's Christianity is a purely rhetorical fervor, a matter of mere words. Words like *angels* and *God,* in fact, are used here only as Humpty Dumpty uses words—and Arnold pays the very high price of producing a strained and unconvincing elegy.[51]

"Rugby Chapel" shows by negative example why the agnostic poetry of the wilderness is, at its best, a poetry of wandering and uncertainty. It presents the quest as absolutely purposeful, but only by a kind of poetic bad faith, a deliberately misleading use of words to suggest more than they could mean to the author. Even Arnold's account of the poem to his mother suggests that it was intended not as a strict expression of truth but as the perpetuation of a myth. Like "The Scholar-Gipsy," it was written to "fix" something—in this case not experience but a pious legend: "I think I have done something to fix the true legend about Papa, as those who knew him best feel it ought to run."[52] With no genuine faith to refer to, the poem's language, seeking plenitude, achieves only a profound emptiness, and the questing poet, seeking truth, achieves only hollow rhetoric. "Rugby Chapel" is a moving poem, but moving in its demonstration of how hard Arnold was willing to work to find conviction in language, and how impossible that task was. The irony is that even if the poem's conclusion carried genuine conviction, it would not enable the poet to write better poetry. Even if Arnold heard the voice of God setting a clear goal, the poetry would be only more flat. By declaring a goal—the "City of God"—the poem eliminates the possibility of an interesting quest. Since the end has already been defined, the quest has nothing to discover.[53] However agonizing, the uncertainties underlying "The Scholar-Gipsy" produce a far more exciting poetry than "Rugby Chapel" because they result in a poetry that is still seeking, still struggling with language, still capable of surprises.

Arnold never fully reconciled the idea of wandering in uncertainty with the idea of striving ever onward, but he came closest, perhaps, in an unambitious elegy for his brother, "A Southern Night." William Arnold's wife died and was buried in India, and he himself died on his return to England in 1859 and was buried at Gibraltar. The exotic settings of their graves led Arnold to consider the "irony of fate" that led "two jaded English" to such "peaceful graves" (ll. 57–60), and to consider the appropriate graves for the resolute and determined English of Victoria's imperial realm:

In cities should we English lie,
  Where cries are rising ever new,
And men's incessant stream goes by—
  We who pursue

Our business with unslackening stride,
(ll. 61–72) Traverse in troops, with care-filled breast,
The soft Mediterranean side,
  The Nile, the East,

And see all sights from pole to pole,
  And glance, and nod, and bustle by,
And never once possess our soul
  Before we die.

Such purposefulness is the strong disease of modern life, a perpetual but probably pointless business that leads nowhere but to the grave. It is the wandering that mistakes itself for quest, and it is properly associated with the busy modern city. Arnold explicitly contrasts it with the life of a gipsylike sage, a crusading knight, a troubador, a girl with a pirate lover, and asserts that

Such by these waters of Romance
  'Twas meet to lay.

(ll. 111–16) But you—a grave for knight or sage,
  Romantic, solitary, still,
O spent ones of a work-day age!
  Befits you ill.

But for this once Arnold was willing to transfer the language of romance from the exotic to the familiar:

And what but gentleness untired,
    And what but noble feeling warm,
Wherever shown, howe'er inspired,
    Is grace, is charm? (ll. 129–32)

By simply not fixing too rigid and definitive meaning on words, by letting the words shift and assume new meanings in new contexts, Arnold could find a poetry and a beauty in modern life. But the stanza ends with a question mark, with a hint of uncertainty about the real meaning of words like *grace* and *charm,* perhaps about the possibility of words ever to mean precisely what we want them to mean. In any case the graves of William and Frances Arnold are invested with the same verbal beauty as those of Tristram and Iseult, and the nobles at Brou, and their lives with the same grace and charm as that of the Scholar-Gipsy. But it is all very much a matter of words, and perhaps the slackness of the poem, the lack of energy or intensity, is a result of no longer struggling with language, no longer trying to force ultimate truths out of words. The bulk of Arnold's very late poetry consists of trivial sentiments about dead pets, as though he no longer saw the point of trying to say anything genuinely significant. But his finest and most ambitious poetry resulted always from his attempts to reconcile verbal beauty with the apparently conflicting truths of objective, scientific reality. In romance, verbal beauty was enough, but in elegy the need for sincerity, for conviction, put an added pressure on the language, a pressure to reconcile words with truth.

IV

Love Poetry: Sincerity and Subversive Voices

THE CONVENTIONS and consolatory purposes of elegy put enormous pressure on poetic language to say the utmost that can be said about life, death, and the hereafter. Indeed, elegy tempts the poet to say more than can be justly said, excuses the flattering fictions and the consoling lie. Similarly, love poetry involves sets of conventions that may tempt the poet to excess, to flattery, seductive deception of the beloved, and even self-deception. The love poem is, in one tradition, a tissue of transparent fictions, specious logic, and false spirituality designed seriously to woo or playfully to seduce—the beloved is a divinity, love is eternal, union is paradise. An important convention of love poetry, of course, is that both author and reader recognize and accept the hyperboles as pleasant fictions, exercises in troping on the simple idea of being in love. But the hyperbolic descriptions of love can be taken seriously as an attempt to express insatiable desire and aspiration, especially when no higher ideal than human love is to be found. Consequently, for many nineteenth-century writers, love comes to replace religious faith as the primary source of value and meaning in life. Agnostic poets eager to find and utter the largest possible truths about human life wrote a good deal of love poetry in the nineteenth century, attempting to use the old conventions with a new earnestness and sincerity, attempting in love poetry even more than in the elegy to utter absolute truth, to communicate genuinely in language. Without a divine word to order the phenomenal world and give its expression meaning, Byron, Shelley, and Keats among the romantics, and Swinburne, Rossetti, and Arnold among the Victorians persistently attempted to look within, to read the language of the heart. Shelley, in the brief essay "On Love," described love in part as a desire that one's language be precisely understood, that one be able to escape isolation in the self by perfect communion with another human being.

Other Victorian poets were more obviously love poets than Arnold was, but for none was it so absolutely clear that love presented the ultimate challenge to sincere self-expression. "The Buried Life" is from beginning to end concerned with whether "even lovers" can "reveal / To one another what indeed they feel" (ll. 14–15), and the poems of the "Switzerland" series examine the possibilities of escaping isolation within the self through passionate love. But over and over again the poems arrive at the conclusion that even love cannot enable the speaker to say what he means, to find an effective—let alone a magical or definitive—language. As E. D. H. Johnson said, Arnold's love poetry makes clear "that in the modern world there no longer exists any channel for communication between one individual and another on the level of the deeper sensibilities. The impossibility of true love is thus emblematic of a general breakdown in human intercourse."[1] With the notable exception of "Dover Beach," Arnold's best love poems are preoccupied with the failure of language to express honest feelings, to utter the most important truths of human relationships. But even beyond the thematic expression of the difficulty, the poems necessarily enact the failure of language that they only partially understand and describe—not because Arnold planned it that way, but because he was right in his sense of the incapacity of language, and especially of highly conventional poetic language, to express unmediated truth. That is, the poems cannot simply speak "from the heart"—to achieve any meaning or significance at all, they must refer to the whole Western discourse about love, must accept, reject, qualify, or in any case *respond* to prior utterances about love and the language of love. The poems are particularly interesting as studies in intertextuality because they so clearly seek to transcend discourse while engaging in it, a feat as impossible as picking oneself up by the seat of the trousers. Because they are, as poems, deliberately placed within a tradition of obviously artificial conventions, they of course make the effort to speak "naturally" all the more clearly futile. For this reason T. S. Eliot said that the proper language of love is prose, not the public and artificial language of poetry[2]—but of course Eliot was further than Arnold from the romantic notion that poetry is the natural language of the passions. Yet to be natural, poetic language must avoid its unavoidable conventionality. Robert Browning, faced with this difficulty, adopted the unusual idea that if the artist is to speak sincerely to his love, he must do so in a language of which he has not mastered the conventions:

no artist lives and loves, that longs not
Once and only once, and for one only,
(Ah, the prize!) to find his love a language
Fit and fair and simple and sufficient—
Using nature that's an art to others,
Not, this one time, art that's turned his nature.

("One Word More," ll. 59–64)

But a language that is "sufficient" (Arnold would have preferred "adequate") is not to be had—there are simply no words (or signs of any other kind) to denote the fine shades of individual feeling. And a language that is "simple" cannot be had, since to be comprehensible at all language must take its place in the increasingly complex discourse of a chaotic civilization. The poems of the "Switzerland" series, "The Buried Life," and "Dover Beach" are all relatively short lyrics, and evidently less ambitious than *Empedocles on Etna,* or *Sohrab and Rustum,* or *Merope,* but they represent in its clearest and most urgent form Arnold's longing to find an authentic and authoritative language, and they demonstrate emphatically the impossibility of doing so.

"Switzerland"

Over the past quarter-century it has become critical standard practice to lament the inordinate amount of biographical criticism of Arnold's two series of love lyrics and to wish the poems could be treated as works of art. Critics complain that, for our understanding of the poems, it does not matter whether the "Marguerite" of the "Switzerland" poems was a real woman, let alone who she was, and that it similarly does not matter whether the five poems of "Faded Leaves" describe a crisis in Arnold's courtship of Frances Lucy Wightman. Perhaps now that the biographical events behind the poems have been somewhat sorted out in Park Honan's masterful biography, critics will no longer feel the need to scrutinize "Switzerland" for clues to Arnold's life.[3] Yet it is important to note that it *does* very much matter to our understanding of the poems whether Arnold was writing autobiography or was generating a fictive construct out of whole cloth. If we assume, as William Buckler does, that each poem is to be read on New Critical grounds, divorced from biographical considerations, we are likely to argue—as Buckler does—that the "Switzerland" series is a monodrama analogous to Tennyson's *Maud* and that "Arnold places at the center of this drama a hero so fallible that he brings to his lyrics the exacerbated stresses suggestive of a species of madness."[4] The interest of the poems in such a case, and Buckler draws this out very well, is in the controlled dramatization and analysis of certain morbid states of mind, and in the skill with which Arnold manipulates the ironic distance between author and speaker. It is assumed that the poet controls his language absolutely. But if the poems are at all self-analytical, as the biographical evidence strongly suggests, Arnold and his speaker are less easily disentangled, ironic distances diminish, and the gap between what is said and what the poet feels is a function of the "sad incompetence of human speech" not of controlled authorial detachment. The argument is not whether Arnold was a great poet who knew what he was doing or a poor one who could not handle his materials but whether the poems transcend the romantic ideology they dramatize or enact the entrapment within that ideology of a major poet. Reading the lyrics from a New Critical perspective that would have been alien to Arnold makes him seem a more "modern" poet but obscures our sense of the controlling personal, historical, and ideological pressures that frame and control his discourse. And among these was the belief, fostered by Wordsworth in particular and romanticism in general, that the poet should speak sincerely and from his own experience. Arnold shifted his ground on this point, but in 1848, not long before writing the "Switzerland" poems, he was praising Goethe (and, to a lesser extent, Wordsworth) for "his thorough sincerity—writing about nothing that he had not experienced."[5] The poems are best understood not as autonomous artifacts dislocated in time but as manifestations of how a particular mind at a particular historical time and place could enter the vast and complex Western discourse about love.

Nevertheless, Buckler is undoubtedly right to the extent that whatever autobiographical materials the poems may discuss, the finished "Switzerland" series is indisputably a work of art in which speaker and author cannot be simply identified. Transforming personal experience into art necessarily involves a certain aesthetic distance precisely because the personal and idiosyncratic must be rendered conventional in order to be understood. But it is important to realize that this need to conventionalize and so to falsify personal experience is not just a speaker's problem but Arnold's. Still, the poems do take their place within a well-established literary tradition of attempting to analyze and understand fundamental human problems through a series of love lyrics. In a general sense the tradition can be traced to the lyric sequences of the Italian *stilnovisti* or the sonnet sequences of the English Renaissance, though G. Robert Stange finds more immediate precedents in Wordsworth's "Lucy poems" and the German *Liedercyklus*.[6] As Stange and others have argued, Arnold's careful arrangement and rearrangement of the sequence make it clear that he was attempting to fuse them into an aesthetically satisfying whole, and not just to pour out his soul in heartfelt utterance, and this is yet more evidence that the speaker is not *simply* Arnold, but at most a tidied up, orderly, more conventionalized Arnold.[7] Still, there is no doubt that though the speaker is not precisely Arnold, his problems are profoundly Arnoldian, and chief among his problems is the impossibility of direct communication through efficient speech, the impossibility, in a sense, of Arnold's presenting himself as unequivocal, unadulterated, unmistakable Arnold.

Among the most fundamental Arnoldian difficulties, as we have repeatedly seen, is the ever-frustrated need to find an authoritative voice, a voice that can utter truth. Perhaps more conspicuously than anywhere else in Arnold's poetry, the feebleness and inadequacy of human speech is illustrated in the "Switzerland" series by the sudden intrusions of an infallible utterance from on high. In "Meeting," for example, the speaker begins the poem, and the series, with calm self-assurance:

> Again I see my bliss at hand,
> The town, the lake are here;
> My Marguerite smiles upon the strand,
> Unaltered with the year.
>
> I know that graceful figure fair,
> That cheek of languid hue;
> I know that soft, enkerchiefed hair,
> And those sweet eyes of blue.

The tranquil tone is achieved partly by the very first word, "Again," which suggests the comfortable continuation of a smooth, continuous discourse (even without knowing what was before, the reader accepts as a poetic convention that there *is* a "before") and by the direct appeals to experience, "I see," and to certainty, "I know . . . I know." But as soon as contemplation gives way to action, a more authoritative voice breaks in to destroy the confidence of the earlier one:

> Again I spring to make my choice;
> Again in tones of ire
> I hear a God's tremendous voice:
> "Be counselled, and retire."
>
> (ll. 9–12)

Here as elsewhere in Arnold's poetry the voice of God rings hollow. It is not even really the voice of God but of a vague, unspecified divinity, "*a* God," and however "tremendous," it is utterly unconvincing except as a projection of the speaker's own latent reservations. Simply by representing an unconvincing voice of God the poem suggests that there is no genuine, authoritative voice but only the wish for one. Yet even this specious authority is enough to collapse the calm of the previous lines, and looking back at them we see how vulnerable they are. The appeal to experience, "I see," is unfounded—he *sees* Marguerite, but perhaps is indulging in an unfounded assumption when he translates this into the language of love: "I see my bliss." Bliss, to make the obvious point, cannot be seen. Further, the possessive, even proprietary "My Marguerite" and the implication that she is "unaltered" in affections as well as in appearance make unsupported claims about the relationship, and even the repetition of "I know . . . I know" turns out to assert no more than superficial recognition. Not surprisingly, the poem that began with the calm of simple indicative sentences ends with an open question to mysterious powers and an exclamatory plea for peace:

> Ye guiding Powers who join and part,
> (ll. 13–16) What would ye have with me?
> Ah, warn some more ambitious heart,
> And let the peaceful be!

The poem, understood most simply, is about a sense of foreboding that erupts into a too complacent anticipation of bliss, but it is also the enactment of the eruption of one inadequate form of discourse into another to generate, in the final stanza, a rhetoric of nervous uncertainty.

It is too simple, however, to say that the mysterious "God" and the "guiding Powers" are simply metaphoric projections of the speaker's forebodings. In "Human Life," which was never a part of the "Switzerland" series but was written at about the same time and involved similar concerns, the "guiding Powers" reappear as "some unknown Powers" (l. 26) that guide us, even against our will, to some predetermined end. These "Powers" do not simply "warn," but rule, and they deny us

> The joys which were not for our use designed;
> (ll. 28–30) The friends to whom we had no natural right,
> The homes that were not destined to be ours.

In the "Switzerland" poems, as is anticipated in "Meeting," the "Powers" will eventually deny the speaker his beloved. In "To Marguerite—Continued" the "Powers" appear once again as "a God," not to warn, but to decree:

> (ll. 19–24) Who ordered, that their longing's fire
> Should be, as soon as kindled, cooled?

Who renders vain their deep desire?—
A God, a God their severance ruled!
And bade betwixt their shores to be
The unplumbed, salt, estranging sea.

The authoritative presence of the God provides a concise explanation of human misery, but within the emotional context of the poems it even more clearly provides an excuse for the speaker's failure in love. Since all is destined and decreed, the individual is not responsible for his actions. If the love affair with Marguerite went wrong, it was not the speaker's fault—it just was not meant to be. The God is presented as an absolutely authoritative voice, but this voice emerges from the thoroughly questionable source of the speaker's psychological need for justification. Ultimately this God cannot be taken seriously as more than the wish for certainty, the wish for absolute dictates to explain and justify human behavior. Once again he is only "*a* God," asking to be understood as definitive but remaining vague and unconvincing. The more authoritative the discourse attempts to become, the more hollow it in fact becomes. The introduction of a mysterious God as an explanation of human suffering becomes a cheap and easy evasion—not transcendence—of the difficulties and uncertainties of unauthorized human discourse.

The evasions are, to be sure, the speaker's, and the speaker is not simply Arnold, so it would be wrong to conclude that Arnold in fact believed in "a God" as more than a metaphoric simplification of all the unknown, indescribable forces that obstruct human happiness. Nevertheless, the simplification is itself an evasion that enables Arnold as well as the speaker to make pithy, resonant, seemingly authoritative statements about the human condition. Yet this evasion is essential to the inner dramatic tension of both "Meeting" and "To Marguerite—Continued." The generation of transcendental terms from a cry of desire indicates the hollowness of those terms as the poems enact the development and dependence on essentially empty words. Also, the sheer desperation to find a definitive form of utterance demonstrates the perceived inadequacy of ordinary, referential speech. In "Meeting" the seemingly authoritative transcendental speech forced a reassessment of the seemingly empirical discourse that preceded it. In "To Marguerite—Continued" the "God" confirms rather than contradicts the preceding ideas about the inevitability of human isolation, but even so the evident need to introduce a new, supposedly more authoritative, mode of discourse implies that the preceding mode had been perceived as insufficiently authoritative. In both cases the juxtaposition of human utterance with purportedly divine truth results in a tension that calls into question the adequacy of *both* modes of speech.

The "divine" confirmation of human utterance at the end of "To Marguerite—Continued" is all the more remarkable since the poem begins—as the title implies—as a continuation and confirmation of a still earlier discourse. It begins, in fact, with an emphatic "Yes!" presumably in response to the preceding poem, "Isolation. To Marguerite."[8] The need for such doubly emphatic confirmation of the initial poem would seem to suggest a lack of confidence in it as an authoritative statement. As in the opening stanzas of "Meeting," the discourse in "Isolation" is apparently based on empirical evidence, though in this case the poem analyzes experience more fully. The first two stanzas establish the "lesson" of the poem, and explain how it was learned:

> We were apart; yet, day by day,
> I bade my heart more constant be.
> I bade it keep the world away,
> And grow a home for only thee;
> Nor feared but thy love likewise grew,
> Like mine, each day, more tried, more true.
>
> The fault was grave! I might have known,
> What far too soon, alas! I learned—
> The heart can bind itself alone,
> And faith may oft be unreturned.
> Self-swayed our feelings ebb and swell—
> Thou lov'st no more;—Farewell! Farewell!

The diction and syntax are simple, straightforward, declarative. The speaker had been able to communicate with his own heart ("I bade my heart . . . I bade it . . .") but not with that of his beloved. He had presumptuously assumed a union of hearts, a sympathetic and corresponding constancy, but he has learned from experience that love is not always reciprocated, that love does not necessarily enable one to escape isolation in the self by communion with the beloved. The movement, from innocence to experience, naiveté to disillusionment, implies that the lesson learned and the discourse engaged in are based empirically. Cultural illusions about two hearts beating as one are jettisoned in the face of contradictory personal experience. But of course the empirical evidence is woefully insufficient, since the evident fact that the speaker's love is unreciprocated can hardly prove that love is *never* reciprocated, and the overblown romantic posturings that follow demonstrate that the speaker has not been chastened by experience, but seduced by another set of conventional cultural assumptions. Like Byron or Obermann, he bids a dramatic "Farewell!" to the world of deceived mortals and bids his "lonely heart" (l. 13) retreat: "Back to thy solitude again" (l. 18). Literary and cultural imitation, not unmediated experience of life, now informs the poem's language, and leads it even to what Buckler has called the "superbly literary moment" when the speaker compares himself to the mythically personified moon: "Back! with the conscious thrill of shame / Which Luna felt" (ll. 19–20) when she longingly gazed on Endymion.[9] The language of the poem, at first so simple, becomes increasingly inflated as the speaker justifies and magnifies his cosmic sorrow. The mythic interlude, rather like the eruption of a divine voice in other poems, indexes the speaker's dissatisfaction with a language based merely on experience, but it is almost irrelevant to his real situation. In the first place, Luna is described as moving *toward* love, not away from it, and in the second place, as the speaker soon recognizes, she can hardly be used as an analogy to his experience because she has never experienced human love. With this realization the speaker moves once more, with greater urgency, back to the empirical basis of his discourse:

Yet she, chaste queen, had never proved
(ll. 25–30) How vain a thing is mortal love,
Wandering in Heaven, far removed,

But thou [his heart] hast long had place to prove
This truth—to prove, and make thine own:
"Thou hast been, shalt be, art, alone."

The desire for *proof* is of course characteristic of Arnold's poetry, and here it is interestingly based on experiential evidence—but also on the ambiguity of the word *prove*. In the first line "proved" means "experienced" but in the next two uses "prove" equivocally means both "try" and "definitively confirm." The experiential evidence remains extremely limited, but the verbal quibble leads to an authoritatively stated, dogmatic maxim about human isolation. Empirical language has not described the way *things* are in life but has become enmeshed in ideological and cultural assumptions and in vacillating, uncertain meanings of words. Consequently, the seemingly definitive maxim does not hold up even for the duration of the poem but is immediately qualified: "Or, if not quite alone" (l. 31), he will have the company of nature and of those "happier men" who

at least,
Have *dreamed* two human hearts might blend
In one, and were through faith released
From isolation without end
Prolonged; nor knew, although not less
Alone than thou, their loneliness.
(ll. 37–42)

The ending does not reverse the empirically grounded observation that all men are alone, but severely qualifies it. Even the speaker may have the "love, if love, of happier men" (l. 36), and others at least *seem* to escape their isolation. The speaker's assertion that they are lonely but do not know it seems almost absurd since one can hardly be said to *be* lonely but not *feel* lonely. The dream is dismissed as an illusion, but the illusion is most people's reality. And of course, the speaker's "reality," as we have seen, is at least as culturally determined as the "dream" of "happier men." Buckler is convinced that Arnold is manipulating a self-deluded speaker throughout this poem, and to an extent that is undoubtedly true, but the uncertainties about what is empirically verifiable and what is not are characteristically Arnoldian, and the fruitless attempt to achieve a clear, authoritative statement epitomizes Arnold's continual struggle for a univocal utterance.

The problem is even more obvious in another "Switzerland" poem, "Parting," in which two different lyric forms and voices confront each other and eventually issue in yet a third. The poem is not exactly a dialogue of Arnold's mind with itself—it cannot be, because he is unable simply to express his mind. Rather it is a dialogue of different culturally determined voices. One is the voice of Sturm und Drang romanticism, as Byronism at its stormiest impels the speaker to seek the mountain solitudes:

> There the torrents drive upward
> Their rock-strangled hum;
> There the avalanche thunders
> (ll. 29–34) The hoarse torrent dumb.
> —I come, O ye mountains!
> Ye torrents, I come!

The next presents an ideal of gentle romance, the sweetly domestic charms of the angel in the house:

> But who is this, by the half-opened door,
> Whose figure casts a shadow on the floor?
> The sweet blue eyes—the soft ash-coloured hair—
> The cheeks that still their gentle paleness wear—
> (ll. 35–42) The lovely lips, with their arch smile that tells
> The unconquered joy in which her spirit dwells—
> Ah! they bend nearer—
> Sweet lips, this way!

And the final voice ultimately opts for the solitude of a Byron or Obermann, not by resolving the conflict between the prior perspectives, but by introducing the stern patriarchal tones of a puritanically repressive ideology:

> To the lips, ah! of others
> (ll. 67–70) Those lips have been pressed,
> And others, ere I was,
> Were strained to that breast.

It is this fastidious sentiment that leads to the poem's sententious moral:

> Far, far from each other
>   Our spirits have grown;
> And what heart knows another?
>   Ah! who knows his own?
>
> (ll. 71–74)

The rhetorical questions suggest the idea of isolation, estrangement from others and even from oneself, that dominates the "Switzerland" poems, but it has been unearned. More clearly than in "Isolation. To Marguerite" the lesson supposedly learned from experience in love is actually based on juxtaposed and unreconciled literary representations of stock romantic and Victorian attitudes. Yet the poem does demonstrate formally that the speaker does not know his own heart—it is self-ignorance that leads him into the various inadequate poses and patterns of speech. The disjunctive discourse can hardly be said to prove that true knowledge of ourselves or of others is impossible, but it dramatically enacts the plight of a mind divided against itself and unable even to differentiate between superficial, imitative posing and a "true" self. In strictly literary terms, the poem illustrates its entrapment within the inherited codes and conventions of poetic discourse—it can bounce among various forms of conventional discourse but cannot escape or transcend them. Of course the speaker is never simply Arnold, if only because the poet can never be simply himself. The failure of the poems to find a unified, coherent discourse is, in a sense, a measure of the poet's, or speaker's, creditable recognition that the "true" self, like the "best self" of Arnold's prose, is a merely hypothetical construct representative of the desire for an impossible wholeness. The incoherence of these love poems is movingly analogous to Arnold's recognition that consciousness itself is inevitably fragmented, that the various components of the self can never be fully grasped. Indeed, neither Arnold nor anyone else could ever succeed in accurately representing himself if only because, as Jacques Lacan argues, the attempt to construct the self verbally is paradoxically self-alienating: in the labor that one "undertakes to reconstruct *for another,* he rediscovers the fundamental alienation that made him construct it *like another,* and which has always destined it to be taken from him *by another.*" The danger of attempting to construct the self in language is that all that can be caught of the shifting complexities of consciousness would be an imaginary "objectification . . . of his static state or of his 'statue,' in a renewed status of his alienation."[10] Ironically, it is Arnold's failure to present such a neatly packaged self that saves the Switzerland poems—and "The Buried Life"—from suffering the fate of his inert attempts in classical form.

"Parting" and "Isolation. To Marguerite" both demonstrate the extreme difficulty of speaking of personal experience rather than writing variations on literary themes. "To Marguerite—Continued" is evidently intended to be read as a confirmation of the preceding poem's dictum that individuals are hopelessly alone, estranged from their fellows, but in demonstrating a need to bolster the argument it also demonstrates the perceived weakness of the empirical argument. Interestingly, "To Marguerite—Continued" completely abandons the appeal to personal experience and evolves a stronger, more resonant voice than the individual can muster by bolstering itself with countless echoes from the literary tradition. Kathleen Tillotson, who finds echoes of Horace, Lucretius, Donne, Coleridge, Thackeray, Keble, Carlyle, Browning, Collins, and Foscolo in the poem, has argued that the opening "Yes!" is not a reaffirmation of reality felt along the pulses but is, "finally, something like 'I know now the truth of what so many have written,' " and she argues that "some part of the poem's power consists in its waking of echoes from our reading, and that these also lay within Arnold's reading."[11] Similarly, Roper declares that the poem is characterized by an "imprecise allusiveness" so that "while no one gloss is especially pertinent, the whole complex of glosses—analogues, sources, allusions, reminiscences—greatly contributes to the almost majestic inevitability" of the work.[12] In some sense "imprecise allusiveness" is characteristic of every poem, since literature inevitably gains its significance by generalized intertextualized reference to the codes and conventions established in the entire body of literary work and, indeed, of language generally, but such poems as "To Marguerite—Continued" draw deliberate attention to the tradition by an ostentatiously literary allusiveness, by echoing literary images so familiar as to have almost become clichés.[13] In "Isolation" the most obviously "literary" exclamations, the Byronic posturings, tended accidentally to displace the speaker's direct experience, but in the opening of "To Marguerite—Continued" the speaker does not even try to describe individualized experience but fuses complex echoes of traditional voices to generalize about human experience:

> Yes! in the sea of life enisled,
> With echoing straits between us thrown,
> Dotting the shoreless watery wild,
> We mortal millions live *alone*.
> The islands feel the enclasping flow,
> And then their endless bounds they know.

Pointing out specific possible allusions would be redundant after Tillotson's essay, and would be almost beside the point, since the passage is characterized by "imprecise allusiveness" and no one citation can serve as a gloss or even a source—Arnold may or may not have had any of the possible sources in mind when he exploited the general tradition. But it is important to note, as Tillotson has, that Arnold's resonant statement is achieved by implicit refutation of some possible predecessors (Donne's "No man is an *Iland*," for example), confirmation of others (most clearly Thackeray's "How lonely we are in the world! . . . you and I are but a pair of infinite isolations, with some fellow-islands a little more or less near to us"),[14] and qualification and variation of yet others. The contentious voices of his predecessors are subdued to Arnold's purposes and seem to speak univocally with the ponderous weight of the whole literary tradition. The passage epitomizes what Arnold later called the "grand style severe," which "comes from saying a thing with a kind of intense compression, or in an allusive, brief, almost haughty way, as if the poet's mind were charged with so many and such grave matters, that he would not deign to treat any one of them explicitly" (1:189).

Yet this near perfect blending of multitudinous voices seems somewhat to counter the stanza's premise—such grand concord contrasts with, or at least greatly qualifies, the prevailing idea that "We mortal millions live *alone*," in total isolation. The description of "echoing straits between us thrown" reinforces the sense that the islands are not wholly desolate—like Prospero's, these islands are "full of noises, / Sounds and sweet airs that give delight and hurt not." The second stanza confirms the idea that human isolation is eased by communication in song, for on each island

The nightingales divinely sing;
(ll. 10–12) And lovely notes, from shore to shore,
Across the sounds and channels pour.

The nightingale is among the most traditional of images for the solitary, grieving singer, but it is a symbol of the transmutation of pain to beauty, not of barren isolation. Arnold's own later "Philomela," of course, makes use of the traditional and mythic symbol in this sense, and in "To Marguerite" the song is evidently itself a "balm," even a "divine" alleviation of mortal pain, and a form of communication among the scattered isles of human misery. The song of the nightingale, like the perfectly blended voices of the cultural inheritance, suggests that human beings must have some deep primal connection to one another, that once we were "Parts of a single continent!" (l. 16). In short, both the comprehensive allusiveness of Arnold's "grand style" and the symbolic implications of the traditional images imply that the lost human solidarity is recoverable.

The discourse that makes use of the tradition to find a language of plenitude tends toward the contradiction and refutation of the lone individual voice of "Isolation" as "To Marguerite—Continued" develops, but the blending of disparate voices into a univocal utterance may be perceived in a less reassuring way. One may, after all, perceive the hubbub and Babel of countless suppressed, misinterpreted, disagreeing individual utterances beneath the apparent serenity of the poem's unruffled surface—taking only the voices that make themselves most insistently heard, one can argue that Donne, Keble, Horace, Thackeray, and Carlyle can hardly be brought into agreement. The univocity of the grand style is, in this sense, an illusion brought about by ignoring, not reconciling, the vast and perhaps unbreachable differences among isolated individuals. The serenity disguises but does not wholly conceal the tensions brought about by conflating different ideologies, tensions that are most obviously and nakedly present in "Isolation" when the ideal of Byronic solitude is pitted against the ideal of blended human hearts. Further, the manifest reliance on intertextual echoes for resonance and a full range of implication may be seen as evidence that the poem can be no more than "conventional," and so cannot express the fully personal feelings of the speaker, who therefore is indeed isolated. The allusive method is strangely double-edged—it seems to break down the barriers between individuals, to draw all humanity together in a common voice and sentiment, but at the same time it seems to deny the possibility of simple self-expression. The pessimistic outlook is dominant in the poem, of course, since the evident loss of human solidarity results not in hope for reunion but only in a "longing like despair" (l. 13), an unsatisfiable desire to escape the confines of the self, to communicate with another human being.

The failure, ultimately, of the allusive style to provide a satisfying and definitive form of expression accounts for the sudden eruption of a God's voice into the poem. The ambiguity and ambivalence of merely mortal language is swept aside and replaced by divine fiat: "A God, a God their severance ruled!" But the God is an empty signifier, and his decrees are hollow, so his insertion at this point is only an index of the poet's "longing like despair" for a language that expresses truth. Taken together, the "Switzerland" poems epitomize Arnold's various efforts to find an authoritative voice. The personal voice of "Parting" and "Isolation," speaking from the heart of anguished experience, can never be genuinely personal, and gives way to the fuller, more freely literary speech of "To Marguerite—Continued." Liberally drawing on traditional symbols and echoing past voices enabled Arnold to produce one of his greatest, weightiest, most apparently authoritative poems. But this lyrical grand style gives way, as the personal style of "Meeting" did, to an attempt at a still more authoritative speech when a divine decree, a voice of God, is introduced. The effect of bringing in what can only be an empty signifier for the agnostic is jarring not only because it is abrupt and unwarranted but because it shows a lack of confidence in the humanistic mode that would draw strength from the tradition. The various modes of discourse, then, do not reinforce one another, as would seem to be the design, but deconstruct one another, leaving Arnold without an effective language.

The highly allusive condensed style of "To Marguerite—Continued" would certainly seem to be Arnold's strongest and the best suited to his later ideas about the soothing and saving powers of the literary tradition. But one further example, from a mediocre poem, will reveal some of the dangers involved in awaking echoes of dead poets. In Arnold's first arrangement of "Marguerite" poems into a series for "Switzerland" (1853), the opening poem was "To My Friends," which was later dropped from the series and retitled "A Memory Picture." The original title of the poem when it was first published in 1849, however, was "To my Friends, who ridiculed a tender Leave-taking." The original title suggests a specific biographical origin, and Honan's reconstruction indicates that the source of the poem was Arnold's romantic disappointment with Mary Claude ("Marguerite"), and his friends' mockery upon seeing the usually serene and supercilious dandy put down.[15] The epistolary title, moreover, suggests that the poem is a justification or a self-defense, that at least in a general way the poet is portraying himself in the speaker. The theme reinforces Arnold's projected image of a sophisticated young man, able to rise above even heartbreak—he has been wounded in love but wisely realizes that time erases all wounds and obliterates even the occasion of them, and so he attempts to sketch his beloved in verse in order to avoid forgetting her entirely. The cultured, poised stance is communicated by the poem's most notable feature, an allusive refrain that concludes all but one of the eight stanzas: "Ere the parting hour go by, / Quick, thy tablets, Memory!" The unmistakable allusion is to Hamlet, who sought his "tables" to set down the message of the Ghost. The speaker's reference to Hamlet, another superior man in disarray ("Th' observ'd of all observers, quite, quite down!") not only invites a flattering comparison but shows a cultivated mind solacing itself with the best that has been said and thought in the world. But the danger of awaking echoes is that they may stir an uncontrolled chain of associations by summoning their larger context. Hamlet's words are in response to a revelation from beyond the grave, a revelation that negates the easy wisdom to be had by a cultivated reading:

> Yea, from the table of my memory
> (1.5.98–101) I'll wipe away all trivial fond records,
> All saws of books, all forms, all pressures past,
> That youth and observation copied there.

What Arnold sets down on his tablets is a picture of a human countenance that transparently reveals the inner goodness of his beloved:

> Paint, with their impetuous stress
> (ll. 43–46) Of inquiring tenderness,
> Those frank eyes, where deep I see
> An angelic gravity.

But Hamlet records just the reverse: "My tables! Meet it is I set it down, / That one may smile, and smile, and be a villain" (1.5.107–8). The allusion superficially supported the self-image projected in Arnold's poem, but at a deeper level, in context, it flatly contradicts Arnold's premises and his stylistic recourse to "all saws of books." And as an extra fillip, the Shakespearean context is precisely about the untrustworthiness of the images people project.

It would seem highly unlikely that Arnold intended his allusion to be read as a subversive subtext, but it nevertheless sets up uncontrolled chains of association. All language has a life of its own in triggering endless series of associations, but Arnold's highly allusive language demonstrates with special force that attempts to channel those associations may lead to unexpected hazards. "To My Friends" is a slight poem and perhaps not too much should be made of it, but its evidently accidental generation of a subversive subtext provides a model with which to compare Arnold's most ambitious attempts to write wholly sincere love poetry in "The Buried Life" and "Dover Beach."

Sincerity and Buried Voices

"The Buried Life" and "Dover Beach" are Arnold's clearest and most earnest efforts to find an entirely sincere poetic language. Without the dramatic framework and romantic posturings of "Switzerland," they present themselves as direct addresses from a speaker to his beloved. Indeed, the presence of such an auditor in the poems, as Dorothy Mermin points out, creates a situation "in which the speaker can speak absolutely freely" and unselfconsciously.[16] But his language, however sincere, is not unmediated utterance from the heart. Rather, as in "Switzerland," it is highly allusive, mediated by other texts that are evidently meant to strengthen the language, to provide authority. The two poets most interestingly echoed in the poems, in fact, are Wordsworth and Milton, authors of sublime authority—Arnold had only half-jokingly written to Clough that "those who cannot read G[ree]k sh[ou]ld read nothing but Milton and parts of Wordsworth: the state should see to it."[17] Arnold's invocations of earlier poets, however, are often for the purpose of debunking them. His elegies, as Culler has argued, do not call the dead back to some form of life, but rather attempt to lay the spirits (Arnold once defined *spirit* as "influence" [6:290]) of the threateningly undead to deprive even the surviving words of their potency.[18] And as John Hollander and Harold Bloom have both noted in passing, Arnold's allusions and echoes frequently empty the predecessor's language of its meaning.[19] At their most extreme, Arnold's deflating allusions call into question the status of his own language, of poetic language generally; they generate uncontrolled intertextual reverberations and become subversive subtexts that undermine his ostensible purpose but add a deeper pathos to his poetry. They may constitute, in fact, a kind of demonic buried life beneath the surface stream of his diction.

Even more clearly than in "Switzerland," Arnold's most ostentatiously allusive discourse in "The Buried Life" erupts into a discourse in which the speaker is evidently struggling for an austere, plain diction that can strip words down to pure denotation and so arrive at unadorned truth and avoid any illusions in love. "The Buried Life" is overtly concerned with the limitations of language from its opening lines:

Light flows our war of mocking words, and yet,
Behold, with tears mine eyes are wet!
I feel a nameless sadness o'er me roll.
Yes, yes, we know that we can jest,
We know, we know that we can smile!
But there's a something in this breast,
To which thy light words bring no rest,
And thy gay smiles no anodyne.
Give me thy hand, and hush awhile,
And turn those limpid eyes on mine,
And let me read there, love! thy inmost soul.

The speaker's dissatisfaction with "mocking words" is sufficiently evident in his injunction to his beloved to "hush." But the inefficacy of language is also enacted through a kind of imitative form in the presumably accidental bathos of "Behold, with tears mine eyes are wet!" and the reiterative assertions ("Yes, yes" and "we know . . . / We know, we know") that seem to protest too much. The problem is not in the levity of "light words" but in a general incapacity of language to name emotional states, to communicate feeling—the "sadness" is "nameless" and the language that states only what it can honestly name is able to state almost nothing: "But there's a something." The difficulty is that Arnold is seeking a language purged of metaphorical or connotative meanings as he attempts to describe not what the sadness, or the soul, or the something is *like* but what it *is*. Such a purely denotative language might describe an object as in itself it really is, might even describe an object that inspires a state of feeling (Wordsworth, in an analogous situation, had been able to say "But there's a Tree"),[20] but can hardly describe a feeling.

The speaker is quick to admit his failure, in a pair of rhetorical questions:

Alas! is even love too weak
To unlock the heart, and let it speak?
Are even lovers powerless to reveal
To one another what indeed they feel?
(ll. 12–15)

The questions signal a change in linguistic procedure formally as well as thematically precisely because they are rhetorical (they must be—as in "Thyrsis" the sole auditor, having been hushed, is not expected to reply). The figure of rhetoric as well as the sudden burst of metaphor—apparent in the personification of love, the lock on the heart, and the potentially speaking heart—both indicate that the speaker is willing to try a figurative language. Unfortunately the slightly mixed metaphor anticipates the considerable confusion that metaphoric language will encounter in this poem, and the section ends with an assertion that manages simultaneously to be a platitude, and to be unconvincing: "and yet / The same heart beats in every human breast!" (ll. 22–23). Ironically, the assertion would be hopelessly trite if it made sense within the context of the poem, but as Alice Stitelman has noted, it "contradicts the emphasis of all which has preceded it, and gains its emotional impact by standing as a desperate plea against the weight of the speaker's documented experience."[21] Or put another way, the statement, in the middle of a poem that is trying to establish a completely honest, sincere language, is effective precisely because it is untrue, a lie. Metaphoric language had led to an emotionally effective poetry, but only by betraying truth, or as the poem later puts it, it "Is eloquent, is well—but 'tis not true!" (l. 66).

The dubious assertion leads to the central metaphor of the poem, that of the "buried life," and significantly, the central metaphor, based on a lie, leads to a tangled web. In what follows it is not clear whether our hearts and voices are benumbed by a magical "spell" (ll. 24–25) or are enchained (ll. 26–27), and what we most assuredly cannot know is stated with absolute assurance: "that which seals them hath been deep-ordained!" (l. 29). As always, the ordinance is unauthored; the passive voice allows Arnold to avoid strict mention of a God's voice, but does not provide any other authoritative legislator. The horror of emotional and verbal incapacity is set forth as a boon:

> Fate, which foresaw,
> How frivolous a baby man would be—
> (ll. 30–44) By what distractions he would be possessed,
> How he would pour himself in every strife,
> And well-nigh change his own identity—

That it might keep from his capricious play
His genuine self, and force him to obey
Even in his own despite his being's law,
Bade through the deep recesses of our breast
The unregarded river of our life
Pursue with indiscernible flow its way;
And that we should not see
The buried stream, and seem to be
Eddying at large in blind uncertainty,
Though driving on with it eternally.

The cluttered syntax of this one long sentence, the numerous qualifications, the seven lines between the subject and the predicate, the clashing metaphors of the buried self and the river of life—all of this almost, but not quite, conceals the remarkable central statement: fate decreed that we should not know ourselves so that we cannot betray ourselves. My point, however, is not to sort through the tangle of these lines but only to note how the attempt at absolute honesty, apparent in the qualifications and explanations, leads not to an austere, plain diction and a lucid statement but to an absurd assertion uttered by a disembodied voice and couched in a language that approaches inarticulateness as its complex structures begin to collapse under their own weight.[22]

The poem does not, however, end with a bang as the tower of Babel collapses, but—and this is the important point—just as it approaches inarticulateness, it becomes densely allusive, and far more lucid:

But often, in the world's most crowded streets,
But often, in the din of strife,
(ll. 46–49) There rises an unspeakable desire
After the knowledge of our buried life.

The language unmistakably summons Wordsworth's "Tintern Abbey": "But oft, in lonely rooms, and 'mid the din / Of towns and cities"[23] and just a few lines later, the speaker's "longing to inquire / Into the mystery of this heart which beats" (ll. 51–52) may call to mind Wordsworth's famous phrase "the burthen of the mystery" in conjunction with his efforts to lift the burdens that "Have hung upon the beatings of my heart" (ll. 38, 54). Further, as the speaker listens carefully for some sound of his buried life, he hears strange resonances:

> vague and forlorn,
> From the soul's subterranean depth upborne
> (ll. 72–76) As from an infinitely distant land,
> Come airs, and floating echoes, and convey
> A melancholy into all our day.

The echoes are echoes of echoes, recollections of Wordsworthian recollections:

> Those shadowy recollections,
> Which, be they what they may,
> Are yet the fountain-light of all our day.[24]

As in "Isolation. To Marguerite," the allusiveness introduces a new, weightier level of discourse, and the authoritative presence of Wordsworth, especially, in the poem's subtext is at least initially reassuring. Wordsworth's experience would seem to confirm the possibility of easing "the burthen of the mystery" and, more, his reassuring resonance within the breast reveals that the buried life and language, especially poetic language, may not be incompatible after all. Also, Wordsworth is the poet best suited to help the speaker, for as Arnold stated in "Memorial Verses," Wordsworth's "soothing voice" (l. 35) had the "healing power" (l. 63) to set free just such benumbed souls and enchained hearts:

> He found us when the age had bound
> (ll. 45–47) Our souls in its benumbing round;
> He spoke, and loosed our heart in tears.

Certainly with Wordsworth's "soothing voice" running in a deep subtextual stream, the surface currents of "The Buried Life" smooth out—the syntax becomes clear and the rhythms are no longer tortuous. It would seem that Arnold is indeed using allusions, as one might have conjectured, to provide voices of reassurance and authority, to give resonance and plenitude to his language.

Allusions are rarely so unambiguously reassuring, however, and a brief consideration of Arnold's responses to Wordsworth's influence reveals how troubled the subtextual stream of "The Buried Life" is likely to be. Arnold, of course, had known Wordsworth as a neighbor in the Lake district, and respected him as the greatest English poet since Milton, but as his numerous critical comments on the matter reveal, he was in some ways ambivalent about the older poet's achievement. Wordsworth had "natural magic," could show a "grand style," and often showed "moral profundity," but his "eyes avert their ken / From half of human fate," presumably because like the other romantics he did not "know enough," had not read enough books.[25] Arnold's complex response to Wordsworth's work has been exhaustively studied, and it is not necessary to review it here in detail, but a look at how he laid Wordsworth's perturbed spirit to rest in "Memorial Verses" will help to show how Arnold's having read enough books complicates his allusions to Wordsworth in "The Buried Life" and in "Dover Beach." The allusions in fact open up general problems of intertextuality that complicate matters far beyond, for example, a Bloomian agon in which Arnold combats his ghostly predecessor face to face.

The sense that Wordsworth's voice in Arnold's poem might be reassuring is encouraged by a passage from "Memorial Verses" in which Wordsworth is said to restore our innocence:

> He laid us as we lay at birth
> On the cool flowery lap of earth. . . .
>
> (ll. 48–49, Our youth returned; for there was shed
> 54–57) On spirits that had long been dead,
> Spirits dried up and closely furled,
> The freshness of the early world.

Since Arnold consistently blamed the complexities of the age—its "multitudinousness," its rush, its "unpoetrylessness"—for benumbed senses and failures of communication, this return to Eden would seem a perfect cure for the ills of "The Buried Life." Moreover, the return to Eden is still more suggestive when read in conjunction with Arnold's somewhat later comments on "natural magic" as a kind of Adamic naming that accomplishes the goal of the speaker in "The Buried Life" by perfectly expressing its object. The idea that Wordsworth's language has "magical" restorative powers associated with a kind of hidden, underground life is, moreover, strengthened by Arnold's association of it with "the clear song of Orpheus" in Hades. Once again, such words of power drifting upward from the buried life ought to be heartening.

And yet the full implications of "Memorial Verses" raise disturbing questions about echoes of Wordsworth elsewhere. In the first place, Orpheus almost, but only almost, redeemed Eurydice from Hades—he was able to get only himself out of hell, and not to help others. Also, "natural magic" names only the "outward world" (3:33) so that Wordsworth's ability to say "But there's a Tree" will not provide an alternative to the feeble utterance of the man looking inward, who can still say only "but there's a something." Further, "Memorial Verses," as Culler has argued, does not ultimately affirm the continued potency of Wordsworth's voice but rather denies it by characterizing Wordsworth as "the last survivor of an idyllic age which has long since passed away."[26] Wordsworth can no longer restore the freshness of the early world; he is left well dead and, as the opening lines of the poem make clear, well silenced: "The last poetic voice is dumb— / We stand today by Wordsworth's tomb" (ll. 4–5). The notion of a dumb and entombed voice rising from its buried life begins to take on macabre implications, and the flat statement that Wordsworth's "voice is dumb" seems a direct answer to the fundamental question of "The Buried Life": "But we, my love!—doth a like spell benumb / Our hearts, our voices? must we too be dumb?" (ll. 24–25).

Intriguingly, and pertinently, "Memorial Verses" has a buried life of its own that still further erodes the possibility of genuine poetic communication. In the very lines that seem to place Wordsworth in a primal state of innocence, the subtext reaches back to a still earlier predecessor. Arnold's lines "He laid us as we lay at birth / On the cool flowery lap of earth" recall Gray's description of

Shakespeare, a still earlier, still more magical voice: "Far from the sun and summer gale, / In thy green lap was Nature's Darling laid."[27] And the general sentiment of the whole, that the age of poetry is past partly because, benumbed, we can no longer feel deeply, recalls eighteenth-century lamentations of the loss of feeling and lyric power, and in particular Collins's "Ode to Fear," in which the belated poet echoes Milton's "Il Penseroso" as he seeks from Fear the emotional intensity of Shakespeare: "Hither again thy fury deal, / Teach me but once like him to feel" (ll. 68–69). Collins's lines are a subversive undercurrent beneath Arnold's lament that in these latter days "Others will teach us how to dare" and how to bear, "But who, ah! who, will make us feel?" (ll. 64–67). Arnold does not summon the voices of Shakespeare and Milton to show that those reassuring voices do indeed survive; rather he echoes fruitless pleas for the return of those potent spirits. But their absence indicates that they are silenced, as Wordsworth is. The voices that do survive are the ineffectual voices of Gray and Collins, Arnold's kindred spirits as the talented victims of an unpoetical age.[28]

The displacement of Milton by Collins is especially disturbing since Arnold apparently considered his poem in some sense Miltonic, for he wrote (albeit somewhat facetiously) to Clough that he had "dirged W. W. *in the grand style*,"[29] a style that he associated almost exclusively, in English poetry at least, with Milton. Further, the Miltonic grand style, as Arnold defined it, is the perfect vehicle for a modern poetry that should be able to overcome the problem of belatedness and the consequent unavailability of natural magic by resorting to extreme allusiveness. Arnold divides the grand style into two types, the "simple" and the "severe," of which the "simple" is the more "magical" but is unfortunately not available to modern poets. The "grand style severe," best seen in Milton, "is much more imitable" (though "this a little spoils its charm") and it "comes from saying a thing with a kind of intense compression, or in an allusive, brief, almost haughty way" (1:189–90). Still more pertinently, Arnold described Miltonic style in 1849 as designed "to compose and elevate the mind by a sustained tone, numerous allusions, and a grand style."[30] The style would seem to enable the poet to make a positive use of the "multitudinousness" of his age, the "height to which knowledge is come," rather than being burdened by it.[31] And, indeed, Arnold suggested in a letter to Clough that he was making an effort to achieve such a style: "The poet's matter being *the hitherto experience of the world, and his own,* increases with every century. . . . For me you may often hear my sinews cracking under the effort to unite matter." Yet within the same letter he made two observations that suggest why Milton and Shakespeare are not heard in "Memorial Verses," in his version of the grand style. In the first place, they are too "*curious* and exquisite" because they did not have to contend with "the multitude of new thoughts and feelings" that "a modern has" (they are, presumably, like Wordsworth in this), and second, imitation of the great masters is to be avoided as a sign of "the Decadence of a literature": "One of the factors of its decadent condition indeed, is this—that new authors attach themselves to the poetic expression the founders of a literature have flowered into, which may be *learned* by a sensitive person, to the neglect of an inward poetic life."[32] To save his own "inward poetic life" from decay, the modern must keep out the spirits (influences!) of the dead. The weaker spirits of Collins and Gray may be allowed in as reassurance that the ghosts of Wordsworth and Milton have been well laid.

All of this leads us back to the disturbing implication of Wordsworth's voice suddenly entering into "The Buried Life" to save it from inarticulateness and even to introduce a loftiness that seems to approximate a grand style. Wordsworth's resurrection in the buried life ought surely to constitute not a healing power but a threat to the speaker's "inward poetic life." A closer look at the passage shows that this is so:

> But often, in the world's most crowded streets,
> But often, in the din of strife,
> There rises an unspeakable desire
> After the knowledge of our buried life.

Wordsworth's presence seems, at first, innocent enough. The passage from "Tintern Abbey" describes how the inward life of the mind is restored to tranquility as the remembered past, a kind of buried life, wells up into present consciousness. But in opening up his verse to Wordsworth's voice, Arnold's "inward poetic life" suddenly begins to be crowded out by other, possibly more dangerous voices. The next voice, in fact, is Satan's, as the Father of Lies speaks of his "Unspeakable desire to see and know / All these his wondrous works, but chiefly Man."[33] The lines occur as Satan is lying to Uriel, in an incident that Milton used to emphasize the dangers of hypocrisy, of dissembling words. The situation is peculiarly akin to the echo of Hamlet's horror of hypocrisy in "A Memory Picture"—in both cases the speaker is aiming at complete sincerity while his language is ineluctably summoning references to hypocrisy as a hidden, often indiscernible evil. Even the most sincere speech may veil a lurking evil. Within Arnold's poem about his desire to speak the unspeakable, to name what is nameless, Satan's precedent must be unsettling.

Perhaps Milton's voice drowning out Wordsworth at this point should not be surprising since Arnold argued, much later, that Wordsworth had "no assured poetic style of his own, like Milton" (9:52) but often seemed to take on Milton's style. Written long after Arnold had himself stopped writing poetry, long after he had ceased to be troubled by the anxieties of poetic influence, Arnold's comment betrays no sense that Wordsworth's poetic integrity might have been threatened by Milton's influence. Yet the young poet of "The Buried Life," aware that he did not have Wordsworth's power of natural magic, of writing as though "Nature not only gave him the matter for his poem, but wrote his poem for him" (9:52), might well have felt threatened by the spectacle of one poetic voice welling up from his buried text only to be inundated by yet another. Indeed the Miltonic voice does not merely follow the Wordsworthian, but from the first is a still more deeply buried subtext beneath the Wordsworthian subtext, for the Wordsworthian lines may have conjured in Arnold's mind the famous simile that compares Satan in Eden to "one who long in populous City pent" (*Paradise Lost* 9.445) has temporarily, but only temporarily, escaped from hellish confinement to pastoral innocence and freedom. It is impossible to say to what extent any of these echoes are deliberate, but certainly in this case the Miltonic lines had made an impression on Arnold, who once jokingly wrote to Clough that his "present Labours may be shadowed forth under the Figure of Satan, perambulating, under the most unfavorable circumstances, a populous neighborhood."[34] The reference, however submerged it may be in "The Buried Life," is extremely telling, for like the echo of Satan's hypocrisy, it calls to mind the last moments before the language of the "early world" is corrupted, the last moments before Satan's convincing lies seduced Eve and put an end to the simplicity and magic of Adamic naming. Further, the particular lines from Milton were especially apt to set a chain of echoes dinning in Arnold's ear for, as John Hollander has shown, the lines resound through Coleridge and Keats and, significantly, become explicitly associated with writers in crowded cities as Coleridge addresses "Bards in city garret pent" ("To the Nightingale") and Charles Lamb pining for nature while "In the great City pent" ("This Lime-Tree Bower My Prison").[35] The moment Arnold chooses to tap the grand style of allusive poetry, the moment he allows poets and poetry to surface in his text, he is inundated by lies and a Babel of ancestral voices. In the next fifty lines he will repeatedly echo the voices of his poetic forefathers, Coleridge and Wordsworth and, possibly, even Thomas Arnold.[36]

My allusion to the ancestral voices of "Kubla Khan" is, of course, deliberate, for "Kubla Khan" emerges as yet another precursor of "The Buried Life." The central metaphor of both poems is a subterranean river that casts up mysterious voices. In both poems the river seems harmless so long as it can be placed in a comfortable pastoral setting—"meandering with a mazy motion" in "Kubla Khan" and gliding through the meadows with a "winding murmur" in "The Buried Life"—on its way to a reassuringly quiet end in a "lifeless ocean" in Coleridge's poem and in "the sea where it goes" in Arnold's. But also in both poems the river is associated with a frightening underworld that casts up disturbing voices. In "Kubla Khan" the sounds are of a "woman wailing for her demon lover!" and of a general "tumult" in which can be discerned "Ancestral voices prophesying war!" The Arnoldian river murmurs less dramatically, but disturbingly nevertheless:

(ll. 72–76)

vague and forlorn,
From the soul's subterranean depth upborne

As from an infinitely distant land,
Come airs, and floating echoes, and convey
A melancholy into all our day.

Further, both poems are ultimately concerned at a deep level with the speaker's capacity to control these voices, and so to be able to express himself fully, even magically.

Like the other voices making themselves heard in the poem, Coleridge's dishearteningly suggests that mankind is fallen away from the state in which perfect language is possible, that poetic language is fallen, a hubbub of contending voices from the underworld. Also, to make room for his own voice, Arnold must clear away Coleridge's by revising the prior poem, by showing that it is not the ultimate statement that would make Arnold's redundant. Arnold swerves from the Coleridgean perspective in a fundamentally important respect. Coleridge's speaker considers the demonic voices of the underworld as the sources, if only he could revive them, of a visionary power; Arnold's, with a Victorian distrust of the visionary, hears them as seductively attractive lies that can only bring "A melancholy into all our day."

The extent to which Arnold rejected the demonic lies of poetry, and the consequence of this rejection, can best be appreciated by considering his conclusion, which claims a triumph, but in such carefully honest language that it undoes itself. The speaker claims to have found a language that perfectly expresses inward states ("And what we mean, we say, and what we would, we know" [l. 87]), but in fact he makes no attempt to communicate his feelings. Rather he simply returns to the metaphor of the buried stream, spells it out as his "life's flow" (l. 88), and affirms that he can now not only hear it but even "sees / The meadows where it glides, the sun, the breeze" (ll. 89–90). The actualization of the metaphor is forced, since the speaker is not willing to let it stand as an objective correlative for a state of feeling but insists on placing the physical stream inside the breast. Obviously the speaker does not in fact see such a stream, even though his eyes are apparently turned around in his head ("the eye sinks inward" [l. 86])—and in fact the pretense at seeing is betrayed by the forced rhyme that obliges him to claim even that "he sees . . . the breeze." The closing section, unable to build on such a shaky basis, claims much less:

> And there arrives a lull in the hot race
> Wherein he doth for ever chase
> That flying and elusive shadow, rest.
> (ll. 91–98) An air of coolness plays upon his face,
> And an unwonted calm pervades his breast.
> And then he thinks he knows
> The hills where his life rose,
> And the sea where it goes.

Though this ending has been called a "moment of joy and insight,"[37] it seems to me far from joyful. The lines achieve their calm not by coming to terms with the murmurs of the buried life but by silencing them. Unlike the speaker of "Kubla Khan," who wants to become the vehicle for the subterranean song, to achieve a language of plenitude and redemptive power, the speaker here wants only to silence it and so, by implication, to empty language of its seductive poetical delusions. The calm is not achieved through a full inner life, but rather through an acceptance of death. The goal of life is the "elusive shadow, rest," and the poem ends with the anticipation of life itself and the buried stream emptying themselves into the sea, into the final calm of death. Further, the speaker, fighting to be honest, cannot claim to have achieved even the minimal goal of rest, but only a "lull in the hot race," and cannot claim knowledge of his origin or end, but only that "he thinks he knows." In short, there is no insight, and there certainly is no joy, only calm. The most that can be said of such calm is said at the close of "Youth and Calm":

> Youth dreams a bliss on this side death.
> It dreams a rest, if not more deep,
> More grateful than this marble sleep;
> (ll. 19–25) It hears a voice within it tell:
> *Calm's not life's crown, though calm is well.*
> 'Tis all perhaps which man acquires,
> But 'tis not what our youth desires.

"Calm," here, is found "in the tomb" (l. 15), and the calm of "The Buried Life" is not much better. What is more, the speaker, as has been frequently noted, has completely abandoned the attempt to read his lover's "inmost soul" (l. 11), and in his futile attempt to understand even his own soul he is left entirely alone, isolated by his failure to find an adequate language. In spite of itself, the poem expresses a sense of solipsistic entrapment, or entombment, and anticipates Pater's famous assertion that "each one of us" is bound within "that thick wall of personality through which no real voice has ever pierced on its way to us, or from us to that which we can only conjecture to be without."[38] Emptying the language of his predecessors of its power, Arnold ends by emptying his own, ends with a return to silence. Seeking a calm of Wordsworthian repletion, the poem ends with a calm that, fully examined, is far more akin to the Tennysonian calm of deep grief, or death:

> And in my heart, if calm at all,
> If any calm, a calm despair;
>
> Calm on the seas, and silver sleep,
> And waves that sway themselves in rest,
> And dead calm in that noble breast
> Which heaves but with the heaving deep.

(*In Memoriam,* section 11)

I am by no means contending that Arnold intended to deconstruct his own poem, or intended to include a subtextual current of allusion that would undermine his own language and poetic language generally. Indeed, Arnold presumably saw "The Buried Life" as a fairly tranquil poem about the power of love to unlock the heart and lips. But poetic language has a life of its own, and beneath the surface the poem becomes a subtextual battle that ends in universal casualties. "The Buried Life" is consequently a confused poem that gains its genuine pathos in large measure by its valiant, if losing, struggle for a language of affirmative power. But Arnold's greatest lyric, "Dover Beach," exhibits none of this confusion because, though it fights the same battle as "The Buried Life," it never assumes a victory.

Like "The Buried Life," "Dover Beach" is addressed to a

beloved in a situation that demands, and seems to make possible, sincerity. According to Mermin's excellent discussion of the poems from this perspective, in "The Buried Life" the speaker realizes that "all he can sincerely say is that he would like to be sincere," but in "Dover Beach," she argues, Arnold produced his "one poem in which he shows communication from speaker to auditor as open, direct, complete, and wholly unproblematic."[39] I will argue, however, that like "The Buried Life," "Dover Beach" ends with a desolating sense of aloneness, and that its attempted austerity of diction is similarly undermined by the subtextual voices of Wordsworth and Milton. Also like "The Buried Life," it is a poem that in subtle ways is about its own decomposition. In what is probably the best essay to date on "Dover Beach," Ruth Pitman has convincingly argued that even the landscape—the cliffs and the shoreline—is not as solid as it at first appears. The opening description of the cliffs "glimmering," the light that "gleams and is gone," and the "grating" of pebbles on the shore suggests an erosion of the shoreline, a reminder of what the geologists had been telling the Victorians about the impermanence of the solidest features of the earth itself. The passage is analogous to Tennyson's description of geological transformations in *In Memoriam*:

The hills are shadows, and they flow
(section 123) From form to form, and nothing stands;
They melt like mist, the solid lands,
Like clouds they shape themselves and go.

Further, Pitman argues, the physical decomposition of the landscape suggests an analogous decomposition of meaning in the Victorian worldview—the changed sense of time, the general sense of impermanence, the idea of living in a world in a constant state of flux and decay not only undermined Christian faith but left nothing at all solid to lean on. The decaying shoreline is precisely the spot to ponder the withdrawal of faith from the world, and the loss of a stable worldview. And finally, Pitman adds, erosion of the land and the decay of faith are both reflected in an analogous erosion of poetic form. The poem, she points out, "is made up of a series of incomplete sonnets: erosion of form matches erosion of meaning."[40]

I will not recapitulate her perceptive and thorough analysis of the poem's prosody to support this claim, except to note the obvious. The first two sections each consist of fourteen lines that suggest but do not achieve strict sonnet form, and except for a short (three foot) opening line, the last section emulates the octave of a sonnet, but closes with a single, climactic line instead of a sestet—as though the final five lines had been eroded.

Not only is the form decomposing but, as in "The Buried Life," the poem's metaphors tend to be self-destructive. As Elizabeth Gitter has pointed out, Arnold introduces Sophocles' metaphorical interpretation of the sea only to reject it and replace it with a thought independent of the actual sound: "The vehicle of this new metaphor is not the 'tremulous cadence' of the waves of Dover Beach, but a steady, 'melancholy, long, withdrawing roar.' And the metaphor of the continuously ebbing Sea of Faith is suggested to the poet by the meaning of the note of sadness he hears, not by the way it sounds."[41] Though Gitter's interpretation of her excellent observation is different from mine, it seems to me that this severance of the mind's metaphoric creation from external actuality, this breakdown of metaphoric connection of mind and other, signals the same kind of solipsistic isolation as in "The Buried Life." Arnold's speaker listens to the rising sound of distant waters but hears only what is already within him. He contrasts sharply with the figure of Wordsworth on Mount Snowdon, hearing in the rising sound of waters a proof of a universally and benevolently meaningful world outside of the self. Indeed, as U. C. Knoepflmacher has pointed out, Arnold draws Wordsworth into the poem from its very first lines. And this time the allusion is so sustained, and so pertinent, that Arnold must surely have intended it to be noted.

The allusion in the opening section is to Wordsworth generally and, as Knoepflmacher has noted, is in particular to the sonnet "It Is a Beauteous Evening."[42] Within his sonnet Wordsworth is describing the sounds and significance of the sea to a child (though it is not mentioned in the poem, the setting is, significantly, the shore of the English Channel, though on the French side):

> It is a beauteous evening, calm and free,
> The holy time is quiet as a Nun

Breathless with adoration; the broad sun
Is sinking down in its tranquillity;
The gentleness of heaven broods o'er the Sea:
Listen! the mighty Being is awake,
And doth with his eternal motion make
A sound like thunder—everlastingly.

The echoes in the opening lines of "Dover Beach" are immediately obvious:

The sea is calm to-night.
The tide is full, the moon lies fair
Upon the straits; on the French coast the light
Gleams and is gone; the cliffs of England stand,
Glimmering and vast, out in the tranquil bay.
Come to the window, sweet is the night-air!
Only, from the long line of spray
Where the sea meets the moon-blanched land,
Listen! you hear the grating roar
Of pebbles which the waves draw back, and fling,
At their return, up the high strand,
Begin, and cease, and then again begin,
With tremulous cadence slow, and bring
The eternal note of sadness in.

The opening "calm," the stylistic recourse to flat copulative verbs, the importance of the sea's sound, and especially the request to the companion to "Listen!" are all caught up in Arnold's lines. In the diction, the choice of such words as "calm," "full," "sweet," and "tranquil," the lines invoke a general Wordworthian sense of epiphany. But the undertow is treacherous. The "grating roar" calls in a note of sadness utterly unlike the Wordsworthian undersong of the "sad music of humanity" that, Knoepflmacher notes, is described in "Tintern Abbey" as "Nor harsh, nor grating."[43] Further, in this particular context, the meaningless "grating roar" displaces the powerful and holy presence of a "mighty Being" whose bang is replaced with a whimper, whose eternal motion and everlasting thunder are replaced by an "eternal note of sadness." For this reason—because the world and Wordsworth are emptied of their mythic presence—the calm of Arnold's lines is, as in "The Buried Life," a calm not of repletion but of emptiness. In fact, even the simplest words are emptied of their meaning in Arnold's poem. Wordsworth's serenity is characteristically achieved by the plenitude of his verbs of being—in the first six lines of his octave the word *is* is used four times, and is reinforced by the word *Being*. The word *is* is not a mere linking verb, but an affirmation of divine presence, a transcendental signifier. It is akin, indeed, to the word *broods* that summons up the transcendent and creative presence of the Holy Spirit. But Arnold's four uses of *is* in his opening six lines cannot have this force. As we have seen, Arnold later scorned the idea that *is* and *be* were meaningful metaphysical terms, and he mocked the notion that "*being* was supposed to be something absolute, which stood under all things,"[44] but even within "Dover Beach" it is clear that *is* is not informed with transcendental presence but simply links nouns to adjectives, making the minimal verbal statement. Indeed, in three cases, "The sea is calm," "The tide is full," and "sweet is the night-air," the verb is unnecessary and the adjectives could be used directly: the calm sea, the full tide, the sweet night-air. And in the fourth case the *is* signifies not presence, but absence: "the light . . . is gone." The metaphysical emptiness of Arnold's language is, of course, analogous to the poem's general description of the emptiness of faithless Victorian life, an emptiness most emphatically stated near the end of the poem in a desolating series of denials:

the world, which seems
To lie before us like a land of dreams,
(ll. 30–34) So various, so beautiful, so new,
Hath really neither joy, nor love, nor light,
Nor certitude, nor peace, nor help for pain.

As John Hollander has recently argued, verbal echoes may be a sign not of repletion but of reverberations in hollow or empty landscapes,[45] and certainly the resounding of Wordsworth's voice in the meaningless landscape of "Dover Beach" seems to be just that.

Even in these negations the voices of Milton and Wordsworth

reverberate hollowly. The "world, which seems / To lie before us," Ronald A. Sharp has recently noted,[46] is a skeptical, attenuated version of Milton's

(*Paradise Lost*, 12.646–49)

The World was all before them, where to choose
Thir place of rest, and Providence thir guide:
They hand in hand with wandring steps and slow,
Through *Eden* took thir solitarie way.

Not surprisingly, by this time, mediating between Milton and Arnold is the voice of Wordsworth from the 1850 *Prelude*: "the earth is all before me" (1.14) and "the road lies plain before me" (1.641). But these voices and visions from the grand style are denied; Arnold is cut off not only from Providence, and from the clarity of Wordsworthian purpose, but also, of course, from the language of affirmation that contributes to their grandeur. Yet the prior voices do make themselves heard, and not always to be simply rejected. Whether deliberately or not, the voice of Milton—or more accurately Milton's Satan—is heard in a devastatingly subversive subtext. As Martin Bidney has recently pointed out, the words "neither joy nor love" are lifted directly from *Paradise Lost*. The loss of Wordsworthian joy[47] is associated with Satan's description of Hell as he enviously sees the embrace of Adam and Eve, who

(4.507–11)

shall enjoy their fill
Of bliss on bliss, while I to Hell am thrust,
Where neither joy, nor love, but fierce desire,
Among our other torments not the least,
Still unfulfill'd with pain of longing pines.

Bidney effectively notes the significance of this: "Now that the world has become Hell, the embrace of two lovers stranded amid the dark expanse of aimless fury is a very precarious Eden indeed—an Eden internal, vulnerable, isolated, intermittent at best. The poet tenderly holds out to his beloved the prospect of hope, but in the same sentence, almost in the same breath, he depicts their earthly world in the very words used by a despairing Devil to describe an eternal Hell."[48] The allusion also has a dark significance for the possibilities of language. Arnold, who in a very different context once asked where, in a contaminated language, he could "find language innocent enough" to express the "spotless purity of [his] intentions" (3:275), now cries "Ah, love, let us be true / To one another!" (ll. 29–30) and ironically mouths the words of the Father of Lies, of an archfiend agonizing over the frustration of an unsatisfied sexual desire. Once again, though the Wordsworthian voice may be neutralized, demonic voices will continue to rise from the abyss and subvert the language.

But anterior even to the voice of Satan is another voice, yet more devastating in its implications. As Culler and Pitman have both noted, the speaker of "Dover Beach" is not actually situated on the beach, but on the cliff known—and known to Arnold—as "Shakespeare's cliff" after the cliff scene in *King Lear.*[49] The cliff scene has been lurking in the background all along, but *King Lear* is brought into the verbal texture of the poem by only one word—though a highly charged poetic one—in the closing simile:

And we are here as on a darkling plain
(ll. 35–37) Swept with confused alarms of struggle and flight,
Where ignorant armies clash by night.

Pitman, who notes how thoroughly the closing lines are a tissue of poeticisms, how the plain is "made up of literary allusion and [is] itself a simile," sees a faint hope in the speaker's ability to use the literary tradition to rebuild after all other meaning has been lost: "All that is left is what the mind can construct, from *King Lear,* perhaps, or from Thucydides, not a secure or certain physical place: 'And we are here as on a darkling plain.' The coast lights, gleaming or glimmering, have gone out, like the Fool's candle and left us without a guide, unable to discern the perspective of landscape outside ourselves, confined to the 'darkling plain' of our own minds. ('So out went the candle, and we were left darkling'; *King Lear* 1.4.226)."[50] But the situation is even grimmer than this, for the subtext of the poems has consistently implied that our building blocks, those fragments of the tradition, may be all we have, but they are lies.

Indeed, the situational allusion to the cliff scene makes this painfully clear. Arnold has been listening to the "grating roar / Of pebbles which the waves draw back" but Edgar has told Gloucester that

The murmuring surge
(4.6.21–23) That on th' unnumber'd idle pebble chafes
Cannot be heard so high.

Arnold has once again echoed a precursor to correct his lie—and of course Edgar *is* a liar. He was not at the top of a cliff, but was standing on a flat plain, a "darkling plain" for poor blinded Gloucester, weaving an elaborate poetical lie to save the inhabitant of the darkling plain from utter despair and suicide. Gloucester, of course, thinks he is on the cliffs of Dover, and after he thinks he has jumped off them, he presumably thinks he is on Dover Beach—but in fact there is no escape from his plight, from his darkling plain. The implication of Arnold's allusion is that the lies of poetry may save us from despair, as they saved the deluded Gloucester, but lies they remain and cannot alter our existential state, which is always "as on a darkling plain." The allusiveness of "Dover Beach" helps to make it one of the most powerful and compelling poems in the language, but not because the voices of past poets provide the kind of authoritative language Arnold usually sought. Rather, the poem is compelling in its courageous struggle to set aside the lies, the false consolations of such precursors as Wordsworth (a kind of Edgar figure) and to battle for a true standing ground, however barren and desolate. Even if he is "as on a darkling plain," the speaker wants to be able to state, with an existential truth unavailable to the blind and duped Gloucester, that "we are here."

In his 1863 essay on Maurice de Guérin, Arnold quoted a passage that demonstrates his awareness of the extreme difficulties of finding a language unadulterated by the words of previous authors: "'When I begin a subject, my self conceit,' (says this exquisite artist) 'imagines I am doing wonders; and when I have finished, I see nothing but a wretched made-up imitation, composed of odds and ends of colour stolen from other people's palettes, and tastelessly mixed together on mine.' Such was his passion for perfection" (3:35). The problem is not with deliberate allusions, but with a language so overused that uncontrollable echoes and chains of association are inevitable. And perhaps Arnold's turn from poetry to prose resulted in part from his recognition of an element of "wretched made-up imitation" in his poetry, of his inability to forge a language entirely his own. Certainly when he made a point of deliberately exploiting the tradition by mimicking past poets in such works as *Sohrab and Rustum, Balder Dead,* and *Merope* he was able to achieve little more than lifeless pastiche. The echoes and allusions in his love poetry, however, are extremely vital, uncontrollably so. Nevertheless, Arnold does not use the voices of the poetic tradition as words of power and authority to confirm his own vision. In fact, "Dover Beach" contrasts sharply with such a poem as Swinburne's "On the Cliffs," also about hearing the sea and other voices on an eroding cliff by a "distant northern sea," for whereas Swinburne heard the voices of Sappho—and of Wordsworth, and even of Arnold's "Dover Beach"—as filling the landscape with meaning, Arnold heard the voices of Sophocles and Wordsworth only to reject and deny them, to empty the landscape of their presence. Paradoxically, in his greatest poem the greatest of all defenders of the poetic tradition found himself encumbered by it, and struggled to clear it away. But perhaps it was precisely the resistance against a living and recalcitrant language, the battle to control intertextual echoes and subordinate them to his own purposes, that enabled Arnold to produce his finest poems. The model for Arnold's battle with his poetic forefathers, then, is not a Bloomian agon, an armed battle against a single combatant, but a much harder, less glorious encounter with the protean, many-voiced forces of a seductive and betraying poetic tradition.

Conclusion

IN MANY respects Arnold's poems are the record of his failures to accomplish what he believed—or hoped—poetry could accomplish. The early poems consistently seek an authoritative voice that would make poetic utterance meaningful, and they consistently fail to find it. Later poems founder on the impossibility of finding a language sufficiently uncontaminated by earlier works to allow the poet's utterance to seem wholly his own, and so call into question even the possibility of authenticity and sincerity, let alone authority. He could never find an "Idea of the world" that would enable him to write in an assured, univocal style. In fact, when he came closest to a high literary style that accorded with his idea of the rules, the "wholesome regulative laws" of poetry (1:15), as in the classical imitations (especially *Merope*), it was only by attempting to separate literature from life, even to the extent of producing nearly dead works in a nearly dead language. Characteristically, the more Arnold failed to exclude the multitudinousness of his age and of his own divided mind, the more successful his poems tended to be, the more seemingly "alive." In what may well be the most critically astute comment he ever made, Arnold himself noted that what would make his poems memorable—make them alive—was not their aesthetic or formal accomplishment, and certainly not their authoritative tone, but rather their accurate reflection of the multitudinous mid-Victorian Zeitgeist: "My poems represent the main movement of mind of the last quarter of a century, and thus they will probably have their day as people become conscious to themselves of what that movement of mind is, and interested in the literary productions which reflect it."[1] His poems would be remembered not for their absolute value but for their historical value because he had applied his energies and talents "to the main line of modern development." Consequently, to judge Arnold by his own standards, as laid down in "The Study of Poetry," his poems cannot be considered great art, though they may nevertheless be found moving and, in the most profoundly Arnoldian sense, historically interesting.

Arnold's failures and limited successes reflect the inescapable conditions of his age, and our own—for his "literary productions" necessarily had to fail in their search for a univocal, authoritative voice if they were to "reflect" a multitudinous, skeptical Zeitgeist. Possibly the most pervasive and important characteristic of the mid-Victorian sensibility was the sense of living in an age of transition, a condition most famously epitomized in Arnold's description of "Wandering between two worlds, one dead, / The other powerless to be born." Victorians—or at least Victorian intellectuals—were suspended between the ages of faith (an exploded medieval religion) and the coming age of scientific revelation, so that as Arnold's poetry repeatedly reveals, the emotional consolation of religion and even of poetry was at odds with truth. Certainly it is no novel or startling observation that this perplexed wilderness between a past that he cannot return to and a future he cannot arrive at is the locale of all of Arnold's poetry and provides most of its themes, but it has not been generally noted that the historical moment is embodied in the language itself and consequently in the very conditions of literary production. Language itself, as we have since come to realize, was in a state of "wandering," of perpetual errantry in error. Since the triumph of the scientific outlook, language did not seem to embody truth, but only to reflect uncertainties, doubts, aspirations. Arnold could, and did, make a case for literary "wandering" as a way to a kind of truth, but both the value and the limitations of such wandering are well characterized by Bakhtin:

> *The artist has a keen sense for ideological problems in the process of birth and generation.*
>
> *He senses them in* statu nascendi, *sometimes better than the most cautious "man of science," the philosopher, or the technician. The generation of ideas, the generation of esthetic desires and feelings, their wandering, their as yet unformed groping for reality,*

> *their restless seething in the depths of the so-called "social psyche"—the whole as yet undifferentiated flood of generating ideology—is reflected and refracted in the content of the literary work.*[2]

This sense of the seething Zeitgeist even as it comes into being, this reflection of multitudinous ideologies ("Ideas of the world") in the literary work, is precisely what Arnold claimed he would be remembered for, and it is possibly the most that a modern poet can hope to accomplish, but it is not what the young Arnold set out to accomplish. It makes poetry a fascinating historical barometer, but does not give it an authoritative power to transcend the clash of ideologies, to arrive at truth.

The problem for the poet in the modern wilderness is that the past can no longer press meaningfully into the present. Because past beliefs are regarded as simply false in the light of modern thought, the tradition is simply a tradition of error—as Shelley said, our tradition teaches us to assign false values to words and signs so that "our whole life is thus an education of error."[3] Yet Arnold's impulse was not to break with the tradition and so achieve a fresh start at the expense of falling into poetic and cultural anarchy, but to find ways to salvage the tradition. His use of traditional forms, his insistence on adhering to the established "laws" of poetry, his devotion to and imitation of classical form, his attempts to define and preserve a "canon" of the greatest works, all were attempts to sustain a saving tradition even in the wilderness. This fundamental impulse is nowhere more evident than in the peroration of his 1853 Preface: "Let us not bewilder our successors: let us transmit to them the practice of Poetry, with its boundaries and wholesome regulative laws, under which excellent works may again, perhaps, at some future time, be produced" (1:15). Arnold's criticism of the Bible reveals clearly enough that he did not mistake tradition for truth, yet he nevertheless insisted on tradition as a source of authority in the modern world. In a comment on Kafka that could be applied with equal justice to Arnold's desire to "transmit" a tradition he knew to be rife with error, Walter Benjamin lamented that "he sacrificed truth for the sake of clinging to its transmissibility." Geoffrey Hartmann, who regards this as "one of the saddest sentences"

Benjamin ever wrote, observes that for the modern thinker "truth and tradition ('transmissibility') are now in opposition. We are reminded not only of Bloom's analysis of this bind in the relation of later to earlier poet but of all contemporary criticism that presents itself as commentary on a received text yet cannot be called submissive to it."[4] Arnold's poetry falls constantly into this bind as it attempts to continue the tradition, to gain authority from it, and yet inevitably (at least at its best) refuses to be submissive to it. His best poetry, consequently, is always implicitly criticism, revising and rejecting traditional works even as it resonates with them. It should not, therefore, be surprising that he ultimately came to regard criticism, not poetry, as the proper literature of the wilderness, since only criticism could properly *transmit* the practice of poetry to future generations. The central argument of Hartmann's *Criticism in the Wilderness* is that, since Arnold, literature must necessarily be criticism, and criticism ought certainly to be regarded as literature: "The wilderness alluded to in my title is Arnold's. . . . Arnold identifies the critics, of whom he is one, with the generation that was destined to perish in the Sinai desert. But this wilderness is all we have. Arnold's fiction of presence was that our errand in the wilderness would end: that a new and vital literature would arise to redeem the work of the critic. What if this literature is not unlike criticism, and we are forerunners to ourselves? Perhaps it is better that the wilderness should be the Promised Land, than vice-versa."[5] Surely Arnold ought to have the benefit of such a shift in perspective, and we ought now to be able to see him as a forerunner to ourselves and in Hartmann's sense as a forerunner to himself. His poetry is critical of the tradition and his rhetorically lively criticism, full of reminiscence, allusion, and quotation is poetical—both the poetry and the criticism epitomize the literature of the wilderness.

Such a shift in perspective, however, misses the most significant fact about Arnold—his *unwillingness* to live in a world where all questions are left open, all conclusions are provisional, all ideals are open to criticism. The point is well made by George Levine, who sees that Arnold is more an unwitting forerunner than an alternative to contemporary critical theorists: "When we look back at Arnold as an alternative to any of the advanced theories of our time, we are looking back toward his own touching inability to live with the irresolution and the subversion of authority that his very critical procedure, his own willingness to turn back upon himself, dramatized and enabled."[6] The crucial problem for Arnold, then, is that he could not avoid corrosive criticism of authority, but he was unwilling to do without authority. As Hannah Arendt has argued in her provocative meditations on tradition and authority in the modern age, this is the crucial problem for all intellectuals and artists living "between past and future"—or "wandering between two worlds." Arendt traces the origins of the modern loss of authority and break with tradition to the mid-nineteenth century, when Kierkegaard, Marx, and Nietzsche "were the first who dared to think without the guidance of any authority whatsoever; and yet, for better and worse, they were still held by the categorical framework of the great tradition." In celebrating the modern movement beyond even these revolutionary thinkers, Arendt is dismissive of the tradition and of its Arnoldian upholders, " 'educated philistines,' who all through the nineteenth century tried to make up for the loss of authentic authority with a spurious glorification of culture. To most people today their culture looks like a field of ruins which, far from being able to claim any authority, can hardly command their interest."[7] The description, I think, accurately fits Arnold's efforts, though both the ruins and the effort to redeem them must continue to command our interest.

Certainly Arnold's lifelong effort was, precisely, to find some way "to make up for the loss of authentic authority." He constantly advocated the authority of right reason, of the state, even of academies, and the special status he accorded to the Bible and to the classics was designed to preserve them as authoritative, a stay against anarchy. For the poet and critic, of course, the crucial question is how, or whether, literary language can gain authority. As Huxley and other scientists argued, truth no longer resided in words or traditional wisdom, but in things—without truth, religion becomes merely poetry, and poetry becomes merely entertainment, pleasant but not important, and certainly not authoritative. Arnold's ambition, of course, was to save religion as poetry ("The strongest part of our religion to-day is its unconscious poetry"

[9:161]), with the result that poetry becomes a kind of religion with its own body of "sacred" texts, a "canon." David Daiches makes the point that

> *if religion is saved as poetry, and is still seen as something central in civilization, then poetry must take on the prestige of religion and be valued as something central in civilization, and the task of defining what Arnold called the "best" poetry becomes the high function of the priest-critic. This line of thought eventually leads us to F. R. Leavis's concept of the "great tradition" in a national literature, to be interpreted and transmitted by the dedicated apostle of literary culture. Just as the biblical canon was distinguished from the Apocrypha, so there was a literary canon from which everything not in the "great tradition" was to be excluded.*[8]

Arnold's outlook was broader than this, and involved more than what he would have called the "merely literary," but his insistence on the transmission of culture, on the role of the critic to winnow out the "best that has been thought and said in the world," is very much in this spirit. The role of the critic is to find this "best," to define it as a part of the "culture" that is a stay against chaos, a stay against anarchy. If the modern world could not have the absolute truth of religion, it could at least have the best that has been thought and said. Northrop Frye, one of the greatest spokesmen for the value and authority of humane letters since Arnold, rests his case, with admirable force and lucidity, on purely Arnoldian principles: "The conception of the Classical in art and the conception of the scriptural or canonical in religion have always tended to approximate one another; . . . the closer the approximation, the healthier it is for both religion and art; . . . on this approximation the authority of humane letters has always rested."[9] And of course academic critics, who naturally want to believe in the value and authority of what they teach and study, have not been averse to seeing themselves in the almost priestly way these assumptions would lead to, as moral instructors improving their students with the true religion of the humanist canon.

Unfortunately, Arnold's description of how the critic can determine the "best" tends to remove him from this socially purposeful role. The "best" can be found only by the "disinterested" critic, the critic removed from the give and take of the bustling, multitudinous world. The paradox, then, is that in order for culture, and especially literature, to attain its authority within society, it must be removed from society. Literature, once canonized as classical, becomes sacralized, removed from the temporal and mundane realm of common life. The result, as Foucault has argued, is that literature, especially poetry, became folded in upon itself in the mid-nineteenth century. Removed from both religious truth and the social referentiality of language as it is actually spoken, literature becomes self-referential, enclosed within its own autonomous form and able to generate meaning only in relation to prior literary works. Not surprisingly, the harder Arnold tried to write poetry that would be canonical, that was uncontaminated by the vices and living voices of the age, the harder he tried to write by the guidance of "disinterested" criticism, the more sterile and academic his poetry became. *Sohrab and Rustum, Balder Dead,* and *Merope* do not regain the "authentic authority" of the tradition, but only become monuments on a "field of ruins which, far from being able to claim any authority, can hardly command [our] interest."

To be convincingly authoritative, to fulfill something like the function of a religious oracle, the poem must be univocal. The "dialogue of the mind with itself" could only reflect vacillation and uncertainty, whereas the "unity and profoundness of moral impression, at which the ancient poets aimed" (1:12) can offer certainty and security. Arnold believed that poetry—rather than criticism or novels, say—could have a religious force because he perceived it as by nature powerfully univocal. Bakhtin, discussing the distinction between the unified discourse of poetry and the "heteroglossia" of the novel, defines poetry in a way that epitomizes Arnold's aspirations for it: "The world of poetry, no matter how many contradictions and insoluble conflicts the poet develops within it, is always illumined by one unitary and indisputable discourse. Contradictions, conflicts and doubts remain in the object, in thoughts, in living experiences—in short, in the subject matter—but they do not enter into the language itself. In poetry, even discourse about doubts must be cast in a discourse that cannot be doubted."[10]

Arnold wanted to preserve the "boundaries and wholesome regulative laws" of poetry, to avoid crossing those boundaries and engaging in a corrosive dialogue that would contaminate the purity of the word in poetic discourse. Again, as Bakhtin points out, poetry, narrowly conceived, aspires to do just this. In poetry "the word is sufficient to itself and does not presume alien utterances beyond its own boundaries. Poetic style is by convention suspended from any mutual interaction with alien discourse, any allusion to alien discourse."[11] To retain its presumed authority, poetry must avoid other forms of discourse, must fold in upon itself or, as Bakhtin well says, "the language of poetic genres . . . often becomes authoritarian, dogmatic and conservative, sealing itself off from the influence of extraliterary social dialects. Therefore such ideas as a special 'poetic language,' a 'language of the gods,' a 'priestly language of poetry' and so forth could flourish on poetic soil."[12] But as we have seen, when Arnold wrote in the authoritarian style he advocated in the Preface, his works were monolithic but inert. In general, the effort to reduce the "heteroglossia" of a multitudinous language to a unified poetic utterance that excludes the untamable associations of other levels and types of discourse is an attempt to reflect in language a unified and authoritative ideology. It is, in short, an attempt to erect a monolithic "culture" against anarchy, a unified ideology (or "Idea of the world") against multitudinousness. Unfortunately, Arnold did not have a unified ideology to convey in poetic form, so his medium became his message in such a work as *Merope*—the conventional form, hermetically sealed from the life of society and its living languages, was everything. Art became separated from society and Arnold's efforts to give poetry the centrality of religion ended with a notion very like that of art for art's sake, with poetry relegated to the margins of society. In a perverse way, the poetic canon, the body of revered texts, engages in a dialogue with itself because it is deliberately cut off from dialogue with all other forms of discourse.

Arnold turned to criticism, presumably, because he recognized his failure to produce the kind of poetry that could have a genuine, and positive, influence on the life of his times. Criticism could engage in genuine dialogue with alien ideologies, and yet through the artistic control of the author could draw them into a kind of unity. Arnold could quote directly from the cheerfully mindless paeans to England of Roebuck and Adderley ("The best breed in the whole world" [3:273]), from the brutally barren observations of the newspapers ("Wragg is in custody" [3:273]), from topics of parliamentary debate (the deceased wife's sister act), from an anonymous M.P. ("That a thing is an anomaly, I consider to be no objection to it whatever" [3:265]), even from the unpoetical stock of English surnames ("Higginbottom, Stiggins, Bugg!" [3:273]), and yet draw all into an artistic whole by achieving an urbane transcendence of the Babel of discourses. By achieving a polished, unruffled urbanity of tone, he could ultimately assert an ideology of culture that would seem to include other forms of thought and speech rather than cutting itself off from them. And in achieving something like a univocal style, the criticism, at its best, could aspire to the condition of poetry. Conversely, Arnold's most ambitious late poetry aspired to the condition of criticism. "Heine's Grave" is not unlike a chopped prose version of the essay on Heine, and "Obermann Once More" is a peculiar dialogue in which the author of Obermann returns from the dead to abandon his melancholy writings and turn to the more hopeful doctrines of Arnold's criticism.

Of course Arnold could never write the authoritative, pure poetry he aspired to. Poetry as univocal discourse, as a pure form of speech, can only be aimed at, not achieved. Bakhtin argues that the "historically existent poet, as a human being surrounded by living hetero- and polyglossia," can never be immune to contaminating influences from other forms of speech, but his relationship to the living language of his time must be excluded from his poetic style: "This relationship could not find a place in the *poetic style* of his work without destroying that style, without transposing it into a prosaic key and in the process turning the poet into a writer of prose."[13] This, I think, is precisely what happened to Arnold. He certainly did want to find a pure form of poetic discourse separated from and authoritative over the anarchic "polyglossia" of the living language, but he also wanted to be directly engaged with that language. Consequently, after his increasingly unsuccessful efforts with a pure, classical poetic style, his poetry became increasingly prosaic, even conversational, and his literary ambitions shifted to critical prose. A passage addressed to Heine, for example, is hardly characteristic of a priestly poetic language:

> But was it thou—I think
> Surely it was!—that bard
> Unnamed, who, Goethe said,
> *Had every other gift, but wanted love*;
> Love, without which the tongue
> Even of angels sounds amiss.
>
> ("Heine's Grave," ll. 97–102)

The conversationally meditative language is anything but authoritative—the question raised is not in itself a deeply significant one, and the answer is couched in the terms of merely personal opinion: "I think / Surely it was." The passage awkwardly brings in the authoritative voice of Goethe, but here even Goethe's voice is critical rather than bardic. Finally, the direct quotation of Goethe gives way to the more compelling authority of the Bible, in an allusion to St. Paul: "Though I speak with the tongues of men and of angels, and have not charity, I am become as a sounding brass, as a tinkling cymbal" (1 Cor. 13.1). And even this authority speaks of the difficulty of speaking. But the point here is that Arnold is not even attempting to write in a priestly poetic style. He is writing verse criticism in the same mode as his prose criticism—an urbane, knowledgeable tone supported by quotation and allusion. Arnold provides perhaps the clearest example to support Hartmann's claim that much "post-Miltonic or post-visionary writing" (that is, writing that no longer assumes its own authority) "tends toward the condition of quotation, attenuated allusion and paraphrase."[14] Both Arnold's critical prose and his late critical verse become a kind of bricolage, or patchwork, of resonant phrases.

In his later work, of course, Arnold deliberately and ostentatiously used a style of "reminiscence and quotation" to incorporate what Walter Benjamin would call the "aura" of past works into his own writing. Arnold never went as far as Benjamin, whose ambition was to write a complete work consisting wholly of quotations, but he did, as we have seen, often regard great phrases as talismanic, magical touchstones, so it is perhaps not entirely surprising that his late literary works did not strive for pure poetic style, or the natural magic of Adamic naming in an uncontaminated language, but rather adopted a style that accommodated itself to a well-used language, attempting to benefit from its resonances, its aura. But his best early poetry also depends for its effectiveness on allusion and quotation, although less consciously, and even apparently against the will of the poet and speaker. Bakhtin argues that the poet achieves a "unitary language" by "stripping all aspects of language of the intentions of other people, destroying all traces of social heteroglossia and diversity of language" with the result that a "tension-filled unity of language is achieved in the poetic work,"[15] but Arnold, despite his efforts, never stripped his language this bare, and so his poetry always tended, as Bakhtin would have it, to become prosaic. In *Tristram and Iseult,* for example, he would not keep the archaic discourse of romance free of the more recent ideology of romanticism or of the contemporary ideology of Victorian home and family. In *Empedocles on Etna* he was so far from achieving a unitary style that he came to regard the work as a dialogue of competing discourses, contentious and irresolvable. The classical poetic style of Callicles could not transcend, incorporate, or exclude the Victorian common sense and credulity of Pausanias or the strange, unresolved mix of romanticism, agnosticism, and rationalism of Empedocles. The "Switzerland" poems, similarly, consist of a clash of romantic, sentimental Victorian, and literary-critical discourses that cannot be resolved in an ideologically unified discourse even in the beautiful "To Marguerite—Continued"—a poem so far from achieving a purity of language that it seems to consist almost wholly of "the intentions of other people." Even "The Buried Life," Arnold's most deliberate effort to strip his language down to a univocal, absolutely sincere vehicle, is contaminated by the bathetic discourse of conventionally sincere lovers, and by the past literary efforts of, among others, Milton and Wordsworth. And even "Dover Beach," as moving and sincere a poem as the language seems capable of producing, consists of literary criticism, deliberate allusions, and reminiscence and quotation of subversive texts.

Paradoxically, the very failure of Arnold's efforts to eliminate such "contamination" or to refute alien intentions effectively is the source not only of the tensions in his poetry that generate emotional power and energy but even of such authority, or at least authenticity, as the poems may claim. They are authentic because they reflect, in all its richness and diversity, the living language of Arnold's historical moment in precisely the way that Bakhtin associates solely with prose: "The living utterance, having taken meaning and shape at a particular historical moment in a socially specific environment, cannot fail to brush up against thousands of living dialogic threads, woven by socio-ideological consciousness around the given object of an utterance; it cannot fail to become an active participant in social dialogue."[16] A purely objective poetry is impossible because the object can never be perceived let alone described as "in itself it really is"—it can never be disentangled from the "living dialogic threads." Arnold tried, in his quasi-classical poems, to avoid this living language, and in these poems he failed not only to gain authority but even to reflect the life of his times—its "main movement of mind." Such poetry, as I have argued, aspires to the condition of a dead language, but Arnold's best poetry is in a language so very much alive that it could not be controlled in an unambiguous, univocal, monolithic style. The language itself is multitudinous, anarchic, caught between an age of certainties in which poetic style could express a unified ideology of faith and an uncertain future, in which no such unified discourse could be meaningful. To say that Arnold's poetry is prosaic, in the sense that it embodies the complexities of the living language, is only to praise it.

Nevertheless, the crucial point is that Arnold did not intend to betray the grand style of poetry to the living language of a more prosaic style. His ambition was to find a poetic language with the authority of religious utterance, and failing that, he sought at least a poetic language "innocent enough" to "make the spotless purity of [his] intentions evident" (3:275), a language at least uncontaminated enough to allow him to speak sincerely, with his own voice. As is apparent in his later practice of limiting the range of words by precise definitions, he wanted to appropriate words for his own purposes, to use them as if all their authority resulted from his intentions. Bakhtin's description of the usual consequences of such an effort sounds almost like a summary of my analysis of Arnold's difficulties in appropriating language for his own purposes. Language

> *exists in other people's mouths, in other people's contexts, serving other people's intentions: it is from there that one must take the word and make it one's own. And not all words for just anyone submit equally easily to this appropriation, to this seizure and transformation into private property: many words stubbornly resist, others remain alien, sound foreign in the mouth of the one who appropriated them and who now speaks them; they cannot be assimilated into his context and fall out of it; it is as if they put themselves in quotation marks against the will of the speaker. Language is not a neutral medium that passes freely and easily into the private property of the speaker's intentions; it is populated—overpopulated—with the intentions of others.*[17]

The quotation marks are usually quite visible in Arnold's prose, around the works of Bishop Wilson, or Bishop Butler, or Roebuck, or Adderley, or Sir Charles Gooch, or Goethe, or Wordsworth, and they are visible around Goethe's words in "Heine's Grave" and around Sénancour's supposed words in "Obermann Once More." But words seem to "put themselves in quotation marks against the will of the speaker" in "To Marguerite—Continued," "The Buried Life," and "Dover Beach"—that is, in Arnold's best poems. Arnold failed in his desire to appropriate words to his own unified poetic style, to eliminate the contamination of other people's intentions, but in that failure he produced a few remarkable poems that demonstrate the inevitable condition of literature in the wilderness. In a language so overused, so overpopulated, so teeming with multitudinous life, any poetry not written in a positively dead language must tend "toward the condition of quotation, attenuated allusion and paraphrase," must tend toward a bricolage dense with the traces of other writings and other forms of discourse.

To be sure, Arnold's poetry draws a semblance of authority from its echoes of the tradition, from its resonance of intertextual echoes, but these echoes subvert at least as much as they support his apparent purposes. The echoes tend to be demonic voices that come even when they are not called. But as Hartmann points out, to characterize this region of echoes as demonic "matters less than to recognize its verbal power"—the language that calls spirits from the abyss may not have the authority of truth, may not have any authority at all, but it does seem to have a kind of power. In saying this, however, I come to an Arnoldian turn upon myself, and realize that though we have become expert at showing why poetry should not have power over us, we have not gone much beyond Arnold's account of why it nevertheless does seem to exercise such a power. My language, like Hartmann's, flaunting that word *power,* assumes what it cannot demonstrate. We can, indeed, excise the religious functions of poetry, doubt that its apparent power is necessarily a power for good, demonstrate the impossibility of an effective yet pure poetic style, show the inevitable intertextuality of all poetic utterance, and deconstruct all of Arnold's poetry—but still we cannot account for the mysterious power somehow inherent in words. It is true that we can now appreciate Arnold's language in historical terms, as a peculiarly rich embodiment of the mid-Victorian Zeitgeist, and can be interested in his works as the "literary productions which reflect" the age's uncertainties, but still we cannot fully account for the emotional power that "Dover Beach" has over us. Like Arnold, we are left wondering *how* language can have the power that we seem to experience in it, and answering with the Preacher that "though a man labour to seek it out, yet he shall not find it; yea, farther, though a wise man think to know it, yet he shall not find it." Like Arnold, and like his Scholar-Gipsy, we are wanderers still, still seeking, though now more hopelessly than ever, for sources of power and authority in language, and still engaged in a critical enterprise that can only empty language of its authority. We are still wandering in a postromantic wilderness, and our philosophical criticism can only show us that the Promised Land will not be found, that language itself is now condemned to wandering in its own historical error. But to Arnold is due the credit that he was among the first to recognize the modern wilderness, that if his poems failed by his own standards, it was only because the wilderness was inescapable. The literature of the wilderness, Hartmann argues, may well be criticism—but as Hartmann realizes, Arnold was there before him, and not only by turning from poetry to criticism. He was there before him by demonstrating, however unwillingly, that poetry in an overpopulated language must also be criticism, must constantly criticize and refute its own intertextual resonances, and its own aesthetic premises. Contamination—stray voices and associations—may be the source of power in Arnold's best poetry because it represents what must be and cannot be overcome, what must be and cannot be appropriated and shaped into the univocal poetic utterance. Failure to overcome it generates pathos, of course, but it also generates, if not power, at least the sense of a vivid, powerfully living language that lies beneath and around the poetic text, and that refuses to be overcome. George Levine has observed that "we continue to read Arnold because of the sheer power of his invention. His language has entered ours."[18] Arnold continues to "live" as a poet and critic because his words and phrases, his poems and essays, have, as he would put it, entered the great tradition, or as we might put it, have entered into and forever altered the tissue of the living language.

Notes
Index

Notes

Introduction: The Betrayals of Language

1. Douglas Bush, *Matthew Arnold: A Survey of His Poetry and Prose* (New York: Macmillan, 1971), p. 187.

2. The passage from "The Study of Poetry" paraphrases the concluding passage of "On Poetry," his Preface to *The Hundred Greatest Men,* 9:63.

3. ApRoberts, *Arnold and God* (Berkeley: Univ. of California Press, 1983), pp. 281, 226.

4. Bush, p. 185.

5. Fulweiler, *Letters from the Darkling Plain: Language and the Grounds of Knowledge in the Poetry of Arnold and Hopkins* (Columbia: Univ. of Missouri Press, 1972), p. 29.

6. Miller, *The Disappearance of God: Five Nineteenth-Century Writers* (Cambridge: Harvard Univ. Press, 1963), p. 265.

7. Shaw, "The Agnostic Imagination in Victorian Poetry," *Criticism* 22 (1980): 127.

8. "Obermann Once More," l. 28.

9. The phrase is Oscar Wilde's, from "The Critic as Artist," in *The Portable Oscar Wilde,* ed. Richard Aldington (New York: Viking, 1946), p. 87.

10. Huxley, in *Autobiography and Essays,* ed. Brander Matthews (1919; rpt. New York: Kraus, 1969), p. 227.

11. Ibid., pp. 226–27.

12. See Hans Aarsleff, *The Study of Language in England, 1780–1860* (Princeton: Princeton Univ. Press, 1967), pp. 224 ff.

13. "Nature," in *Selected Writings of Ralph Waldo Emerson,* ed. William H. Gilman (New York: New American Library, 1965), pp. 201, 200.

14. Richard Chenevix Trench, *The Study of Words* (New York: Redfield, 1852), pp. 13, 23–24, 25.

15. Müller, *Lectures on the Science of Language, Delivered at the Royal Institution of Great Britain in April, May, and June, 1861,* 2d ed., rev. (New York: Scribner, 1863), pp. 377, 384. Arnold expressed his general agreement with Müller in a letter to him in 1878: "The line [of *Literature and Dogma*] was, I knew, in some sort the same as your own—the pursuit of the thread of *natural history* in all those religions and theologies; but it was followed in so peculiar a way that it might well displease. I am very glad, however, that it pleased you." The letter is in the Bodleian Library.

16. Coleridge, *Principles of Genial Criticism: Essay Third.*

17. The comment is from *St. Paul and Protestantism,* but see also his comment in *Literature and Dogma* that the idea of the Logos is not authorized by Jesus: "Jesus did not give any scientific definition of [the word *Christ*],—such as, for instance,

that Christ was the Logos. He took the word Christ as the Jews used it" (6:307–8). See also 6:297.

18. The proper way to understand the Bible is to study it "with a fair mind, and with the tact that letters, surely, alone can give. For the thing turns upon understanding the manner in which men have thought, their way of using words, and what they mean by them" (6:196).

19. ApRoberts, p. 226.

20. Reprinted in *Matthew Arnold: Prose Writings, the Critical Heritage,* ed. Carl Dawson and John Pfordresher (London: Routledge & Kegan Paul, 1979), p. 291. Arnold gave an answer, of sorts, in his Preface to *Last Essays:* "Finely touched souls have a presentiment of a thing's natural truth even though it be questioned, and long before the palpable proof by experience convinces all the world" (8:157).

21. Brown, *Matthew Arnold: A Study in Conflict* (Chicago: Univ. of Chicago Press, 1948), p. 154.

22. Shaw, p. 126.

23. Ibid., p. 121.

24. Quoted in Aarsleff, p. 231.

25. Aarsleff, pp. 24–25.

26. Müller, p. 391.

27. "Nature," *Selected Writings of Emerson,* p. 199.

28. Trench, pp. 33, 36.

29. See Elizabeth K. Helsinger, *Ruskin and the Art of the Beholder* (Cambridge: Harvard Univ. Press, 1982), pp. 257–64.

30. The letter to Müller, dated January 20, 1871, is in the Bodleian Library. According to John Holloway, "Arnold's definitions are often textbook definitions; they are dull; they are diaphanous. It is not merely that they cannot facilitate interesting inferences; they preclude them, and this is their job" (*The Victorian Sage: Studies in Argument* [1953; rpt. New York: Norton, 1965], p. 221).

31. ApRoberts, p. 120.

32. Ibid., p. 228.

33. *The Letters of Matthew Arnold to Arthur Hugh Clough,* ed. Howard Foster Lowry (London: Oxford Univ. Press, 1932), p. 135.

34. "The Nigger Question," in *Carlyle: The Nigger Question; Mill: The Negro Question,* ed. Eugene R. August (New York: Appleton-Century-Crofts, 1971), p. 29.

35. *Letters to Clough,* pp. 100–101.

36. Arnold frequently suggests a mysterious or sacred power in language, but perhaps nowhere more clearly than in his description of Wordsworth's inspiration: "To give aright what he wishes to give, to interpret and render successfully, is not always within Wordsworth's own command. It is within no poet's command; here is the part of the Muse, the inspiration, the God, the 'not ourselves.' In Wordsworth's case, the accident, for so it may almost be called, of inspiration, is of peculiar importance. No poet, perhaps, is so evidently filled with a new and sacred energy when the inspiration is upon him; no poet, when it fails him, is so left 'weak as is a breaking wave' " (9:51).

37. Burke, *A Rhetoric of Motives* (Berkeley: Univ. of California Press, 1969), p. 41.

38. *Letters to Clough*, p. 126.

39. Foucault, *The Order of Things: An Archaeology of the Human Sciences*, trans. from the French (London: Tavistock, 1974), p. 298.

40. Ibid., p. 44.

41. Ibid., p. 89.

42. Pater, Preface, *The Renaissance: Studies in Art and Poetry*, ed. Donald L. Hill (Berkeley: Univ. of California Press, 1980), p. xix; Wilde, p. 87.

43. D. G. James, *Matthew Arnold and the Decline of English Romanticism* (New York: Oxford Univ. Press, 1961), pp. 26–27, 102.

44. Bloom, "The Breaking of Form," in *Deconstruction and Criticism* (New York: Seabury, 1979), pp. 4–5.

I: The Early Poetry: Distant Voices

1. G. Robert Stange, *Matthew Arnold: The Poet as Humanist* (Princeton: Princeton Univ. Press, 1967), p. 15.

2. Quoted in *Poems*, p. 680.

3. Quoted in Graham Hough, *The Last Romantics* (1947; rpt. London: Methuen, 1961), p. 42.

4. *Letters to Clough*, p. 65.

5. Ibid., p. 97.

6. Ibid., p. 130.

7. *Unpublished Letters of Matthew Arnold*, ed. Arnold Whitridge (New Haven: Yale Univ. Press, 1923), p. 18.

8. E. D. H. Johnson, *The Alien Vision of Victorian Poetry: Sources of the Poetic Imagination in Tennyson, Browning, and Arnold* (Princeton: Princeton Univ. Press, 1952), p. 159; W. Stacy Johnson, *The Voices of Matthew Arnold: An Essay in Criticism* (New Haven: Yale Univ. Press, 1961), p. 13. Others, however, have defended Arnold's consistency. Stange, for example, insists on "the *consistency* of Matthew Arnold. The word consistency is meant to connote those realizable qualities of Arnold's poetry which I have tried to understand and define, and also to suggest the tendentious purpose of this study—to affirm that Arnold's whole imaginative enterprise is a *consistent* effort to apply ideas to life" (p. 11).

9. Johnson, *Alien Vision*, p. 152.

10. Johnson, *Voices*, p. 6.

11. Speaking of Victorian poetry generally, Dorothy Mermin notes that poetic "use of language shows a constant awareness that against the novelistic ethos of humaneness, moderation, relativism, and common sense . . . poetry was apt to sound selfish, absolutist, even violent—and worst of all, just silly" (*The Audience in the Poem: Five Victorian Poets* [New Brunswick: Rutgers Univ. Press, 1983], p. 12).

12. *Letters to Clough*, p. 57.

13. Quoted in *Poems*, p. 3.

14. "Reply to a declaration that he would not live by the Sea, made in verse by H.H.," ll. 13–20.

15. Stephen M. Parrish, *A Concordance to the Poems of Matthew Arnold* (Ithaca:

Cornell Univ. Press, 1959). I am including the variations "voiceless," "voices," "voicings."

16. John Henry Cardinal Newman, "Literature," in *University Subjects* (Boston: Houghton Mifflin, 1913), pp. 64–65, 67.

17. Roper, *Arnold's Poetic Landscapes* (Baltimore: Johns Hopkins Univ. Press, 1969), p. 129.

18. *The Sermons and Devotional Writings of Gerard Manley Hopkins,* ed. Christopher Devlin, S.J. (London: Oxford Univ. Press, 1959), pp. 200–201.

19. See Walter J. Ong, S.J., *Interfaces of the Word: Studies in the Evolution of Consciousness and Culture* (Ithaca: Cornell Univ. Press, 1977), pp. 121–26.

20. Quoted in *Poems,* p. 36.

21. *Letters to Clough,* p. 140.

22. Johnson, *Voices,* p. 24.

23. *Poems,* p. 27.

24. See Alan Grob, "Arnold's 'Mycerinus': The Fate of Pleasure," *Victorian Poetry* 20 (1982):1–20.

25. *Letters to Clough,* p. 107.

26. See Warren D. Anderson, *Matthew Arnold and the Classic Tradition* (Ann Arbor: Univ. of Michigan Press, 1965), pp. 20–21.

27. Quoted in Stange, pp. 110–11.

28. *Selected Writings of Emerson,* p. 202.

29. *Poems,* p. 113.

30. Ibid., p. 112.

31. Culler, *Imaginative Reason: The Poetry of Matthew Arnold* (New Haven: Yale Univ. Press, 1966), p. 23.

32. Miller, p. 234.

33. Christ, *The Finer Optic: The Aesthetic of Particularity in Victorian Poetry* (New Haven: Yale Univ. Press, 1975), p. 33.

34. The point has been often and ably discussed. See especially Leon Gottfried, *Matthew Arnold and the Romantics* (Lincoln: Univ. of Nebraska Press), pp. 219–23, and U. C. Knoepflmacher, "Dover Revisited: The Wordsworthian Matrix in the Poetry of Matthew Arnold," *Victorian Poetry* 1(1963):18–21.

35. *Letters to Clough,* pp. 81, 98–99.

36. Ibid., p. 99.

37. Allott points out that lines 265–68 recall Wordsworth's "There was a boy . . .":

> "the visible scene
> Would enter unawares into his mind
> With all its solemn imagery, its rocks,
> Its woods, and that uncertain heaven received
> Into the bosom of the steady lake." (ll. 21–25)

And he notes that the phrase "turf we tread" occurs in Wordsworth's "The Brothers," l. 14 (*Poems,* p. 99).

38. Knoepflmacher, pp. 20–21.

39. "Nature," *Selected Writings of Emerson,* p. 200.

40. Quoted in Anne Taylor, *Magic and English Romanticism* (Athens: Univ. of Georgia Press, 1979), p. 93.

41. Johnson, *Voices,* p. 47.

42. Allott hears another echo of "The Mermaid" elsewhere in the poem, and notes also a significant "imitation of Byron"—of a passage of magical incantation from *Manfred* (*Poems,* pp. 103–5).

43. See especially Roper, pp. 123–27.

44. *Poems,* p. 67.

45. Hickman, "A New Direction for 'The Strayed Reveller,'" *Victorian Poetry* 21 (1983):140.

46. Ibid.

47. *Poems,* p. 68. In an 1854 review in the *Westminster Review* J. A. Froude quoted lines 130–70 as a prose paragraph with the comment that "whatever be the merits of the 'Strayed Reveller' as poetry, it is certainly not a poem in the sense which English people generally attach to the word, looking as they do not only for imaginative composition but for verse;—and as certainly if the following passage had been printed merely as prose . . . no one would have suspected that it was composed of an agglutination of lines" (in *Matthew Arnold: The Poetry, the Critical Heritage,* ed. Carl Dawson [London: Routledge & Kegan Paul, 1973], p. 87).

48. P. N. Medvedev/M. M. Bakhtin, *The Formal Method in Literary Scholarship: A Critical Introduction to Sociological Poetics,* trans. Albert J. Wehrle (Baltimore: Johns Hopkins Univ. Press, 1978), p. 47.

49. Bloom, *The Ringers in the Tower: Studies in Romantic Tradition* (Chicago: Univ. of Chicago Press, 1971), p. 10.

50. "Nature," *Selected Writings of Emerson,* pp. 199–200.

II: Romantic Voices and Classic Form

1. Mermin, p. 95.

2. Ibid.

3. Ibid. And for an excellent discussion along these lines see Johnson, *Voices,* pp. 25–33.

4. *Letters to Clough,* p. 95.

5. Sénancour was in fact born in 1770, the same year as Wordsworth. Goethe was born in 1749.

6. Kenneth Allott, "A Background for 'Empedocles on Etna,'" *Essays and Studies,* vol. 21 (London: John Murray, 1968), p. 87.

7. *Letters to Clough,* pp. 63, 126.

8. Quoted in C. B. Tinker and H. F. Lowry, *The Poetry of Matthew Arnold: A Commentary* (New York: Oxford Univ. Press, 1940), pp. 287, 291.

9. Ibid., p. 287.

10. Houghton, "Arnold's 'Empedocles on Etna,'" *Victorian Studies* 1 (1958): 325.

11. The notable exception to the chorus of dispraise for the ode is Swinburne, who referred to it as the "long and lofty chant of Empedocles" (*Arnold: The Poetry, the Critical Heritage,* p. 164).

12. Quoted by Allott in "A Background for 'Empedocles on Etna,'" p. 96.

13. Shaw, "The Agnostic Imagination," p. 127.

14. Johnson, *Voices,* p. 118. Warren D. Anderson is even more emphatic about the impossibility of resolving the dialogue: "Two opposed outlooks have been set forth by means of a dramatic device, not at all classical but thoroughly Victorian, which rules out any possibility of set debate or philosophical dialogue. Arnold deliberately chose this method of presentation, and it may be suggested that he did so to demonstrate the impossibility of communication between the inner worlds represented by Callicles and Empedocles. The introspective man of thought brooding upon his wrongs and the barrenness of the time, ill at ease in solitude as in society, has no common language with the poet, whose thought radiates outward. Arnold himself embodied this dilemma" (*Arnold and the Classic Tradition,* p. 45). See also Paul Zietlow's comment that the various voices "comprise the heritage of mid-nineteenth-century culture, yet somehow they cry out ineffectually as if in isolation from one another, unheeded, misunderstood, or rejected by the listener" ("Heard but Unheeded: The Songs of Callicles in Matthew Arnold's *Empedocles on Etna,*" *Victorian Poetry* 21 [1983]:255).

15. Mermin, p. 95.

16. See Houghton, p. 327; Roper, p. 204.

17. Zietlow, p. 252.

18. Ibid., p. 255.

19. See Culler, p. 159.

20. Friedrich Nietzsche, *The Birth of Tragedy,* in *The Birth of Tragedy and The Genealogy of Morals,* trans. Francis Golffing (New York: Doubleday, 1956), p. 137.

21. Ibid., p. 132.

22. *Letters to Clough,* p. 130.

23. Nietzsche, p. 93.

24. Ibid., pp. 132, 134–35.

25. Ibid., p. 31.

26. Ibid., p. 60.

27. *Poems,* p. 183.

28. Buckler, *On the Poetry of Matthew Arnold: Essays in Critical Reconstruction* (New York: New York Univ. Press, 1982), p. 140.

29. Zietlow, p. 249.

30. *Letters to Clough,* p. 111.

31. Buckler, p. 140.

32. Anderson, p. 42.

33. Johnson, *Alien Vision,* p. 178.

34. Culler, p. 176.

35. ApRoberts, p. 19.

36. *Letters to Clough,* p. 122.

37. According to Frank Kermode, "Empedocles is the Romantic poet who knows enough; Callicles the Romantic poet who does not know enough" (*Romantic Image* [New York: Macmillan, 1957], p. 13).

38. Nietzsche, p. 28.

39. *Letters to Clough,* p. 124.

40. Eliot, "Matthew Arnold," *The Use of Poetry and the Use of Criticism* (London: Faber and Faber, 1933), p. 119.

41. Even Clough, in a composite review of Arnold, Smith, Sydney Walker, and William Allingham, seemed to express a preference for Smith's contemporary settings and themes, and his forthright manner. Smith's *Life-Drama* "has at least the advantage, such as it is, of not showing much of the *litterateur* or connoisseur, or indeed the student; nor is it, as we have said, mere pastoral sweet piping from the country. These poems were not written among books and busts" (*Victorian Scrutinies: Reviews of Poetry 1830–1870,* ed. Isobel Armstrong [London: Athlone, 1972], p. 156).

42. Dietrich, "Arnold's *Empedocles on Etna* and the 1853 Preface," *Victorian Poetry* 14 [1976]:323.

43. [Masson], "Theories of Poetry and a New Poet," *North British Review* 19 [American ed., vol. 14] (August 1853):157–84. "Goethe's theory of poetical or creative literature was, that it is nothing else than the moods of its practitioners objectivized as they arise. . . . Scheming out some plan or story, which is in itself a sort of allegory of his mood as a whole, he fills up the sketch with minor incidents, scenes, and characters, which are nothing more, as it were, than the breaking up of the mood into its minutiae, one by one, into the concrete" (p. 170). And it was this that he had in mind when he said, "A true allegory of the state of one's own mind in a representative history, whether narrative or dramatic in form, is perhaps the highest thing that one can attempt in the way of fictitious art" (p. 180).

44. Mermin, p. 160; Miller, pp. 222–23.

45. "A Defence of Poetry," in *Shelley's Poetry and Prose,* ed. Donald H. Reiman and Sharon B. Powers (New York: Norton, 1977), p. 483.

46. In the *Christian Remembrancer,* April 1854; reprinted in *Arnold: The Poetry, the Critical Heritage,* p. 105. Coventry Patmore repeated the same sentiment in the *North British Review* of August 1854: "By devoting his efforts to subjects of this kind, Mr. Arnold has of necessity confined himself to the small circle of scholars, and though he may succeed in pleasing *them,* he has cut himself off from that general popularity which true poets have sooner or later commanded" (ibid., p. 118).

47. Masson, pp. 166, 175.

48. Ong, p. 25.

49. Nietzsche, p. 136.

50. Ibid., p. 137.

51. The letter, dated May 15, 1857, is in the National Library of Scotland.

52. Nietzsche, p. 137.

53. *Letters of Matthew Arnold 1848–1888,* 2 vols., ed George W. E. Russell (New York: Macmillan, 1896), 1:35; *Letters to Clough,* p. 146.

54. Buckler, p. 151.

55. Culler, p. 214.

56. Ibid., p. 212.

57. Anderson, p. 53; Roper, pp. 245–46.

58. Pearson, "The Importance of Arnold's *Merope,*" in *The Major Victorian Poets: Reconsiderations,* ed. Isobel Armstrong (Lincoln: Univ. of Nebraska Press, 1969), pp. 235–36.

59. Buckler, p. 150.

60. Culler, p. 214.

61. Review in *Fraser's Magazine,* February 1854, reprinted in *Arnold: The Poetry, the Critical Heritage,* pp. 138–39.

62. Buckler, p. 152. But see Lionel Trilling, *Matthew Arnold* (1939; rpt. New York: Harcourt Brace Jovanovich, 1954), pp. 134–35 and Kenneth Burke, *A Rhetoric of Motives* (Berkeley: Univ. of California Press, 1969), p. 8.

63. Culler, p. 207.

64. Ibid., p. 208; Roper, p. 243; Johnson, *Alien Vision,* p. 190.

65. J. A. Froude in the *Westminster Review,* January 1854, suggested that "it seems as if Teutonic tradition, Teutonic feeling, and Teutonic thought had the first claim on English and German poets" (in *Arnold: The Poetry, the Critical Heritage,* p. 95).

66. Pearson, p. 241.

67. *Letters,* 1:69.

68. Culler, p. 227.

69. "Story of the Drama," in *Poems,* p. 433.

70. Pearson, p. 243.

71. Ibid., p. 229.

72. Nietzsche, p. 112.

III: The Poetry of the Wilderness

1. Bloom, *A Map of Misreading* (New York: Oxford Univ. Press, 1975), pp. 10, 40.

2. Jameson, "Magical Narratives: Romance as Genre," *New Literary History* 7 (1975):158.

3. Frye, *Anatomy of Criticism: Four Essays* (Princeton: Princeton Univ. Press, 1957), pp. 190–91.

4. Parker, *Inescapable Romance: Studies in the Poetics of a Mode* (Princeton: Princeton Univ. Press, 1979), p. 224.

5. See Allott's note in *Poems,* p. 304.

6. William E. Buckler has argued that "in a strange, ambiguous way, this pilgrim from the present to the past, from now to then, this outcast of the contemporary universe, is in search of a metaphor of paternity—of a fatherhood that will keep faith with a future that is now in part the speaker's past, of a hospice that, despite its cold severity, will serve as a substitute home." The problem, however, seems not that the speaker cannot find a father, but that he can find too many. Buckler's argument is, however, far stronger when he asserts that "the poets had been his 'fathers' and from them there is no real escape," pp. 113, 112.

7. *The Works of Thomas Carlyle,* 30 vols., vol. 28, *Critical and Miscellaneous Essays* (New York: Charles Scribner's Sons, 1900), pp. 29–30, 31.

8. For a discussion of what Arnold might in fact have seen, see Charles T. Dougherty, "What Arnold Saw and Heard at *La Grande Chartreuse,*" *Victorian Poetry* 18 (1980):393–99.

9. Buckler, p. 126.

10. For an excellent discussion of Iseult's major role in the poem, see Barbara Fass Leavy, "Iseult of Brittany: A New Interpretation of Matthew Arnold's *Tristram and Iseult,*" *Victorian Poetry* 18 (1980):1–22.

11. A less ambivalent reading of the poem's layerings of fantasy and dream is provided by Beverley Taylor, "Imagination and Art in Arnold's 'Tristram and Iseult': The Importance of 'Making,'" *Studies in English Literature* 22 (1982):633–45.

12. The allusion is noted by Leavy, p. 18.

13. Victorian painters frequently did just that. Most notably, Burne-Jones painted a remarkable series of Merlin and Vivian pictures in which the intricate drawing makes the enclosing thicket a thing of beauty. The series is analogous to his *Briar Rose* series, in which a sleep like death is made beautiful, and even to his *Pygmalion* series, in which the statue is as beautiful as the living flesh it becomes, and the living flesh is as placid as the statue. Also analogous are the many Victorian paintings of dead or dying women, such as Millais's *Ophelia* and Waterhouse's *The Lady of Shalott*.

14. Allott notes allusions to Byron's *The Siege of Corinth*, ll. 620–27, to Keats's "The Eve of St. Agnes," ll. 358–59, and to Tennyson's "The Palace of Art," ll. 61–64 (*Poems*, p. 226).

15. Quoted in Tinker and Lowry, *Commentary*, p. 124.

16. "The Scholar-Gipsy," first published in 1853, was probably written in 1852–53; "Thyrsis," composed in a long, drawn-out manner, was conceived by 1862–63, but not completed until January 1866.

17. See Bloom, "The Internalization of Quest Romance," in *The Ringers in the Tower*, pp. 13–35.

18. Johnson, *Alien Vision*, p. 199.

19. Quoted in *Poems*, p. 356.

20. Alpers, "Convening and Convention in Pastoral Poetry," *New Literary History* 14 (1983): p. 287.

21. See Harry Levin, "Notes on Convention," in *Perspectives of Criticism*, ed. Levin (Cambridge: Harvard Univ. Press, 1950), pp. 55–83, and Christopher Ricks, "Allusion: The Poet as Heir," in *Studies in the Eighteenth Century III*, ed. R. F. Brissenden and J. C. Eade (Toronto: Univ. of Toronto Press, 1976), pp. 209–40.

22. Nietzsche, p. 53.

23. Bloom, *The Anxiety of Influence: A Theory of Poetry* (New York: Oxford Univ. Press, 1973), sneers at Arnold for "sneering at Keats while writing *The Scholar Gipsy* and *Thyrsis* in a diction, tone, and sensuous rhythm wholly (and unconsciously) stolen from the Great Odes" (p. 56).

24. *Letters to Clough*, p. 146.

25. Roper, p. 224.

26. Arnold's prose was, of course, effective, but it was not genuinely "disinterested"—his urbanity and irony could give the impression of critical detachment, but at the same time enable him to preach with moral fervor. The idea of "disinterested criticism" is effective as a rhetorical strategy for committed engagement with certain issues, but that engagement obviously undercuts the principle of disinterestedness.

27. Buckler, p. 170.

28. The exception is from the penultimate to the final stanza, but of course these final two stanzas present a single tableau of their own. The only other stanza that is not end-stopped is the sixth, but there the comma could be changed to a period without damaging the grammar or altering the meaning.

29. *Poems,* p. 363.

30. Culler, p. 185.

31. Ibid., p. 190. Culler's reading is effectively refuted by Roper, pp. 212–14.

32. A. E. Dyson, who sees the Gipsy as deliberately rejected by Arnold because "his place is with the primitive, the uncultured, the unintellectual," notes that the Tyrian's flight from the Greeks is a flight from "the bearers of culture" ("The Last Enchantments: Arnold's *The Scholar Gipsy,*" in *Between Two Worlds: Aspects of Literary Form* [London: Macmillan, 1972], pp. 47,52).

33. Culler, p. 191.

34. Philip Drew, "Matthew Arnold and the Passage of Time: A Study of *The Scholar Gipsy* and *Thyrsis,*" in *Major Victorian Poets,* p. 205.

35. Culler, p. 250.

36. *Poems,* p. 537.

37. *Letters of Matthew Arnold,* 1:380.

38. *Poems,* pp. 543–44. The allusion is to *Comus,* ll. 310–13:

> "I know each lane and every valley green
> Dingle, or bushy dell of this wilde Wood
> And every bosky bourn from side to side
> My daily walks and ancient neighborhood."

Also echoed is Oberon's speech: "I know a bank whereon the wild thyme blows, / Where oxlips and the nodding violet grows" (2.1.249–50).

39. Culler, p. 259.

40. Eliot, "Tradition and the Individual Talent," in *Selected Essays* (New York: Harcourt, Brace, 1950), pp. 4, 9.

41. Culler, p. 259.

42. Roper, p. 228.

43. Ibid.

44. Lewis Carroll, *Through the Looking Glass,* chapter 6.

45. Drew, p. 215.

46. A distinction between wandering and questing is not always clear: the wandering in line 212 is associated with "this happy quest." But this lack of precision, I think, signals only the poet's desire to make the wandering simultaneously carefree and purposeful.

47. "Ulysses," ll. 51–52; for Clough, see *Dipsychus,* 6.166–69:

> " 'Whether there be [a God],' the rich man says,
> 'It matters very little,
> For I and mine, thank somebody,
> Are not in want of victual.' "

The passage also overtly alludes to Milton's Christ prophesying the death of Death: "Death last, and with his Carcass glut the Grave" (*Paradise Lost* 3.259).

48. For an interesting discussion of Victorian images of questing and wandering, see George P. Landow's *Images of Crisis: Literary Iconology, 1750 to the Present* (Boston: Routledge & Kegan Paul, 1982), pp. 47–75.

49. Such hero worship, inspired by Carlyle, was a common recourse for

Victorian agnostics, but for the true skeptic even this is a dubious faith. See Clough's

> "To think that men of former days
> In naked truth deserved the praise
> Which, fain to have in flesh and blood
> An image of the imagined good,
> Poets have sung and men received,
> And all too glad to be deceived,
> Most plastic and most inexact,
> Posterity has told for fact;—
> To say what was, was not as we,
> This also is a vanity." (ll. 1–10)

Though not published until 1869, the lines were written by 1851, and were very likely known to Arnold.

50. The many echoes of Exodus are discussed by L. H. Hornstein, " 'Rugby Chapel' and Exodus," *Modern Language Review* 47 (1952):208–9. For a more general discussion of Victorian uses of the typology of Exodus, see George P. Landow, *Victorian Types, Victorian Shadows: Biblical Typology in Victorian Literature, Art, and Thought* (Boston: Routledge & Kegan Paul, 1980).

51. Not everyone would agree. Buckler praises the poem for the "disciplined thought" of its speaker, who "is determined that the grounds for gratitude, affection, and admiration be scrupulously true" (p. 163). W. S. Johnson, however, notes the "thinness and uncertainty in the allegory and diction of the tribute" and calls it "pep-talking" (*Voices,* pp. 67–68).

52. *Letters to Clough,* p. 164.

53. See Parker, p. 172.

IV: Love Poetry: Sincerity and Subversive Voices

1. Johnson, *Alien Vision,* p. 151.

2. Eliot, "The Three Voices of Poetry," in *On Poetry and Poets* (New York: Farrar, Straus and Cudahy, 1957), pp. 97–98.

3. Honan, *Matthew Arnold: A Life* (New York: McGraw-Hill, 1981), chap. 7. For more on the Marguerite debate, see Miriam Allott, "Arnold and 'Marguerite'—Continued," in *Victorian Poetry* 23 (1985):125–43, and in the same issue, Honan, "The Character of Marguerite in Arnold's *Switzerland,*" pp. 145–59.

4. Buckler, p. 68.

5. *Letters of Matthew Arnold,* 1:11.

6. Stange, p. 222.

7. For the publication history of the poems, see Paull F. Baum, *Ten Studies in the Poetry of Matthew Arnold* (Durham: Duke Univ. Press, 1958), pp. 79–84, and Stange, pp. 216–32.

8. How the two poems were originally related is not entirely clear. "Isolation. To Marguerite" was not published until 1857 (as "To Marguerite"—the present title was not bestowed until 1869), and "To Marguerite—Continued" was not given its present title until 1869 but was originally entitled "To Marguerite, in

Returning a Volume of the Letters of Ortis" (1852), then "To Marguerite" (1853, 1854), and then "Isolation" (1857). Still, the identical stanza forms, the overlapping titles, the publication in sequence from 1857 on, and the final titles all indicate their eventual relationship, and strongly imply an initial connection.

9. Buckler, p. 65.

10. *Écrits: A Selection,* trans. Alan Sheridan (New York: Norton, 1977), pp. 42–43.

11. Tillotson, "Yes: In the Sea of Life," *Review of English Studies,* n.s. 3 (1952):364, 346.

12. Roper, p. 156.

13. The poems thus admirably fit the theoretical model of Michael Riffaterre's *Semiotics of Poetry* (Bloomington: Indiana Univ. Press, 1978), in which the completed poem is seen as a series of variations on a "pre-existent word group" (p. 23) called a "hypogram."

14. Tillotson, p. 347. According to Kenneth Allott, Saintsbury, who first pointed out the reference to *Pendennis,* chap. 16, called the poem "simply an extension of a phrase in *Pendennis.*" Note in *Poems,* p. 129.

15. Honan, pp. 149–58.

16. Mermin, p. 97.

17. *Letters to Clough,* p. 97. According to J. B. Broadbent, Arnold's echoes of Milton, Wordsworth, and the Bible provide, at least in *Sohrab and Rustum,* precisely the desired tone of authority and, moreover, reveal the poet as "a man confident—for all he may say elsewhere—in the value of his own civilization." Broadbent also quotes Arnold's admission that he had indeed imitated Milton's manner, "but Milton is a sufficiently great master to imitate." See his "Milton and Arnold," *Essays in Criticism* 6 (1956):406.

18. See the chapter entitled "The Use of Elegy" in *Imaginative Reason,* pp. 232–86. Culler characteristically remarks of some that "they are not so much elegies as attempts on Arnold's part to exorcise an evil spirit which had formerly dwelt within him" (p. 246).

19. Hollander, *The Figure of Echo: A Mode of Allusion in Milton and After* (Berkeley: Univ. of California Press, 1981), p. 90. Bloom, *Anxiety,* p. 56.

20. "Ode: Intimations of Immortality from Recollections of Early Childhood," l. 51.

21. Stitelman, "Lyrical Process in Three Poems by Matthew Arnold," *Victorian Poetry* 15 (1977):136.

22. Others have commented on this confusion. See, for example, Allott's note in *Poems,* pp. 287–88, and for a more extended discussion, Roper, pp. 173–77.

23. Noted in *Poems,* p. 289.

24. "Ode: Intimations of Immortality," ll. 151–53. The allusion is noted in *Poems,* p. 290.

25. "But surely the one thing wanting to make Wordsworth an even greater poet than he is,—his thought richer, and his influence of wider application,—was that he should have read more books" (3:262).

26. Culler, p. 235.

27. The allusion to Gray's "The Progress of Poesy," ll. 84–85, is noted in *Poems.*

28. The point about Gray is made in "The Study of Poetry" (9:181) and Collins is drawn into it in the essay "Thomas Gray" (9:204), but for an earlier comment to the same effect see Arnold's 1849 letter in *Letters to Clough,* p. 99.

29. *Letters to Clough,* p. 115.

30. Ibid., p. 100.

31. Ibid., p. 111.

32. Ibid., pp. 64–65.

33. The echo of *Paradise Lost* 3.662–63 is noted in *Poems.*

34. Quoted by Culler, p. 52.

35. Hollander, p. 80.

36. For the possible allusion to Thomas Arnold, see *Poems,* p. 291.

37. Stange, p. 176.

38. Pater, Conclusion, *The Renaissance,* p. 187.

39. Mermin, pp. 97, 106.

40. Pitman, "On Dover Beach," *Essays in Criticism* 23 (1973):129.

41. Gitter, "Undermined Metaphors in Arnold's Poetry," *Victorian Poetry* 16 (1978):278.

42. Knoepflmacher, pp. 21–22. Michael Timko also discusses the poem as a response to Wordsworthian poetry and thought—he sees it as "Arnold's strongest poetic declaration of his break with the Romantics, especially Wordsworth, and his most direct and explicit denunciation of Wordsworth's 'Ode: Intimations of Immortality.'" ("Wordsworth's 'Ode' and Arnold's 'Dover Beach': Celestial Light and Confused Alarms," *Cithara* 13 [1973]:53).

43. Knoepflmacher, pp. 21–22.

44. See pp. 15–17.

45. Hollander, p. 12.

46. Sharp, "A Note on Allusion in 'Dover Beach,'" *English Language Notes* 21 (1983):53. Sharp points out the echoes of *The Prelude* as well.

47. In his "Address to the Wordsworth Society," Arnold referred to "what is perhaps Wordsworth's most distinct virtue of all—his power of happiness and hope, his 'deep power of joy'" (10:133). For Arnold's consistent association of Wordsworth with joy, see Gottfried, chap. 2.

48. Bidney, "Of the Devil's Party: Undetected Words of Milton's Satan in Arnold's 'Dover Beach,'" *Victorian Poetry* 20 (1982):89.

49. Culler, p. 39.

50. Pitman, p. 124.

Conclusion

1. *Letters of Matthew Arnold,* 2:10.

2. Medvedev/Bakhtin, p. 17.

3. "On Life," in *Shelley's Poetry and Prose,* p. 477.

4. Hartmann, *Criticism in the Wilderness: The Study of Literature Today* (New Haven: Yale Univ. Press, 1980), p. 80.

5. Ibid., p. 15.

6. Levine, "Matthew Arnold: The Artist in the Wilderness," *Critical Inquiry* 9 (1983):469–82.

7. Arendt, *Between Past and Future: Six Exercises in Political Thought* (New York: Viking, 1961), p. 28.

8. Daiches, *God and the Poets, Gifford Lectures,* 1983 (Oxford: Clarendon Press, 1984), pp. 118–19.

9. Quoted in Hartmann, *Criticism in the Wilderness,* p. 87.

10. Bakhtin, *The Dialogic Imagination: Four Essays,* ed. Michael Holquist, trans. Caryl Emerson and Michael Holquist (Austin: Univ. of Texas Press, 1981), p. 286.

11. Ibid., p. 284.

12. Ibid., p. 287.

13. Ibid., p. 285.

14. Hartmann, "Words, Wish, Worth: Wordsworth," in *Deconstruction and Criticism* (New York: Seabury, 1979), p. 185.

15. Bakhtin, *Dialogic Imagination,* p. 298.

16. Ibid., p. 276.

17. Ibid., p. 294.

18. Levine, p. 471.

Index

Aarsleff, Hans, 15
Adderley, Charles, 212, 216
Aeschylus, 117
Allingham, William, 227 n. 41
Allott, Kenneth, 40, 46, 54, 61, 65, 67, 78, 87, 140, 144, 148, 151, 224 n. 37, 229 n. 14, 232 n. 14, n. 22
Allott, Miriam, 231 n. 3
Alpers, Paul, 136
Anderson, Hans C., 62
Anderson, Warren, 226 n. 14
ApRoberts, Ruth, 2, 3, 4, 10, 12, 19, 21, 92
Arendt, Hannah, 208
Aristotle, 94
Arnold, Frances, 161, 162
Arnold, Matthew, *Poetry*: "Alaric at Rome," 34; *Balder Dead*, 95, 101, 102, 109–12, 113, 114–15, 136, 203, 210; "The Buried Life," 164, 165, 176, 181–88, 191, 193–95, 196, 197, 214, 216; "The Church of Brou," 119, 124, 130, 132, 134, 136; "Cromwell," 34; *The Death of Sohrab*, 107; "Dover Beach," 51, 164, 165, 181, 195–202, 203, 214, 216, 217; *Empedocles on Etna*, 49, 78–94, 96, 102, 106, 109, 113, 114–15, 141, 165, 214; *Empedocles on Etna, and Other Poems*, 72; "The Forsaken Merman," 62–64; "Fragment of a Chorus of a 'Dejaneira,'" 51; "The Hayswater Boat," 56–57; "Heine's Grave," 212, 213, 216; "Human Life," 169; "In Harmony with Nature," 52–53, 54–55, 69; "Isolation. To Marguerite," 171, 175, 177, 179, 186; "Land of the East!" 35; *Lucretius*, 148; "To Marguerite—Continued," 165, 169–71, 176–78, 179–80, 214, 216; "Meeting," 168–70, 179; "Memorial Verses," 74, 186–90; *Merope*, 95, 101, 102, 112–15, 136, 165, 203, 204, 210, 211; "Mycerinus," 37, 45–48, 109; "The New Sirens," 37, 48–51, 62; "Night Comes," 32–34; "Obermann Once More," 212, 216; "Parting," 174, 176, 179; "Philomela," 178; "Quiet Work," 53–54; "Resignation," 57–61, 73; "Rugby Chapel," 119, 157–60; "The Scholar-Gipsy," 51, 75, 110, 118, 119, 124, 134–47, 160, 217, 229 n. 23; "Self-Dependence," 31, 73–74; "Shakespeare," 37, 42–43; "The Sick King in Bokhara," 46, 109; *Sohrab and Rustum*, 95, 101, 102–9, 111, 114–15, 136, 138, 165, 203, 210; "A Southern Night," 161–62; "Stagirius," 3, 37–39, 41; "Stanzas from the Grande Chartreuse," 51, 110, 117, 125, 126, 129, 138, 156; "Stanzas in Memory of the Author of 'Obermann,'" 75, 114, 138;

Arnold, Matthew (*Continued*)
"The Strayed Reveller," 64–69; *The Strayed Reveller, and Other Poems*, 30, 72; "Switzerland" series, 164–81, 214; "Thyrsis," 119, 124, 135–37, 147–56, 229 n. 23; "To a Gipsy Child by the Sea-Shore," 56; "To my Friends," 180–81; *Tristram and Iseult*, 119, 123, 124, 125–34, 136, 214; "The Voice," 37, 39–42; "Written in Butler's Sermons," 35; "Written in Emerson's Essays," 37, 43–45; "Youth and Calm," 194. *Prose*: "Bishop Butler and the Zeitgeist," 20, 35–36; "Doctor Stanley's Lectures on the Jewish Church," 12; "A French Elijah," 21; "The Function of Criticism at the Present Time," 11, 14, 97, 117, 121, 201; *God and the Bible*, 9, 15, 16, 17, 18; "Heinrich Heine," 11, 212; "Literature and Dogma," 9, 11, 12, 13, 14, 182, 221 n. 17; "Literature and Science," 6–7, 10, 21; "A Liverpool Address," 10; "Maurice de Guérin," 4, 5, 7, 24, 188, 202; "Milton," 22; "A Psychological Parallel," 11, 19, 20; *St. Paul and Protestantism*, 9, 10, 13, 18, 19, 20, 21; "On the Study of Celtic Literature," 23; "On Translating Homer," 22, 23, 95, 98, 112, 189; "Preface to *Merope*," 100; "Preface to *Poems*," 77, 93–102, 108, 136, 137, 206, 211; "The Study of Poetry," 1, 44, 205, 233 n. 28; "Thomas Gray," 233 n. 28; "Wordsworth," 21, 191
Arnold, Thomas, 39, 120, 158–59, 192; *The History of Rome*, 147
Arnold, Tom, 101
Arnold, William, 161, 162

Bakhtin, M. M., 68, 205, 210–11, 212, 214, 215, 216
Baum, Paull, 231 n. 7
Benjamin, Walter, 27, 206–7, 213
Bhagavad Gita, 79
Bible, 10, 12, 13, 63, 88, 213, 232 n. 17; Ecclesiastes, 7, 8; First Corinthians, 42; Genesis, 8, 9; Gospels, 20; Gospel of St. John, 9; New Testament, 11; Old Testament, 11, 19; Proverbs, 44–45; Romans, 21
Bidney, Martin, 200
Blake, William, 143
Bloom, Harold, 27, 28, 68, 117, 135, 137, 207, 229 n. 17
Borges, Jorge Luis, 105; "Pierre Menard, Author of the *Quixote*," 105
Bradley, F. H., 3
Broadbent, J. B., 232 n. 17
Brown, E. K., 12
Browning, Robert, 14, 27, 96, 165; "Andrea del Sarto," 14
Buckler, William, 88, 105, 109, 126, 143, 146, 166, 167, 172, 173, 228 n. 6, 231 n. 51
Burke, Kenneth, 24, 109
Burne-Jones, E., 229 n. 13
Bush, Douglas, 3, 4
Butler, Bishop, 36, 216
Byron, George Gordon, 74, 79, 84, 88, 118, 121, 122–23, 126, 132, 163, 172, 225 n. 42, 229 n. 14; *Manfred*, 87, 225 n. 42

Carlyle, Thomas, 18, 22, 54, 120, 122, 143, 176, 178; "Characteristics," 122
Carroll, Lewis, 153; *Through the Looking Glass*, 153
Cervantes, Miguel, 105; *Don Quixote*, 105
Chambers, Robert, 6; *Vestiges of the Natural History of Creation*, 6
Choerilus of Samos, 30
Chapman, George, 98

Chateaubriand, François-René de, 78; *René*, 78
Christ, Carol, 57
Claude, Mary, 180
Clough, Arthur Hugh, 21, 22, 30–31, 33, 55, 59, 60, 78, 80, 85, 95, 102, 108, 137, 147, 148, 157, 189–90, 191, 227 n. 41, 230–31 n. 49
Coleridge, E. H., 30
Coleridge, J. D., 99
Coleridge, S. T., 7, 9, 51, 61, 126, 147, 176, 192–93; "Frost at Midnight," 51–52, 54; "Kubla Khan," 129, 192–93; "This Lime-Tree Bower My Prison," 192; "To a Nightingale," 192
Collins, William, 176, 189, 190; "Ode to Evening," 151; "Ode to Fear," 189
Condillac, Etienne, 15, 16
Cowper, William, 43; "Light Shining Out of Darkness," 43
Curtius, Ernst, 17
Culler, A. Dwight, 91, 103–4, 107, 112, 146, 147, 152, 188, 201, 232 n. 18

Daiches, David, 209
Dawson, Carl, 222 n. 20
Derrida, Jacques, 119
Descartes, René, 15, 16
Dietrich, Manfred, 96
Diodorus Siculus, 147
Donne, John, 151, 176, 177, 178
Dougherty, Charles, 228 n. 8
Drew, Philip, 153
Dryden, John, 69
Dyson, A. E., 230

Eliot, T. S., 95, 151–52, 164–65
Emerson, Ralph Waldo, 4, 7, 8, 16, 44–45, 53, 61, 70; "Nature," 8, 53, 61
Empedocles, 79, 80
Epictetus, 52–53, 120

Firdawsi, 107
Foscolo, Ugo, 176
Foucault, Michel, 25, 26, 210
Froude, J. D., 41, 225 n. 47, 228 n. 65; *Nemesis of Faith*, 41
Frye, Northrop, 118, 209
Fulweiler, Howard, 3

Gitter, Elizabeth, 197
Glanvill, Joseph, 140, 145
Goethe, J. W. von, 74–75, 78, 96, 120, 166, 213, 216, 225 n. 5, 227 n. 43; *Sorrows of Young Werther*, 78
Gooch, Sir Charles, 216
Gottfried, Leon, 224 n. 34
Gray, Thomas, 137, 140, 188, 189, 190, 232 n. 27; "Elegy Written in a Country Churchyard," 136, 144; "The Progress of Poesy," 233 n. 28
Grob, Alan, 224 n. 24
Guérin, Maurice de, 23, 24, 61, 84; "Le Centaure," 65

Hamilton, Sir William, 14
Hartmann, Geoffrey, 117, 201, 206, 213, 217, 218
Hegel, G. W. F., 16
Heine, Heinrich, 213
Helsinger, Elizabeth, 222 n. 29
Herodotus, 46, 147
Hesiod, 94, 151
Hickman, Andrew, 65, 66
Holloway, John, 222 n. 30
Homer, 23, 41, 49, 98, 103, 105, 112, 138; *Iliad*, 109; *Odyssey*, 49
Honan, Park, 166, 180, 231 n. 3
Hopkins, G. M., 38–39
Horace, 176, 178
Hornstein, L. H., 231 n. 50
Houghton, Walter, 79
Huxley, T. H., 5, 6, 8, 9, 10, 14, 17, 20, 23, 208; "Science and Culture," 5

Jameson, Fredric, 118
Johnson, E. D. H., 31, 91, 164
Johnson, Samuel, 151
Johnson, W. S., 32, 45, 62, 231 n. 51
Josephus, Flavius, 35; *The Jewish Wars*, 35
Joubert, Joseph, 19, 42

Kafka, Franz, 206
Keats, John, 24, 31, 54, 60, 61, 84, 95, 96, 132, 137, 140, 145, 163, 192, 229 n. 23; "To Autumn," 140; "Bright Star," 54; "Epistle to John Hamilton Reynolds," 60; "The Eve of St. Agnes," 126, 130, 133, 229 n. 14; "La Belle Dame Sans Merci," 126; "Ode on a Grecian Urn," 65; "Ode to a Nightingale," 144, 145, 151
Keble, John, 176, 178
Kierkegaard, Søren A., 208
King, Edward, 149
Kermode, Frank, 226 n. 37
Kingsley, Charles, 108
Knoepflmacher, U. C., 6, 197, 198, 224 n. 34

Lacan, Jacques, 175–76
Landow, George P., 230 n. 48, 231 n. 50
Leavis, F. R., 209
Leavy, Barbara Fass, 228 n. 10
Levin, Harry, 229 n. 21
Levine, George, 207, 218
Lewis, Matthew "Monk," 122
Locke, John, 15, 18
Lucretius, 120, 176

Macaulay, Thomas, 27
Mansel, Henry, 14
Marcus Aurelius, 79, 84
Marx, Karl, 208
Masson, David, 96, 99, 227 n. 43
Maturin, Charles, 122
Menander, 97
Mermin, Dorothy, 72, 74, 81, 98, 223 n. 11
Millais, J. E., 229 n. 13
Miller, J. Hillis, 3, 4, 57, 98
Milton, John, 23, 25, 137, 138–39, 187, 189–92, 199–200, 214, 232 n. 17; *Comus*, 151, 230 n. 38; "Il Penseroso," 189; "Lycidas," 136, 138, 144, 148; *Paradise Lost*, 191, 200, 233 n. 33
Morris, William, 27, 143
Müller, Max, 8, 16, 18, 221 n. 15

Newman, Francis, 41
Newman, John Henry, Cardinal, 36–37, 39, 45, 68
Nietzsche, Friedrich, 84–86, 90, 94, 101, 115, 137, 208

Ong, Walter, 100, 224 n. 19
Ovid, 87

Parker, Patricia, 119
Pater, Walter, 26
Patmore, Coventry, 227 n. 46; *Angel in the House*, 128
Paul, St., 19, 21, 42, 213
Pausanius, 112
Peacock, Thomas Love, 27
Pearson, Gabriel, 105, 112, 115
Pfordresher, John, 222 n. 20
Pitman, Ruth, 196, 201
Plato, 9, 42
Plotinus, 54
Pope, Alexander, 98, 151
Pound, Ezra, 151
Prayer Book, 20, 62, 63
Prose Edda, 109
Pugin, Augustus, 143

Radcliffe, Ann, 122
Rénan, Ernest, 17
Ricks, Christopher, 229 n. 21
Riffaterre, Michael, 232 n. 13
Roebuck, John, 212, 216

Roper, Alan, 37, 141, 152, 176, 232 n. 22
Rossetti, D. G., 27, 30, 68, 163
Rousseau, Jean-Jacques, 4
Ruskin, John, 18, 143

Schiller, Friedrich, 94
Scott, Sir Walter, 143
Sénancour, Etienne, 75–76, 79, 118, 120, 121, 225 n. 5; "Obermann," 74, 78, 172
Sharp, Ronald, 200
Shakespeare, William, 42, 97, 117, 138, 189, 190; *Hamlet*, 42, 180–81; *King Lear*, 201–2; *Macbeth*, 148; *A Midsummer Night's Dream*, 151, 230 n. 38
Shaw, W. David, 3, 4, 12, 14, 80
Shelley, Percy Bysshe, 40–41, 42, 74, 95, 98–99; "Adonais," 118, 121, 163, 206; "On Love," 163; "To a Skylark," 40–41
Smith, Alexander, 96, 227 n. 41
Socrates, 79, 94
Sophocles, 203
Sappho, 203
Spencer, Herbert, 14
Spinoza, 120
Stange, G. Robert, 52, 167, 223 n. 8, 231 n. 3
Stitelman, Alice, 184
Swinburne, Algernon, 27, 49, 125, 163, 225 n. 11; "On the Cliffs," 203

Taylor, Beverly, 228 n. 11
Tennyson, Alfred, 18, 27, 34, 38, 52, 96, 125, 126, 132, 137, 143, 145, 148; "Break, Break, Break," 64; "The Hesperides," 63; *In Memoriam*, 18, 195, 196; "The Lady of Shalott," 124, 127; "Locksley Hall," 124; "The Lotus-Eaters," 140; *Maud*, 68, 166; "The Mermaid," 63; "The Palace of Art," 38, 229 n. 14; "St. Simeon Stylites," 38; "Ulysses," 82, 157
Thackeray, William, 176, 177, 178; *Pendennis*, 232 n. 14
Theocritus, 136, 137
Timko, Michael, 233 n. 42
Thomson, James, 151; "Summer," 151
Thucydides, 147, 201
Tillotson, Kathleen, 176, 177
Trench, R. C., 8, 17
Trilling, Lionel, 109
Tulloch, John, 11; "Amateur Theology," 11

Virgil, 110, 136, 137; *Aeneid*, 109; "Fifth Eclogue," 136

Wagner, Richard, 125
Walker, Sydney, 227 n. 41
Waterhouse, J. W., 229 n. 13
Wesley, John, 41
Wightman, Frances Lucy, 165
Wilde, Oscar, 26, 221 n. 9; *The Picture of Dorian Gray*, 38
Wilson, Bishop, 216
Wordsworth, William, 4, 7, 16, 26, 34, 46, 54, 55–57, 61, 69, 74, 75, 84, 86, 139, 166, 183, 186–88, 190, 192, 197, 199, 202, 203, 214, 216, 222 n. 36, 225 n. 5, 232 n. 17, 233 n. 47; "Elegiac Stanzas," 77; "Gipsies," 54; "It Is a Beauteous Evening," 197–99; "Laodamia," 46; "Lucy" poems, 167; "Ode to Duty," 46; "Ode: Intimations of Immortality," 233 n. 42; *The Prelude*, 200; "Tintern Abbey," 58–60, 185, 190, 198

Yeats, William Butler, 145

Zietlow, Paul, 83, 88, 226 n. 14

is a series of monographs on literature covering the years from 1830 to 1914. Contributions may be critical (historical or theoretical), biographical, bibliographic, comparative, or interdisciplinary.

DANIEL ALBRIGHT, *Tennyson: The Muses' Tug-of-War*
DAVID G. RIEDE, *Matthew Arnold and the Betrayal of Language*